ROMANCE MONOGRAPHS, INC.

Number 13

LOPE DE VEGA'S

LA DESDICHADA ESTEFANÍA:

A CRITICAL, ANNOTATED EDITION OF THE AUTOGRAPH MANUSCRIPT

D1256645

ROMANCE MONOGRAPHS, INC.
Number 13

LOPE DE VEGA'S

LA DESDICHADA ESTEFANÍA:

A CRITICAL, ANNOTATED EDITION
OF THE AUTOGRAPH MANUSCRIPT

BY

HUGH W. KENNEDY

CALIFORNIA STATE UNIVERSITY, LOS ANGELES

UNIVERSITY, MISSISSIPPI
ROMANCE MONOGRAPHS, INC.
1 9 7 5

PRINTED IN SPAIN

IMPRESO EN ESPAÑA

I. S. B. N. 84-399-3628-1

DEPÓSITO LEGAL: V. 1.250 - 1975

ARTES GRÁFICAS SOLER, S. A. - JÁVEA, 28 - VALENCIA (8) - 1975

Library of Congress Cataloging in Publication Data

Vega Carpio, Lope Félix de, 1562-1635.
   Lope de Vega's La desdichada Estefanía.

   (Romance monographs; no. 13)
   Text in Spanish; introd. and notes in English.
   Bibliography: p.
   1. Spain—History—711-1516—Drama. I. Kennedy, Hugh W., 1934-
ed. II. Title. III. Title: La desdichada Estefanía.
PQ6439.D44 1975   862'.3   75-1049

Dedicated to Joseph H. Silverman, teacher and friend. He embodies the very best qualities of the humanist-scholar, who inspires his students to strive toward a high level of accomplishment, which, from his own humility and generosity, he is sure they are capable.

PREFACE

In September 1962, Señora Primy de Noriega, the widow of the distinguished *lopista* Don Agustín G. de Amezúa, allowed me to obtain microfilm copies of the Ignacio de Gálvez manuscript collection, which her late husband had described in detail some years earlier. [1] I promised Señora de Amezúa that no unpublished materials would be divulged before the manuscripts had been returned to their rightful owner. She agreed, however, that I might make use of the Gálvez manuscripts in my teaching and that copies and variants of known autographs could be made available to Lope specialists. In 1965, my graduate students at UCLA, including Ethel R. Bolton, Thomas Lathrop, Dale E. McCall and James R. MacKenzie Saddler, prepared working editions of *El amor desatinado, La·bella malmaridada, La francesilla* and *El príncipe inocente,* on the basis of the Gálvez transcriptions. And, in 1969, I provided Professor Arnold G. Reichenberger with a microfilm copy of the Gálvez version of *Los Benavides* to use in his edition of Lope's autograph manuscript of the play, which had been acquired by the University of Pennsylvania Library on May 30, 1961. [2] At the present time, the Amezúa family retains possession of volumes 1 and 5 of the Gál-

---

[1] *Una colección manu:crita y desconocida de comedias de Lope de Vega Carpio* (Madrid, 1945). Amezúa had received the collection from the Marquis of Valdeiglesias, who was not the legal owner (p. 8).

[2] Arnold G. Reichenberger, "The Autograph Manuscript of Lope de Vega's Play *Los Benavides,*" *The Library Chronicle,* XXVIII (1962), 106-108. See Lope de Vega, *El primero Benavides,* ed. A. G. Reichenberger and A. Espantoso Foley (Philadelphia, 1973), pp. 6-7, n. 8.

vez collection. Volumes 2, 3 and 4 are now housed in the Biblioteca Nacional in Madrid. [3]

When, in 1964, Professor Kennedy completed his edition of
La desdichada Estefanía, he had worked not only with Lope's
manuscript but also with Gálvez's transcription of the original,
"copiada a la letra [en 1762], corregida y enmendada como su
original, y rayadas quantas cláusulas se encontraron." As Professor Kennedy observes in his Introduction, the Gálvez copy of the
play was of great value in resolving textual obscurities in Lope
de Vega's manuscript.

After the appearance, in 1967, of J. H. Arjona's paleographic
edition of *La desdichada Estefanía,* Professor Kennedy was
tempted to abandon the project of reworking his doctoral thesis
for publication. But, a meticulous analysis of the Arjona text
convinced him that his own work had not been superseded.
Arjona had not seen the Gálvez copy and, in addition to a number
of editorial inaccuracies that he committed — errors in transcription and verse tabulation, for example — he chose not to discuss
the work as a piece of dramatic literature, nor to elucidate the
numerous lexical, historical and literary matters that might offer
difficulty to a modern reader.

Professor Kennedy, on the other hand, has enriched our understanding of the play through 1) a sensitive analysis of its sources
and Lope's extraordinary ability to turn historical narrative into
a tragic dramatic action; 2) a thorough examination of its significance as tragedy and relationship to other plays, such as
Lope's *El castigo sin venganza* and later works on the *Desdichada Estefanía* theme; and 3) a careful tracing and study of
motifs, themes — especially honor — character and plot structure.

As Professor Kennedy convincingly argues, Estefanía, despite
the play's title, is not its main character. From Sandoval's *Historia de los reyes de Castilla y León,* we learn about Fernán
Ruiz de Castro that "le atravessaba el alma la muerte tan sin
culpa de su querida mujer: no hallaba poder tener consuelo jamás,

---

[3] Lope de Vega, *El amor desatinado,* ed. J. García Morales (Madrid,
1968), p. XXXVIII, n. 1.

pues el daño era tan sin remedio." This, of course, is the center of the tragedy. As King Alfonso laments in the final moments:

¡Ay, cómo saben los cielos
poner en el bien templanza!

In the light of Fernán Ruiz's horrible deed, performed in the name of God, one wonders about the number of Lope tragedies and tragicomedies in which Heaven is assigned the duty of defending the honor code and of meting out punishment to its transgressors, with man serving simply as the instrument of Divine Justice. [4] Is it not possible that an implied condemnation of the code lurks behind such barbarity, perpetrated in God's name? [5] To all these "loving killers" — the phrase is A. S. Gérard's — the following remarks by Albert Camus may be applied with varying degrees of appropriateness:

The evil that is in the world always comes of ignorance, and good intentions may do as much harm as malevolence, if they lack understanding. On the whole, men are more good than bad; that, however, isn't the real point. But they are more or less ignorant, and it is this that we call

---

[4]   ... del cielo el castigo te ha venido.
(La desdichada Estefanía, v. 2604)

Cielos
hoy se ha de ver en mi casa
no más de vuestro castigo.
Alzad la divina vara....
Este ha de ser un castigo
vuestro no más....
(El castigo sin venganza, vv. 2834-2843)

Ya te viene a dar castigo
el Cielo.
(Los comendadores de Córdoba, Acad. XI, 296a)

[5] In an unpublished critique of Donald R. Larson's doctoral thesis on The Development of the "Honor Plays" of Lope de Vega (Harvard, 1967), I discussed this aspect of the honor code in terms of Los comendadores de Córdoba, La bella malmaridada, El castigo sin venganza and the novel La (más) prudente venganza, reminding Professor Larson that from Lope's earliest days he was aware of the difference between God's will and human "justice," particularly in the realm of honor. I expect that in the revised version of his thesis, soon to be published by Harvard University Press, Professor Larson will give this subject a more detailed treatment.

vice or virtue; the most incorrigible vice being that of an ignorance that fancies it knows everything and therefore claims for itself the right to kill.

Antonio López de Vega, a brilliant seventeenth-century outsider, undoubtedly of *converso* origin, ridiculed the insane tyranny of the honor code and with righteous indignation he exclaimed: "¡No le faltava más al Cielo que autorizar con su patrocinio los medios errados de que se vale el furor de los hombres!" [6] Professor Kennedy has written suggestively of these matters in his discussions of honor and plot.

       ❋ ❋ ❋

A carefully edited text of a Lope de Vega autograph manuscript is always welcome, particularly when it is accompanied by a perceptive study and illuminating notes. This volume is a valuable addition to the canon of edited Lope de Vega autographs and its critical apparatus will be an important source of information for students of Lope and his *tragicomedias,* wherein those siamixed twins of tragedy and comedy — to steal a phrase from James Joyce — live together in necessary, verisimilar and discordant harmony.

JOSEPH H. SILVERMAN
University of California
Santa Cruz

---

[6] *Paradoxas racionales,* ed. E. Buceta (Madrid, 1935), p. 119. In one of the satellite narratives of *Don Quixote,* Cardenio, an estranged, deeply troubled young man, is miraculously quixotized and liberated from his paralyzing alienation by contact with Don Quixote. As Professor Theodore R. Sarbin has suggested to me, the long embrace between Cardenio and Don Quixote is the initial mechanism of the young man's cure. It symbolizes the warmth and intimate contact that Cardenio missed in his relationship with his father and it has the therapeutic effect that physical contact has proved to have in recent psychological treatment.

When he meets Dorotea and learns of her seduction by Fernando, Cardenio vows, as a gentleman and *true* Christian — even using the knightly rhetoric of a Feliciano de Silva — that he will "desafialle, en razón de la sinrazón que os hace, sin acordarme de mis agravios, *cuya venganza dejaré al cielo,* por acudir en la tierra a los vuestros" (Part I, chapter 29; emphasis added).

TABLE OF CONTENTS

ABBREVIATIONS

A	Text of *La desdichada Estefanía* in *Ac.*, VIII.
Ac.	*Obras de Lope de Vega publicadas por la Real Academia Española,* Madrid, 1890-1913, 15 vols.
Ac.N	*Obras de Lope de Vega publicadas por la Real Academia Española, Nueva edición,* Madrid, 1916-1930, 13 vols.
Amezúa, *Colección*	Agustín G. de Amezúa, *Una colección manuscrita y desconocida de comedias de Lope de Vega Carpio,* Madrid, 1945.
Arte nuevo	Lope de Vega Carpio, "Arte nuevo de hazer comedias en este tiempo," in *Dramatic Theory in Spain,* ed. H. J. Chaytor, Cambridge, 1925, pp. 15-29.
B	*Doze comedias nuevas de Lope de Vega Carpio y otros autores, segunda parte,* Barcelona, 1630.
BAAEE	*Biblioteca de autores españoles,* Madrid, 1846-1880, 71 vols.
BAE	*Boletín de la Real Academia Española.*
BHS	*Bulletin of Hispanic Studies.*
Catálogo	*Catálogo de la Exposición Bibliográfica de Lope de Vega,* organizada por la Biblioteca Nacional, Madrid, 1935.
Covarrubias, *Tesoro*	Sebastián de Covarrubias Orozco, *Tesoro de la lengua castellana,* Madrid, 1611 (edition consulted: Barcelona, 1943).
Fontecha	Carmen Fontecha, *Glosario de voces comentadas en ediciones de textos clásicos,* Madrid, 1941.
G	Ignacio de Gálvez, copyist, *Primera tragedia de Estephania la desdichada,* Madrid, 1762.
H	*Hispania* (journal of the American Association of Teachers of Spanish and Portuguese).
Hoge, *El príncipe*	Henry W. Hoge (ed.), *El príncipe despeñado,* Bloomington, 1955.
HR	*Hispanic Review.*

J	J. Homero Arjona (ed.), *La desdichada Estefanía: edición paleográfica*, Madrid, 1967.
M	*Dozena parte de las comedias de Lope de Vega Carpio*, Madrid, 1619, with Cárdenas coat of arms.
MLN	*Modern Language Notes*.
Morby, *La Dorotea*	Edwin S. Morby (ed.), *La Dorotea*, Berkeley, 1958.
Morley-Bruerton, *Chronology*	S. Griswold Morley and Courtney Bruerton, *The Chronology of Lope de Vega's "Comedias,"* New York, 1940.
Morley-Tyler, *Nombres*	S. Griswold Morley and Richard W. Tyler, *Los nombres de personajes en las comedias de Lope de Vega*, Berkeley, 1961, 2 vols.
PMLA	*Publications of the Modern Language Association of America*.
RAED	*Diccionario de la lengua española*, Real Academia Española, 1956.
RFE	*Revista de filología española*.
RHi	*Revue hispanique*
S	*Dozena parte de las comedias de Lope de Vega Carpio*, Madrid, 1619, *escudo* of centaur.

INTRODUCTION

BIBLIOGRAPHY

I. *The Autograph Manuscript*

THE FULLY AUTOGRAPH MANUSCRIPT OF LOPE DE VEGA's *La des-dichada Estefanía*, dated November 12, 1604 in Toledo, is presently owned by the Real Academia Española. The manuscript is made up of 63 folios, which measure approximately 210 × 152 mm. [1] It has the usual characteristics of a Lope autograph. Act I has 18 numbered folios, Act II 16, [2] ending on the verso of the 17th, unnumbered folio, as does Act III. Only the folios of the text proper are numbered, with separate foliation for each act. Other unnumbered folios are: The title page [r], printed in capitals; the following folio [r], on which appears "y [?] y [?] genaral" in the upper left margin, "es de Antonio Granados, autor de comedias, el parol" (under an ink stain), a *rúbrica* under this writing (which appears in the upper center of the page). Below it is "es de Antonio Granados, autor de comedias por su magest[a]d y el que otra cosa digere mien[te]...... [*rúbrica*] Ge [?];" the next folio [r] has a listing of characters and actors, which will be discussed in the Manuscript Notes; upside down, beginning in the lower right margin, there appears a series of squared numbers, written over the names of actors and their assigned roles; the next folio [v] begins a listing of characters and actors, while [r] has the *reparto* for Act I; the folio numbering

---

[1] *Catálogo*, p. 9, No. 17. The manuscript is described as being composed of 59 folios; the measurements are those of the *Catálogo*.

[2] Except for the unnumbered folios 13 and 15 of Act II.

Act II [r]; that containing the *reparto* for Act II [r]; the folio numbering Act III [r]; the *reparto* for Act III [r]; and the three folios which continue the *licencias* and *censuras* after Act III.

The first act consists of 1019 lines; the second, 909; the third, 880, for a total of 2808 lines. Morley and Bruerton list a total of 2651 lines, [3] due to the numerous deletions and omissions in the texts upon which their count was based. At the top of each page of the text, the title page, and those containing *repartos* (not the folios numbering Acts II and III), Lope wrote a small cross, over which appear the initials JM or JMJ (Jesús, María, José). [4] Lope also used a cross potent in designating the entrance or exit of characters (shown as ✠ in the text). This cross differs from the type found at the top of the pages in that it is much heavier and darker. When speeches have been deleted, underlined, or boxed off to indicate omission by a person other than Lope, a simple cross is often used to indicate the end of the deletion. In many cases *sí*'s and *no*'s abound in the margin next to such passages, indicating changes of opinion, conflicting ideas, or perhaps specific needs of the troupe in staging certain scenes. For example, the scene close to the end of Act II with the *cochero* and the *alguazil* is eliminated entirely, possibly because of a lack of actors for the roles (the taking of several roles by one person is clearly indicated in the cast list on the unnumbered folio preceding the *reparto* for Act I). This autograph has a large number of such alterations and marginal notes, [5] apparently characteristic of the Antonio de Granados troupe. It had in its repertory the autographs of *El cuerdo loco* and *El príncipe despeñado,* both containing an unusual number of alterations. [6]

---

[3] Morley-Bruerton, *Chronology,* p. 24. The 157 missing lines are accounted for by the 155 lines omitted, 2 added of the *Dozena Parte* editions.

[4] See W. L. Fichter (ed.), *El sembrar en buena tierra* (New York, 1944), p. 1, and his article, "New Aids for Dating the Undated Autographs of Lope de Vega's Plays," *HR,* IX (1941), pp. 79-80, for a discussion of these initials in the period 1602-1610. Also A. G. Reichenberger (ed.), *Carlos V en Francia* (Philadelphia, 1962), p. 15, n. 9.

[5] Of 49 passages so marked (728 lines), printed editions omit 101 lines.

[6] Henry W. Hoge, "Notes on the Sources and the Autograph Manuscript of Lope de Vega's *El príncipe despeñado,*" *PMLA,* LXV (1950), p. 824, n. 2, and p. 828, n. 19.

Lope's own deletions are characterized by a series of loops which run through the corrected material, often completely obliterating the original word or phrase. However, an attempt has been made to decipher as many of these *tachaduras* as possible, and the proposed solutions will be found in the Manuscript Notes.

Diego Marín and Evelyn Rugg, in their edition of Lope's *El galán de la membrilla* (Madrid, 1962), have treated extensively the orthography and punctuation of their manuscript (pp. 18-27). Rather than attempt to duplicate their work here, it will suffice to indicate briefly the typical aspects of Lope's orthography which contrast with contemporary spelling conventions.

As initial consonants, *b-*, *v-*, *u-* are all common (though *u-* is less frequent than the others, it is more prominent than was found to be the case in *El galán*. See *uida* 4 and 2063, *ui* 2166 and 2619, *uiue* 23, *uiste* 80 and *uiua* 89). For *b-*: *balor* 43 and 50, *buelba* 167. For *v-*: *verdad* 88, *viue* 136, *vil* 167, *vengo* 18. In an intervocalic position, *-u-* occurs with more frequency than *-b-*. For *-u-*: *reçiuida* 2, *tuuiere* 4, *hauéis* 35, *diuinos* 1561, *viue* 136, *priua* 88; but also: *derribar* 38, *andube* 1405, *llebo* 51, *habéis* 1609, *xabóname* 680. In contact with a consonant, *-u-* and *-b-* occur with equal frequency. See *buelba* 167, *sirbo* 1507, *alborotes* 2079, *desbentura* 2253; *seruiçio* 1493, *aduierte* 1524, *boluí* 2307, *enuidia* 2428, and the interesting contrast *poluo* 1790 and *polbo* 1791.

Initial *ç-* is the rule, rather than *z-*: *çielo* 1294, *Çaragoza* 1299, *çanja* 1579, *çelos* 2425. Within a word, both appear with equal frequency: *obedenzia* 7, *Franzia* 15 (but *Françia* 82 and 151), *lizenzia* 568 (but *liçençia* 941), *alça* 1418.

-ee as a monosyllable appears in *fee* 37 and 681, *vee* 2110.

-ff- is used in *effetos* 787 (but *efeto* 2199); *-ph-* for *-f-* in *filosophando* 1329, and *Estephanía* on the title page.

ge and *gi* for *gue* and *gui* appear with less frequency in this play than is indicated for other Lope autographs: *pluguiera* 2293, *llegué* 1486 (but *llegé* 2424). *güerta* 1319, and *agüelo* 1870, are common.

Initial *h-* and intervocalic *-h-* are often omitted, but conversely are used in many cases: *abrá* 2516, *onor* 198, *onbre* 393, *onesto*

1203, *ola* 2217, *aya* 2688, *aora* 2061; but *hauían* 1237, *honor* 2074, *honbres* 2201, *crehí* 31, *hoy* (for *oí*) 1042, *trahe* 1189.

y for *i* is common: *ygualdad* 44, *yguales* 1934 (but *igual* 64), *yr* 64, *ynçita* 327, *ylo* 2409, *traydor* 240, *ayre* 392. But the reverse is the case in *soi* 2713, *estoi* 2621.

-ss- for *-s-* is frequent: *fuesse* 13 and 148, *passó* 82, *desseo* 157, *perdiesse* 2412.

x for *j*: *quéxate* 960, *dexe* 33, *xabóname* 680, *mexor* 1202 (but *mejor* 1445). *g* for *j* also appears: *lisongera* 1291, *trage* 1388; and the opposite: *escoje* 1517, *cojido* 1769.

s for *x*: *estremo* 1, *estraña* 32.

q for *c*: *quando* 21, *quarto* 1794.

mb and *nb*, plus *mp* and *np* fluctuate: *hombres* 2265 (but *onbre* 2250), *campo* 213 (but *canpo* 407).

Initial *v-* for the vowel *u-* is common: *vn* 471, *vno* 2034 (but *un* 15, *aun* for *a un* 193, *yuna* for *y una* 277). Since there are many cases of initial *u-* as a consonant, and examples demonstrate Lope's use of initial *u-* as a vowel, as above, the *u-* is maintained in the transcript for words which were written as one in the original.

Capitalization shows no consistent pattern. *Dios-dios, rey-Rey, guzmán-Guzmán, amor-Amor,* appear with equal frequency, within and at the beginning of sentences.

The main abbreviations occur with *que* (alone and as part of a word), as in *aunq̃* 8, *porq̃* 2223, *aq̃l* 2303, *peq̃ña* 887, but not in forms of *quedar*: *quedaras* 240, *quedo* 1975; nor *buscar*: *busqué* 186; *quexar*: *quexa* 1642. *Que* is sometimes written out (vv. 267, 405, 1442), as it is in *aquesto* 6, *aquella* 391, *aquestas* 716. All instances of *q̃* are resolved as *que*. Other abbreviations are *vro* for *vuestro* 5 (and its variations), *gras* for *graçias* 1230, *ymporta* for *ymportançia* 2450 and 2518, *tpo* for *tiempo* 1488, *mto* for *muerto* 2641, *sra* for *señora* 2633, *pa* for *para* 2251, *nro* for *nuestro* 1930 (and variations), *xpiano* for *cristiano* 899, *mrd* for *merçed* 531, *da* for *dama* 1719, *mto* for *muerto* 2641, *mdo* for *mundo* 806, *Pº* for *Primero* in the foliation number for the heading for Act I.

Lope very often wrote two words as one, or attached the last syllable of one word to the beginning of the next: *enestremo* 1, *dela* 2, *deçierto* 137, *condios* 677, *aninguno* 754. Words are sometimes written without regard for etymology: *vitoria* 492 and 1954, *fidedinos* 1487, *defetos* 1336, and *solene* 1730. Also, a vowel ending a word can serve to begin the following word, as in *desta [a]lma* 2320, *he [e]cho* 1553.

Punctuation is scanty, but Lope did use periods, commas, question and exclamation marks (as well as the slash to close a sentence or a speech [see vv. 293, 944, 1094, 2588]). More often than not there is simply an omission of punctuation, with no observable pattern followed in its use.

Insofar as the recent history of the manuscript is concerned, Fichter says that:

> [The Academia Española] acquired the MS less than thirty years ago. It then belonged to Maggs Brothers in London ... It had belonged to Gerald H. Villiers, who sold it through Sotheby's to Maggs Brothers. The first owner, at least in England, had been George William Villiers, the Earl of Clarendon. M. A. Buchanan has a short note on the MS in *HR*, III (1935), 74-75. He mentions Maggs Brothers' Catalogue, *Seventy-five Spanish and Portuguese Books, 1481-1764* (London, 1934), in which the MS was offered for sale, but fails to mention that the MS had already been offered for sale in their ealier catalogue, *A Selection of Books, Manuscripts, Bindings, and Autograph Letters* ... (London, 1931). In both catalogues the price was £ 500. I might add here that so far as I know there are no *sueltas* of the play. [7]

The Academia Española has rectified the situation that J. H. Arjona described in regard to *La desdichada Estefanía* "that the folios of the autograph manuscript are in utter disorder in the binding recently done for the Academia." [8] When examined extensively in July, 1966 by the editor, the manuscript was quite in order.

II. *Editions*

There are five printed editions and a manuscript copy of *La desdichada Estefanía*. The play first appeared in 1619, the elev-

---

[7] Extracted from a letter by William L. Fichter to Joseph H. Silverman, dated February 23, 1963, Brown University, Providence, R. I.

[8] J. H. Arjona. "Defective Rhymes and Rhyming Techniques in Lope de Vega's Autograph Comedias," *HR*, XXIII (1955), p. 114.

enth work (folios 241-262) in the *Dozena parte de las comedias de Lope de Vega Carpio,* [9] "Con Privilegio. En Madrid, Por la viuda de Alonso Martin, A costa de Alonso Perez mercader de libros." The *Parte* carries a dedication, "A Don Lorenzo de Cardenas, Conde de la Puebla, quarto nieto de don Alfonso de Cardenas, Gran Maestre de Santiago," with the Cárdenas coat of arms (two wolves, one shown above the other, with a border of castles and lions, alternated). It is referred to hereafter as M.

A second *Dozena Parte,* appearing the same year, with a different *escudo* (a centaur with a drawn bow, and the encircling legend, "Salvbris Sagita a Deo Missa"), was long believed to be identical to the other edition, or that at most it had only minor differences. [10] It is designated S in subsequent references. It is not known which *Parte* was printed first. After comparing the *Dozena Parte* texts of *Fuenteovejuna* alone, Anibal concluded that there must have been two separate, distinct printings. His conclusions are fully supported in comparing the versions of *La desdichada Estefanía.* Not only are there frequent variations between the two in the text itself, there are also differences in the type which was used (e.g., the *reparto* of M uses a capital *R* with an extended tail in several cases, while S has the regular *R* throughout; in v. 789, M has *cõcierto,* S uses the full form, *concierto;* S erroneously shows folio 259 for the correct M foliation, 256). The major element which both have in common is the vast number of changes made in the text of the play. To quote Arjona, they are "horrendous," with "innumerable omissions, countless transpositions, and just as many alterations. There are very few stanzas of the autograph left untouched." [11] As is usual-

---

[9] Juan Isidro Fajardo, *Títulos de todas las comedias que en verso español y portugués se han impreso hasta el año 1786* (Madrid, 1787), fol. 16 [r], records "*Desdichada Estefanía o Castros y Andrades,* de Lope, en su *Parte* 22". A careful examination of the manner in which Fajardo wrote numbers shows that he did indeed err in his *Parte* designation for the play. Lope's *Peregrino* list does not mention the play, but F. Medèl del Castillo has it in his "Indice general," *RHi,* LXXV (1929), p. 172. La Barrera, *Ac.,* I, p. 319, possibly influenced by Fajardo, gives *Castros y Andrades* as a second title of the play.

[10] C. E. Anibal, "Lope de Vega's *Dozena Parte,*" *MLN,* XLVII (1932), pp. 1-7, discusses these opinions and other ideas relating to *Parte XII.*

[11] Arjona, *op. cit.,* p. 114.

ly the case, these *Parte* changes do nothing to enhance the work, rather they lead to confusion, distortion, and nonsense verse.

In 1630 the *Doze comedias nuevas de Lope de Vega Carpio y otros autores, segunda parte,* was published in Barcelona by Gerónimo Margarit. It is often referred to as an *extravagante* edition. *La desdichada Estefanía* is the eleventh work in the collection. It seems to derive from one or both *Parte* editions, carrying most of their errors and changes. As might be expected, there are further alterations in this version, which the *Catálogo* describes as: "Edición igual a la anterior [*Dozena Parte*], de la que sólo se diferencia en el escudo de la portada y en los preliminares." [12] It is designated B in the list of variants.

Agustín G. de Amezúa reported in 1945 the existence of a manuscript copy of *La desdichada Estefanía,* the fourth work in Volume IV of a collection, signed by the copyist, Ignacio de Gálvez. [13] A photostatic copy of the Gálvez manuscript was fortunately available for study and inclusion in the variants of this work. Of the thirty-two plays of the Gálvez collection, Amezúa states that:

> No todas las obras dramáticas copiadas por Gálvez presentan variantes: ora por tratarse de autógrafos a los que Lope pasó ya las correcciones de su primera redacción, ora por tratarse de copias genuinas y revisadas por él para regalarlas a su señor y mecenas el Duque de Sessa. [14]

Amezúa does not mention *La desdichada Estefanía* as one of the plays showing variants, though a comparison of the Gálvez manuscript with the autograph reveals over fifty changes in the text itself, and many in the stage directions. The copy is designated G in the list of variants. The manuscript has proved very useful in clarifying doubtful readings of the autograph and corroborating others.

Another edition of the play appears in the Academy edition of Lope's *Obras,* with a preliminary study by Menéndez y Pe-

---

[12] *Catálogo,* p. 87, No. 326.
[13] Amezúa, *Colección,* pp. 42-43.
[14] *Ibid.,* p. 79.

layo. [15] This text is based on the 1619 editions, [16] with notes for "las escasas variantes que ofrece el texto de esta tragicomedia en la *Segunda Parte* apócrifa o *extravagante* de Barcelona (1630)." [17] Of the eight *variantes* noted by Menéndez y Pelayo, six are incorrect, and will be duly noted in the Manuscript Notes. No mention is made of the more than fifty other variants between the 1619 and 1630 editions. In an effort to render the unintelligible passages of the 17th-century texts comprehensible, the editor introduced further changes which more often than not only add to the confusion. Arbitrary changes which add nothing to the play were also introduced (e.g., in v. 763 *graues* as *grandes pasos*). This edition is designated A in the list of variants.

The latest version of *La desdichada Estefanía* is a paleographic edition prepared by J. H. Arjona (*La desdichada Estefanía, edición paleográfica*, Estudios de Hispanófila, No. 6, Ed. Castalia: Madrid, 1967), with a brief section of *Observaciones preliminares*. In the main, this version and the present edition are in agreement on the resolution of most transcription difficulties. In those cases where there is a difference of opinion, either a manuscript note is provided, or the variant is listed among the other variant readings. Professor Arjona notes the variant readings only of A, stating that "... resulta innecesario anotar las variantes de la primera edición o repetir la compulsa ya hecha de la segunda" (p. 13). The reader is thus left with the impression that there was only one 1619 edition, and that, by listing A's variants, most cases of divergences from the autograph text will be covered adequately. Even a cursory glance at the listings of variants as noted in the present edition will suffice to show that this is not the case. In addition, Professor Arjona omitted many of the variant readings in A (e.g., vv. 497, 568, 758, 760, 791, 822, 1100, etc.). A further defect in his listing of A's variants consists of his recording the variant reading in italics, and continuing the editor's comments in italics also (see n. 976, p. 45; n. 1750, p. 73). The reverse occurs as well; he notes the variant reading in straight

---

[15] The text of the play is in *Ac.*, VIII, pp. 331-363, with the "Observaciones preliminares" on pp. lxvi-lxxvii.

[16] "Menéndez y Pelayo no pudo aprovechar el manuscrito autógrafo." Amezúa, *Colección*, p. 43.

[17] *Ac.*, VIII, p. 331, n. 1.

type and continues the editor's comment in straight type as well. This situation occurs also in his notes describing the manuscript (see n. 111-130, p. 20; n. 271, p. 25).

In many instances, Professor Arjona's notes deciphering deletions, marginal notations and underlinings are incomplete or are inaccurate (see the Manuscript Notes for vv. 290-302, 521-22, 556, 894, etc.). The solution proposed by Arjona for many of the deletions and alterations is questionable (see the Manuscript Notes for vv. 5, 111-115, 419, 517-522, 556, 895, 1118, etc.).

Although he reports that "Fuera de alguna que otra letra o sílaba que he añadido *(siempre entre corchetes)*", (p. 10, underlining mine), there are several instances where he added words or letters without indicating that he was supplying them (see the Manuscript Notes, vv. 1087, 1586, 1726, 2320, 2467, 2607, etc.).

Arjona's reproduction of Lope's orthography is generally accurate. There are, however, a number of instances where changes in orthography were introduced (e.g., vv. 291, 669, 685, 926, 992, 1069, 1103, 1355, etc.).

Arjona mentions that G was unavailable for examination and inclusion in his study, and does not indicate that the autograph manuscript was examined.

Professor Arjona follows a system of punctuation which is quite different, on occasion, from that used in the present edition. These differences reflect personal preferences, at times, rather than a conflict of interpretation. In the view of this editor, Arjona tends to punctuate as if the play were to be read only, and does not seem to consider the text from the standpoint of what might be expected of the spoken language. This leads to a "choppy" effect in reading verse, instead of aiding the flow of thought. The following passages, which appear at the beginning of Act I, will serve to illustrate this difference in punctuation patterns.

En esta breue distanzia,	En esta breue distanzia,
aunq̄ es grande la gananzia,	aunque es grande la gananzia
q̄ fuesse, no es marauilla,	que fuesse, no es marauilla
corta huéspeda Castilla,	corta huéspeda Castilla,
Luis, para un Rey de Franzia.	Luis, para un Rey de Franzia.
Mal sin regalo os detengo,	Mal sin regalo os detengo,
pues sólo en esta ocasión,	pues sólo en esta ocasión
en q̄ a reçiuiros vengo,	en que a reçiuiros vengo,

he ensanchado el corazón,
donde como a hijo os tengo.
   (Arjona, vv. 11-20)

Déstas tantas ha mostrado
Castilla, q̄ voy, señor,
   (Arjona, vv. 26-27)

Dios y vos lo hauéis de hazer:
Dios, con ayudar el çelo
de vrā. fee contra el moro;
vos, en derribar al suelo
su imperio, y deste tesoro
ofreziendo el quinto al çielo;
q̄ tenéis de ilustre gente,
q̄ en las fiestas han mostrado
tal balor, q̄ no consiente
ygualdad con el pasado
ni fama con el presente.
   (Arjona, vv. 35-45)

¡Q̄ gallardos caballeros!
Conquistar pueden mil mundos,
naciendo entre moros fieros,
en la edad al Cid segundos,
pero en el balor primeros.
   (Arjona, vv. 46-50)

he ensanchado el corazón,
donde como a hijo os tengo.
   (This Edition, vv. 11-20)

Déstas, tantas ha mostrado
Castilla, que voy, señor,
   (This Edition, vv. 26-27)

Dios y vos lo hauéis de hazer:
Dios, con ayudar el çelo
de v[uest]ra fee contra el moro;
vos, en derribar al suelo
su imperio, y deste tesoro
ofreziendo el quinto al çielo.
Que tenéis de ilustre gente,
que en las fiestas han mostrado
tal balor, que no consiente
ygualdad con el pasado
ni fama con el presente.
   (This Edition, vv. 35-45)

¡Qué gallardos caballeros!
Conquistar pueden mil mundos,
naciendo entre moros fieros;
en la edad, al Cid segundos,
pero en el balor primeros.
   (This Edition, vv. 46-50)

In the first passage, Arjona appears to avoid *encabalgamiento,* which tends to produce a "sing-song" effect in speaking the lines.

In the second section, the avoidance of a slight pause after *Déstas* would induce the listener to perceive that *Déstas* is used to modify *tantas,* instead of referring back to *grandezas.*

The third passage, at v. 35, establishes a two-part statement closed by a colon, followed by the two sub-sections amplifying the statement, each separated by a semi-colon. The thought is completed at v. 40, calling for a period, but Arjona uses a semi-colon. The thought of vv. 41-45 amplifies the second sub-section immediately preceding, but also serves as a bridge for the exclamation of v. 46, and is not an integral element of the foregoing two-part statement.

In the fourth passage, Arjona uses a comma at the end of v. 48 instead of a semi-colon. The latter seems more appropriate for a passage which is evenly divided into two sub-sections of two verses each, the first verse in both cases ending with a comma. The sense of the passage calls for a slightly longer pause at v. 48. The construction of this section is parallel with that of vv. 25-45.

There is an unfortunate error in the versification tables prepared by Professor Arjona. He indicates a tabulation of 900 verses for Act III, instead of the correct number of 880, for a total of 2808 lines (p. 12).

His resolution of the *licencias y censuras*, at best a difficult task, provides a number of contrasts with the version of this edition. Rather than list these points one by one, the Arjona transcription is reproduced in the Appendix for comparison purposes.

The Arjona edition is designated J in the list of variants.

In view of the type of defects noted above, the Arjona edition should not be used by investigators as their sole source of contemporary information regarding *La desdichada Estefanía*.

III. *This Edition*

The preparation of this edition follows the norms set forth by William L. Fichter in his Preface to *El sembrar en buena tierra*. [18] That is, Lope's autograph has been transcribed exactly as he wrote it, with the following exceptions:

1) Punctuation, which is erratic in the original, has been used extensively in this edition as an aid in clarifying the meaning of speeches. It is realized that in a number of instances the manuscript offers other possibilities of interpretation.

2) Capitalization has been modernized.

3) Accents have been supplied in accordance with modern practice. In the few cases where Lope omitted a tilde, it has been restored without comment. A *c*, instead of a *ç* (before *e* or *i*) has not been altered. Dieresis is added when it is required for pronunciation (e.g., *agüelo*, v. 666).

---

[18] Fichter, *op. cit.*, pp. vii-ix.

4) Abbreviations have been resolved, and letters supplied are between brackets. Only q̃ for *que* and the abbreviated names of characters are written in their resolved form without brackets. Any letters or words not in the original are bracketed (e.g., *vengo [a] hallarte*, v. 368), as are indications of the verso of each folio. Parentheses enclose the unnecessary repetition of character names.

As previously indicated, the Manuscript Notes contain a transcription of all legible material which has been crossed out. Also in this section is a description of points concerning the actual appearance of the manuscript, marginal notations, etc.

The Notes to the Text contain explanatory information relative to words, ideas, themes, etc., which need clarification or identification for a fuller appreciation of the play. Though not intended to be exhaustive, it is hoped that they will prove sufficient to guide the reader through the areas of difficulty. Annotated material is identified in the text by an asterisk in the right margin of the line in question.

The variant readings of the other editions are found in the footnotes. If further discussion of a variant is deemed necessary, an asterisk indicates that more information will be found in the Manuscript Notes.

Synopsis of the Play

Act I: King Luis of France has come to Spain, ostensibly to make a pilgrimage to Santiago de Compostela, but in reality to ascertain the truth about his wife, Costanza, who is rumored to be the illegitimate daughter of King Alfonso. The latter hastens to assure him that she is, indeed, his legitimate offspring. At this point Fernán Ruiz de Castro, one of Alfonso's nobles, and Fortunio Ximénez (also referred to as Fortún), who serves Luis, exchange insults, Castro accusing Ximénez of originating the rumor. Castro challenges him to a duel, but is refused *canpo*, first by Alfonso, then by Luis. Castro then designates Fez as their meeting ground and leaves after angrily reproaching Alfonso. The scene shifts to the convent where Estefanía, Alfonso's real illegitimate daughter, is swearing her eternal love to Castro. Ximénez arrives to announce the impending visit of the Kings, and almost comes to blows with Castro. The latter again leaves angrily, while Estefanía is presented to Luis, who asks that she be married to Ximénez. Forced to agree, she first requires that Ximénez return victorious from his duel with Castro. Ysabel, her slave, expresses her delight with the prospective marriage, calculating to fulfill her own long-standing love for Ximénez. Next, Castro and Mudarra, his servant (who loves Ysabel), arrive in Fez and are given permission to hold the duel. But a group of Moors, led by Albumasar, plans to murder their ruler and crown Abdelmón king. The drum beat announcing the *desafío* is confused by them with the signal for their revolt. The act closes as Castro urges Mudarra to help in defending the Miramamolín, but Mudarra is more concerned that he may not be able to return to Spain with a monkey for Estefanía and Ysabel.

Act II: Ximénez tells King Alfonso of his attempt to reach Fez for his duel there with Castro, and of the rebellion which prevented him from doing so. He warns the King that Abdelmón is gathering his forces for an invasion of Spain. Alfonso reacts to this news with confidence and orders that Estefanía appear to marry Ximénez. Sadly she is forced to agree to the marriage, but vows to herself that her soul will refuse it. Castro and Mudarra, having learned of the impending marriage, hasten to the King. After denouncing Ximénez for not appearing, Castro reveals that he has courted Estefanía for six years. Alfonso then allows Estefanía to choose between them. After she selects Castro, both Ysabel and Ximénez voice their despair. But Ysabel, still plotting to have Ximénez, informs him that Estefanía really does love him and that she will serve as their go-between. At first Ximénez is suspicious, but she quickly allays his fears, and both express jubilation: she will have him by trickery; he will get his revenge on Castro. A series of three evil omens mar the marriage of the young couple, and both express apprehension, as does the King. Sancho Laynez arrives with the news that the *moros almohades* have invaded the country, taken several cities, and threaten to overrun Spain. Alfonso again expresses confidence, plans to gather his troops, and name his captains. Castro, he announces, is to have the wedding period free of duties while the men assemble from the various provinces.

Act III: Ximénez, accompanied by his servant Olfos, keeps a rendezvous with a woman they believe to be Estefanía, but in reality it is Ysabel. They climb the garden wall by means of a ladder which Olfos has carried. But Bermudo and Ximeno, faithful servants of Castro, see the men talking with a woman they also believe to be Estefanía. Bermudo resolves to kill the couple to protect his master's honor, but Ximeno advises against such action to avoid possible future reprisals. Castro and Mudarra, riding back to Burgos, happily discuss the birth of Castro's son. They are met by Bermudo and Ximeno, who request that Mudarra be sent ahead so they can speak privately with their master. When he has gone, they inform Castro of what they have seen, and ask that he believe not them, but his own eyes. When Castro reaches home, Estefanía's joyous greeting for him is contrasted with his preoccupation as he considers her possible guilt. Fortunio later confesses to Olfos that what at first was a desire for vengeance against Castro has become true love for Estefanía. He plans to keep another rendezvous with her in spite of Olfos's warning. Castro, who has feigned business in Burgos, awaits the arrival of Estefanía and her suitor in the garden, accompanied by Bermudo and Ximeno. When the two lovers are observed, Castro kills Ximénez; Bermudo and Ximeno capture Olfos; Ysabel flees to her mistress's bedroom and hides under the bed. Castro pursues her, and in the darkness stabs the form on the bed. Estefanía, their son in her arms, awakens, dying, protesting her innocence. Bermudo, Ximeno and Mudarra enter, the latter lamenting her murder, also protesting her innocence. Ysabel is discovered and confesses as Estefanía dies. Castro leaves for Alfonso's court, ordering that Ysabel be burned alive. He relates to Alfonso the events leading to his crime and begs that justice be done. Alfonso, stunned, does not himself pass judgement, but rather leaves sentence to his judges. The play ends with an invitation to the public to learn the remainder of the story in a second play, for the thread of the first ends here.

HISTORICAL SOURCES

Menéndez y Pelayo has pointed out in his *Observaciones Preliminares* to the *Academia* edition a number of areas of the play which echo the events of history. [19] This fact bears out the statement by Edwin S. Morby that "Lope does not often flout the tradition that tragedy select its material from historical sources." [20] The designation of *La desdichada Estefanía* as "Tragedia Primera," and again as a *tragedia* in v. 2802 invites a comparison of Lope's scenes with what is available in the records of history. The relevance of such an investigation is subscribed to by Arnold G. Reichenberger, who writes that "it is incumbent upon the editor of a historical play to study the literature available at the writer's time, both for the general concept of the theme and for a possible direct source." [21]

Of the three historical situations in the play (the visit of King Luis VIII of France to Spain, the illegitimacy of Estefanía and her death at the hands of Fernán Ruiz de Castro, the invasion of the *moros almohades* under the leadership of Abdelmón) Menéndez y Pelayo discusses only the first two. He partially reproduces texts of Sandoval, [22] the *Crónica general,* [23] and the *Libro de linajes* [24] which correspond to the situations in the play.

Of Luis's pilgrimage to Santiago, Menéndez y Pelayo writes that "la primera escena de la comedia de Lope es casi una paráfrasis del texto de la *Crónica general.*" [25] Sandoval's report reduces greatly the detail of the *Crónica general.* The latter work's lengthy treatment of Luis's visit in Spain is used only as a point of departure by Lope. Some scenes suggest a stronger influence from the *Crónica* than others, but Menéndez y Pelayo's description of the first scene as almost a paraphrase of the text is not quite accurate. Lope has altered, omitted and invented material,

---

[19] *Ac.,* VIII, pp. lxvii-lxxii.

[20] Edwin S. Morby, "Some Observations on *Tragedia* and *Tragicomedia* in Lope," *HR,* XI (1943), p. 192.

[21] Reichenberger, *op. cit.,* pp. 34-35.

[22] F. Prudencio Sandoval, *Historia de los reyes de Castilla y de León* (Madrid, 1792), II, pp. 314-315. Menéndez y Pelayo consulted the work under the title *Crónica de los cinco reyes* (Pamplona, 1615), p. 210.

[23] *Primera crónica general de España, publicada por Ramón Menéndez Pidal* (Madrid, 1955), II, Sec. 978, pp. 656-58. Menéndez y Pelayo cites a 1604 edition.

[24] D. Pedro de Barcellos, "Os livros de linhagens," *Portugalliae monumenta historica, Scriptores* (Lisboa, 1856), I, pp. 265-67.

[25] Marcelino Menéndez y Pelayo, *Estudios sobre el teatro de Lope de Vega* (Santander, 1949), IV, p. 16.

which in conjunction help constitute a basically different account than that of the *Crónica*. Examples of the play and the *Crónica* follow. The surprise that Luis registers upon seeing the richness of Alfonso's court is expressed thus:

Crónica, 656a-b

Sopo dantes ell emperador aquella uenida del rey don Loys de Francia, et enuio por todos sus ricos omnes et por sus cauallerias muy grandes, et dixoles como el rey de Francia uinie, et yua en romeria a Santyago, et que se guisassen todos muy bien pora salir a recebirle con el, que grand debdo auien todos en fazerlo. Et ellos guisaronse todos muy bien de muchos pares de pannos muy nobles, et de muy buenos cauallos et muy assazonados, et de muy buenas mulas; et segund dize ell arçobispo don Rodrigo et las otras estorias que acuerdan con ell, que era y con ell estonces el rey de Nauarra. Et ayuntaronsse todos en Burgos, et salieron todos muy bien guisados a grand marauilla, et cada unos con sus azemilas muy buenas et muchas dellas, et cargadas de muchos buenos repuestes, cada unos los suyos; et salieron desta guisa a reçebir a don Loys rey de Francia. Aqui dize el arçobispo que, quando el rey de Francia uio aquel reçebimiento que ell rey de Castiella le fazie, et uio tantos omnes buenos et tan onrrados, quien querie en buen cauallo, quien querie en buena mula, et uio otrossi tanta caualleria de caualleros mancebos, todos apuestos et grandes et guisados pora todo buen fecho, et los otros guisamientos tantos et tan grandes, que dize ell arçobispo que quando todo aquello uio esse rey don Loys, que se marauillo tanto que non sabie a que catar, et que en la uista sola esbaherecio.

Lope, vv. 21-52

Quando el huésped que reçiue
es pobre, cunple mostrando
la voluntad con que uiue;
quando es rico, sólo obrando
las grandezas que aperçiue.
Déstas, tantas ha mostrado
Castilla, que voy, señor,
de v[uest]ro reyno admirado.
Justamente Emperador
de España fuistes llamado.
No crehí que tal poder
teníades. ¡Cosa estraña!
Dios os dexe, Alfonso, ver
Rei absoluto de España.
Dios y vos lo hauéis de hazer:
Dios con ayudar el çelo
de v[uest]ra fee contra el moro;
vos en derribar al suelo
su imperio, y deste tesoro
ofreziendo el quinto al çielo.
Que tenéis de ilustre gente,
que en las fiestas han mostrado
tal balor, que no consiente
ygualdad con el pasado
ni fama con el presente.
¡Qué gallardos caballeros!
Conquistar pueden mil mundos,
naciendo entre moros fieros;
en la edad, al Cid segundos,
pero en el balor primeros.
Yo llebo bien que contar
a mis nobles en París.

Concerning the real reason for Luis's visit to Spain, Lope has Luis question Alfonso directly about the legitimacy of Costanza. In the *Crónica*, on two separate occasions, Luis is shown expressing satisfaction concerning this point without specifically questioning Alfonso. The *Crónica* first says:

> ... et todas tan bien guisadas que las siruientas semeiauan unas sennoras. Et alli entendio el rey don Loys muy bien que aquellos auoles omnes quel dixieran que la reyna donna Helisabet su muger que non era fija del emperador et de la emperadriz donna Berenguela, quel mintieran yl dixieran falssedat. ... (p. 656b)

Later, in Toledo, Alfonso speaks of the subject:

> Dixo al rey don Loys assi: "rey Loys, veet et sabet que en la emperadriz donna Berenguella, hermana deste conde de Barçilona, fiz yo la mi fija donna Helisabet, que yo a uos di por mugier et con quien oy sodes casado. (p. 657b)

Lope's dialogue is seen in contrast with another section of the *Crónica*:

Crónica, 656a	Lope, vv. 106-131
... murmuriauan a la oreia a esse rey don Loys, diziendol que su mugier la reyna donna Helisabet que non la ouiera ell emperador don Alffonsso en su mugier la reyna, mas que la fiziera en una su barragana, et non fijadalgo, mas mugier uil. El rey don Loys, diziendol aquellos omnes malos et uiles esta razon muchas uezes, pesol, et ouo de tornar y cabesça et pensso en prouarlo et como lo podrie fazer; et guisosse como rey romero pora uenir et prouar si era assi; et cogiosse daquella guisa, et uenose por Espanna como romero, en uoz que yua en romeria a Santyague et uiniesse por el camino por o los otros romeros uan en su romeria a aquell apostol.	LUIS Tu hija, Alfonso, me diste en casamiento. ALFONSO Es verdad. LUIS Ser legítima dixiste, y ygual a la magestad que en França y sus reyes uiste. ALFONSO ¿Quién lo duda? LUIS Yo, que he sido de lo contrario ynformado, y que bastarda ha naçido Alfonso, y que has engañado quien no te lo ha mereçido. ¿Costanza, bastarda tuya, me das a mí?

ALFONSO

                                            ¿Que a esto vienes
de Françia?

LUIS

... ...
Con esta pena fingí
la romería a Santiago
por informarme de ti,
para no darle mal pago
a quien quiero más que a mí.
Dime, Alfonso, la verdad.

Luis's esteem and affection for Costanza is displayed on several occasions by Lope, while the *Crónica* shows Luis in a somewhat more cynical attitude. After he is sure that his wife is legitimate he is described thus: "Amo a su mugier donna Helisabet muy mas que no solie" (p. 658a). Illustrative passages from Lope and the *Crónica* follow.

Crónica, 657a

Et dalli touo por muy meior et muy mas alto el fecho de donna Helisabet su mugier que no fazie ante, et la preçiaron el rey don Loys et toda Francia, et la onrraron et la ouieron mayor uerguença dalli adelante.

658a

Esto passado et librado todo, espidiosse el rey de Francia por yrse, et dixo de cabo en su espedimiento que se tenie por muy onrrado del casamiento de donna Helisabet, fija del emperador don Alffonsso et de la emperadriz donna Berenguella, et entergado con ella, et que en quanto ell uisquiesse siempre la onrrarie quanto pudiesse, como duenna de tan alta guisa deue seer onrrada.

Lope, vv. 118-125

          La graçia suya
y mil naturales bienes
quieren que su sangre arguya,
mas yo tengo informaçión
de que es bastarda Costanza,
y entre reyes no es razón
engañar la confianza
y ofender la estimaçión.

vv. 268-273

No ay cosa que yo pretenda
como el çierto desengaño
de mi amada y dulçe prenda.
Señor, dadme este contento,
porque sepa yo que ha sido
legítimo el casamiento.

An echo of the *Crónica* is voiced by Fernán Ruiz de Castro as he accuses Fortunio Ximénez of inciting Luis:

Crónica, 656a

Unos omnes malos et auoles et de
mala parte, segunt dize ell arçobispo,
queriendo meter mal et desabenencia
et desamor entrell emperador don
Allffonsso et don Loys rey de Francia, ...

Lope, vv. 156-163

Tu mudable condizión
y el desseo de venganza
ha hecho aquesta inuenzión,
porque tienes esperanza
de tu injusta posesión.
Y mouiendo los que están
en paz a perpetua guerra,
quando las manos se dan ...

One of the major deviations from the *Crónica* text occurs when
Alfonso speaks of his and Berenguela's children:

Crónica, 654b

Pues ouo ell emperador estas dos
mugieres, una empos ell otra et amas
lindas: la primera donna Berenguella,
hermana de conde don Remont de
Barçilona; et en esta fizo all inffante
don Sancho y all inffante don Ffer-
nando, et estas dos fijas: donna Helisabet et donna Baesça. Esta inffante [*sic*] donna Helisabet casaron con
don Loys, rey de Francia.

Lope, vv. 276-283

De Berenguela, mi muger primera,
tube tres hijos y una hija sola:
Sancho, el mayor, Fernando, y don/
                                    Garçía,
y Costanza Ysabel, que todo es vno.
Por dicha, equiuocándose en los/
                                    nonbres,
piensan que os engañé, Rey cris-/
                                    tianísimo,
y que por daros a Ysabel, mi hija,
os he dado a Costanza.

Alfonso thus attempts to provide a possible explanation for the
origin of the rumors Luis has heard. It is simply that Costanza
was also known by the name Ysabel. The use of two names for
one daughter may be purely Lope's invention for the purposes
of Alfonso's explanation, or the combination of names may be
referred to in some writings of the period which are not presently
known to the editor. Angel Gamayo y Catalán speaks of two
daughters, Constancia and Sancha, but he does not refer to
Baesça, named in the *Crónica.* Like the latter work, Gamayo y
Catalán notes only two sons, Sancho and Fernando. [26]

Closely linked to Luis's pilgrimage is the introduction of Estefanía, the illegitimate daughter of Alfonso. The avowal of

---

[26] Angel Gamayo y Catalán, *Crónica histórica de los doce Alfonsos de
Castilla y de León* (Madrid, 1878), pp. 57 and 59.

Costanza's legitimacy by Alfonso allows Lope to present her and her background as a possible factor in Luis's misunderstanding. The *Crónica* says little of her, but as Menéndez y Pelayo indicates, Sandoval's *Chrónica del ínclito emperador de España, don Alonso VII* (Madrid, 1600. See Menéndez y Pelayo, *Estudios, op. cit., p.* 25) was available to Lope, with its translation of Estefanía's lineage directly from *Os livros de linhagens* by don Pedro de Barcellos. The Portuguese version will be found in the Appendix for comparison with the following Spanish text from Sandoval. The *Crónica general's* reference to Estefanía appears first:

Crónica, 655a

Empos esto cuenta don Luchas de Tuy que fizo ell emperador don Alffonsso en una donzella muy fijadalgo, que dizien donna Maria, una fija que dixeron Esteuania, donzella muy fermosa.

Sandoval, pp. 80-81

Esta [Ximena Núñez] fue casada cõ Fernan Lainez, hijo de Diego Lainez, padre de Ruy Diaz el Cid. Hizo en ella à don Aluar Fernandez, y porq̃ tenia à Castro Xeriz del Rey en tenẽcia, è auia alli vn solar de aquellos de donde decendian, que fuera del Conde don Gutierre, llamose por esso el de Castro, porq̃ era Conde, y fidalgo asaz. ... E don Aluar Fernandez fue casado con doña Mencia Assures, hija del Conde don Pedro Assures de Carrion, è ouo en ella vna hija, que se llamò doña Maria Aluarez, que casò con don Fernando, hijo de ganancia del Rey de Nauarra, è ouo en ella tres hijos ... El tercero Gutierre Fernandez: don Fernan Fernandez casò con doña Maria Aluarez, hija del Conde don Aluaro de Hita, è ouo en ella vn hijo y vna hija: el hijo ouo nõbre Martin Fer-

Lope, vv. 284-304

... piensan que os he cassado con/
       la bella
y hermosa Estefanía, a quien agora
veréys para más prueba deste en-/
       gaño.

LUIS

Pues, ¿quién es essa bella Estefanía?

ALFONSO

Vna hija que tuue de vna dama
tan buena como yo, porque fue nieta
del Conde Albar Fernández, el de/
       Castro,
sobrino de aquel Çid, honor del/
       mundo,
y de doña Menzía Ansures, hija
del baleroso Conde Pedro Ansures.
Fue hija doña Sancha, que este/
       nombre
tubo esta dama, de Fernán Garzía,
hijo del Rey Garzía de Nauarra.
Así que Estefanía se pudiera
cassar con qualquier príncipe del/
       mundo,
por ser de tantos reyes sangre ilustre.
Que lo que le faltó de ser legítima,
suple su gran belleza y alto ingenio,
aconpañado de virtudes raras.
Esta es la hija que bastarda tengo,
y no Costanza, Rey...

nandez, è fue muy buen cauallero, è
murio sin hijos de edad de 26 años:
la hija se llamò doña Sancha, cuya
hermosura fue tanta, que el Emperador se aficionò ciegamente à ella ...
tuuo lugar de darse al Emperador, y
fue su amiga, y huuo en ella vna hija
que se llamò doña Estefania, que
casò con Fernan Ruyz de Castro,
gustando dello el Emperador, por ser
Fernan Ruyz de tan ilustre sangre.

Gamayo y Catalán accepts Sancha as the name of Estefanía's
mother, calling her a "dama de ilustre estirpe castellana," [27] but
Flórez de Setién remarks specifically, "también es de notar que
el Tudense llama María a la amiga del emperador, madre de la
infanta doña Estefanía, diciendo que era una señora nobilísima.
... El nombre no concuerda, sino en caso de que doña Sancha se
llamase también María." [28] But Sandoval, in his commentary on
the Portuguese text, states only that "de una dama que se llamó
doña María, hubo el Emperador esta señora doña Estefanía; no
hallo quien diga de qué gente era," [29] pointing out that the history
of Estefanía, as presented by don Pedro de Barcellos, contains
factual errors. Whatever the historical truth may be, it is evident
that Lope followed closely the lineage indicated above, either
from Sandoval's work or from another contemporaneous source.

The *Crónica general*'s account of Fernán Ruiz de Castro has
three sections of particular interest:

> En aquel tiempo era aquel noble uaron Fernando Royz
> de Castro, et por sobre nombre el Castellano ... veno
> aquel noble Ferrand Royç de Castro el Castellano, et dio
> la tierra libre et quita, aquella que el tenie, a su sennor
> don Alffonsso rey de Castiella. Et el fuesse de la tierra,
> et passosse a moros, et tornosse con grand muchadum-
> bre de moros et ueno apriessa alli do es agora Çipdad

---

[27] Gamayo y Catalán, *op. cit.*, p. 59.
[28] P. Enrique Flórez de Setién, *Memorias de las reinas católicas de
España* (Madrid, 1959), I, p. 403.
[29] From the text reproduced by Menéndez y Pelayo, *Estudios, op. cit.*,
p. 28.

> Rodrigo por tomar dantes el logar, et los pobladores como eran nueuos, que se no guardarien . . . (673b)

> Mas este Ffernand Royz el Castellano, non sabiendo estar quedo nin en paç, començo de yr contra los castellanos et de boluer muy de rrezio contienda et batalla contra ellos . . . (674a)

> El rey don Fferrando de Leon tomo a donna Esteuania su hermana de padre, et casola con aquel Ferand Royç el Castellano; et esse Fferand Royç fizo en aquella donna Esteuania un fijo que ouo nombre Pero Ferrandez el Castellano otrossi, que fue despues uaron de grand guisa et que fue muy onrrado con los reyes. (674b-675a)

The first passage probably suggested to Lope Fernán's journey to Africa for his duel with Fortunio Ximénez. Where the *Crónica* shows Fernán in alliance with the Moors, Lope emphasizes his allegiance to Alfonso by the following:

MIRAMAMOLÍN   Ya suena acá
la exçelençia de su nombre.
¿Querráme seruir a mí
si le trata mal su Rey?
LEARÍN   Defiende tanto su ley
que dudo el pensar que sí,
mas yo le hablaré, que el sol
no ha uisto mexor soldado.
MIRAMAMOLÍN   Estimaré que a mi lado
asista vn Castro español.   (vv. 980-89)

The second sample from the *Crónica* helps to explain Lope's characterization of Fernán in Acts I and II as a contentious noble with a penchant for speaking his mind, even to the King. [30] The third establishes that Fernán Ruiz and Estefanía were married, though not by Alfonso (as also noted by Sandoval, *Historia*).

Where Sandoval has suggested emotion or stated fact simply in narrative terms, Lope has expanded and refined, shaping elements to mesh smoothly in his dramatic version of the historical

---

[30] G. Cirot, "Une chronique latine inédite des rois de Castille (1236)," *BHi*, XIV (1912), pp. 248-49, n. 10.1, has reference to Fernán's chronicled battles against his countrymen.

account. Sandoval writes: "Y que en el huerto entraba aquel hombre *saltando las paredes* [italics mine]." [31] This is a motif which, with its echoes from *La Celestina* (Act IV), is developed into several scenes in Act III (vv. 1929-2104, 2487-2544, 2583-2600, etc.). Sandoval says of the servants that: "Zelando su honra, le dixeron que su muger le hazía trayción haziendo lo que está dicho." The description is evolved to give Bermudo a motivation for "zelando su honra" (vv. 1995-2053), and Lope adds to their accounting to Fernán by their hesitation to tell him what they had seen (vv. 2156-2308). Fernán, in Sandoval's words, "creyólo fácilmente," but not so easily that he does not first warn the servants, in Lope's rendition: "Abrí muy bien los ojos" (v. 2217). In the play, Fernán repudiates their story, begins to have doubts, and he gradually comes to suspect that they are telling the truth. Sandoval states: "Ciego Ruy Fernández con la passión de tal caso" and "'ciega y torpemente la maté.'" Lope develops this material into a body of references to *los ojos, el ver*, and the *engaño* they involve, interwoven through vv. 2031-2360.

Sandoval states that: "Le atravessaba el alma la muerte tan sin culpa de su querida mujer: no hallaba poder tener consuelo jamás, pues el daño era tan sin remedio." Here is the nucleus of Fernán's tragedy, the point to which all the elements of the play are subordinated. In the historical account Alfonso pardons Fernán: "Ruy Fernández de Castro, yo os doy por bueno e por leal. Este fecho bien parece fue más caso que otro, y assí sois vos sin culpa." [32] Lope structures his play in such a way that we have a deeper awareness of the real tragedy of Fernán, who "no hallaba poder tener consuelo jamás," by leaving him in that suspended position between crime and punishment, a Limbo from which he is not removed in this play. Lope sensed the dramatic possibilities of the basic situation and, not limiting himself to the historical account, developed it more fully through emphasis and broadening of detail. The following brief example will illustrate this:

---

[31] Menéndez y Pelayo, *op. cit.*, p. 26. References to Sandoval in the following lines can be found on pp. 26-28.

[32] See the section on Honor for a discussion of *caso* as *honor*.

Sandoval, from Menéndez y Pelayo, *Estudios*, IV, pp. 26-27

Lope, vv. 2563-2571

Ciego Ruy Fernández con la passión, arremetió para ellos con un puñal en las manos: y porque el hombre no se le fuesse cerró con él, dándole de puñaladas. Embarazado en esto, tuvo lugar la camarera de huir, que los escuderos, entendiendo que era su señora, no la echaron mano: y assí ella pudo yrse, y a todo correr, como quien escapa de la muerte, volvió por donde había venido, y fuese para el aposento de su señora, y entró passo, que no la sintió como era al primer sueño, y metióse debaxo de la cama.

DENTRO
¡Muerto soy!
FERNÁN
¡Onbre atreuido!
YSABEL
¡Triste de mí! ¿Dónde yré?
Mas debaxo de la cama
me entraré de mi señora.
FERNÁN
¿Adónde está la traydora
que mi noble sangre infama?
BERMUDO
Al aposento se fue
donde duermes, si entendí
bien lo que dixo.

Fernán Ruiz, referred to as Ruy Fernández in several of the above passages transcribed from *Os livros de linhagens* by Sandoval, is noted by him to be the incorrect name used by don Pedro de Barcellos in the Portuguese original, one of the factual errors he calls to the attention of the reader (see above, p. 35). Regarding another error in the history, Flórez points out that:

> Muy lejos de haber muerto doña Estefanía en vida del emperador, su padre, nos dice el epitafio de León que subrevivió veintitrés años, pues, traducida la inscripción dice ... así: 'Aquí descansa la infanta doña Estefanía, hija del emperador Alfonso, mujer del muy poderoso varón Fernán Ruiz, madre de Pedro Fernández el Castellano, la cual murió en 1 de julio de la era 1218.' Esta era 1218 es el año 1180. [33]

Supporting this evidence, Gamayo y Catalán states:

> De doña Sancha Fernández de Castro, dama de ilustre estirpe castellana, tuvo [Alfonso VII] otra hija llamada doña Estefanía, por apodo la *Desgraciada*, no siendo verosímiles los trágicos y novelescos episodios con que

---

[33] Flórez de Setién, *op. cit.*, p. 403.

algún bardo de la época desfiguró la historia con sus romances. [34]

The last historical aspect of the play, that of the *moros almohades*, appears in the *Crónica general* (pp. 568b-659b), but Sandoval's Chapter lvi of the *Chrónica* (pp. 150-152) contains elements which are not mentioned by the *Crónica*, and which appear in the play. Sandoval's text will be found in the Appendix. Lope, reflecting the account of Sandoval, has the *almohades* prepare a full-scale invasion of Spain in an effort to re-take the peninsula, while the *Crónica* indicates no such grand design. Below is just one passage of the text of the *Chrónica* and Lope's version:

Sandoval, p. 151

Mataró có grã crueldad todos los Christianos Moçarabes, q̃ siẽpre auiã viuido entre los Moros guardãdo nuestra Sãta Fè, à otros hizerõ renegar della, y à los q̃ permaneciã firmes en su santa cõfesion, martirizauan, y los que no se sentian con fuerças, pudiendo escapar, huyã, passandose à la tierra de los Christianos. Fue vno dellos Clemẽte Arçobispo de Seuilla, q̃ vino a Talauera, hõbre doctisimo en la lẽgua Arabiga, dõde viuio, y acabo sus dias santissimamẽte. Otro fue Arnugo Santo religioso, el qual vino à la villa de Olmedo ...

Lope, vv. 1885-1900

Ganólas, ganó a Xerez,
de donde a Seuilla parte,
que, aunque de moros, tenía
muchos cristianos muzárabes.
Huyó su santo arçobispo
Clemente, y el docto frayle
Arnugo, y otros varones
fueron esperando mártires.
No ay lengua para dezirte
deste ollero las crueldades,
pero basta que te diga
que ya es su orgullo tan grande
que han jurado de venir
a Castilla, y no dexarte
hasta que como Pelayo,
en las Asturias te guardes.

Scenes involving the Moors appear at the end of Act I, the beginning and end of Act II, and the end of Act III.

---

[34] Gamayo y Catalán, *op. cit.*, p. 59. What gives these arguments importance is not that they disprove the historical veracity of the events reported by don Pedro de Portugal and Sandoval's accounts, but rather that they indicate that somehow the situation entered popular tradition. It is unfortunate that Gamayo y Catalán was not more specific when he mentions "algún bardo de la época." A search of collections of *romances* has thus far proved fruitless in discovering a popular version of the episode.

To sum up, then, Lope certainly had available texts concerning the major historical elements which he developed in *La desdichada Estefanía*. But these accounts did not limit the scope of his utilization of the material contained therein. They served principally as a point of departure, of orientation, the raw material which was then shaped and molded for dramatic presentation. The intricate weaving of history and fiction becomes the more impressive when an attempt is made to separate the two. Yet, fiction has not distorted historical fact — indeed, the discrepancies noted between sources and the play can be termed *verosímiles* in that they do not reflect a historical *impossibility*.

Reichenberger's comment that, "Lope's familiarity with historical facts is rather amazing," [35] certainly applies to that area of this play as well. The detail of the incidents utilized, as well as the psychological implications for characters in the play, reveal not only a grasp of historical fact, but an understanding of human motivations. The three major situations in juxtaposition cease to be mere chronicles of historical events, for context renders them significant on an individual level. Menéndez y Pelayo, of course, saw the important relationship of history to the play, and as far as he went his observations remain pertinent.

VERSIFICATION OF THE PLAY

I. *Tables*

A. Distribution of Verse Forms

Act I.	vv. 1-275	quintillas	275 lines	
	276-320	sueltos	45 lines	
	321-580	redondillas	260 lines	
	581-684	octavas	104 lines	
	685-779	quintillas	95 liens	
	780-825	tercetos	46 lines	
	826-989	redondillas	164 lines	
	990-1019	sueltos	30 lines	1019 lines
Act II.	1020-1179	quintillas	160 lines	
	1180-1283	redondillas	104 lines	

[35] Reichenberger, *op. cit.*, p. 54.

	1284-1417	romance (e-a)	134 lines	
	1418-1461	redondillas	44 lines	
	1462-1587	romance (i-o)	126 lines	
	1588-1717	quintillas	130 lines	
	1718-1773	octavas	56 lines	
	1774-1837	redondillas	64 lines	
	1838-1860	sueltos	23 lines	
	1861-1928	romance (a-e)	68 lines	909 lines
Act III.	1929-2388	redondillas	460 lines	
	2389-2402	soneto	14 lines	
	2403-2486	redondillas	84 lines	
	2487-2544	sueltos	58 lines	
	2545-2600	redondillas	56 lines	
	2601-2712	octavas	112 lines	
	2713-2730	sueltos	18 lines	
	2731-2808	romance (a-a)	78 lines	880 lines

B. Number of Lines of Each Verse Form by Passages

	Soneto	Redondillas	Quintillas	Romance	Sueltos	Octavas	Tercetos
I		260	275		45	104	46
		164	95		30		
II		104	160	134	23	52	
		44	130	126			
		64		68			
III	14	460		78	58	112	
		84			18		
		56					
	14	1236	660	406	174	272	46

Morley-Bruerton, *Chronology* (p. 24), read:

	14	1176	620	371	152	272	46

C. Percentages

Soneto	Redondillas	Quintillas	Romance	Sueltos	Octavas	Tercetos
.498	44.017	23.504	14.458	6.196	9.686	1.638

Buchanan, *HR*, III (1953), pp. 74-75, gives:

(1)	43.5	23.4	11.4	8.4	10.4	1.8

Morley-Bruerton, *Chronology* (p. 24), show:

.5	44.4	23.4	13.9	5.8	10.3	1.7

II. *Verse Form in the Plot*

Act I:

1-275	quintillas	Luis praises the richness of Spain; Alfonso inquires into Luis's lack of contentment; Fernán and Fortunio exchange insults.
276-320	sueltos	Alfonso relates Estefanía's lineage and the legitimacy of Costanza.
321-580	redondillas	Fernán and Estefanía swear their love; Fortunio interrupts and the two men almost come to blows; Alfonso and Luis appear, Castro leaves; Luis has Alfonso give Estefanía to Fortunio, but she demands that he fulfill his obligation to fight Fernán in a duel.
581-684	octavas	Ysabel relates her love for Fortunio. Mudarra complains of having to leave her for Africa, and the two express their mutual love, and they say goodbye.
685-779	quintillas	Albumasar informs Abdelmón that he is to be King of Africa.
780-825	tercetos	Albumasar and the other Moors plot to murder the King and put Abdelmón in his place.
826-989	redondillas	Mudarra and Fernán come to request permission from the Miramamolín to hold the duel, which they receive.
990-1019	sueltos	The plotters confuse Mudarra's *caja* announcing the duel with their signal for the uprising.

Act II:

1020-1179	quintillas	Fortunio returns to claim Estefanía, tells of the uprising which prevented him from dueling with Fernán.

1180-1283	redondillas	Fernán and Mudarra go to the convent, but are told that Estefanía has left to marry Fortún.
1284-1417	romance	Fernán complains of Estefanía's inconstancy; Mudarra cannot console him; he in turn begins to doubt Ysabel's faithfulness.
1418-1461	redondillas	Estefanía shows only sadness in contrast to Fortunio's jubilation; Fernán arrives.
1462-1587	romance	Fernán denounces Fortunio for not appearing in Fez, discloses his long suit of Estefanía, who chooses him. Ysabel is dismayed at the turn of events, but listens to Mudarra's offer of his gift from Africa. Fortunio complains of his misfortune in losing Estefanía.
1588-1717	quintillas	Ysabel, plotting to have Fortunio, tells him that Estefanía really loves him and desires a meeting. Both plan to achieve their respective goals.
1718-1773	octavas	Estefanía falls as the wedding party leaves the church, then as Castro's house is neared, part of it gives way.
1774-1837	redondillas	Mudarra, covered with debris, tells the group that several servants have been killed in the accident. Don Nuño invites the couple to stay at his house. Fernán and Estefanía show their uneasiness.
1838-1860	sueltos	More noise is heard; a *cochero* has killed one of Fernán's servants and is led away by an *alguazil*. Alfonso affirms that the events are *cosas naturales*. Sancho Laynez arrives from his border post.
1861-1928	romance	Sancho tells of the invasion of the *almohades*, Alfonso prepares to organize his troops.

Act III:

1929-2388	redondillas	Fortunio and Ysabel, pretending to be Estefanía, meet in Castro's garden. Two servants observe them and report to Castro, who is just returning to see his recently-born son. Estefanía greets

		him warmly, but he is preoccupied with the news of her infidelity. Mudarra and Ysabel arrange to meet later.
2389-2402	soneto	Ysabel laments that she cannot show her love for Fortunio openly.
2403-2486	redondillas	Olfos hears Fortunio complain of Fernán's return, but Fortunio nevertheless plans to meet with the woman he believes to be Estefanía.
2487-2544	sueltos	Fernán and his two servants await the arrival of the lovers in the garden; they finally appear.
2545-2600	redondillas	Fernán kills Fortunio, Ysabel flees to Estefanía's bedroom; Olfos tells Fernán that it was Fortunio whom he killed, and Bermudo and Ximeno kill Olfos.
2601-2712	octavas	Fernán stabs Estefanía while she sleeps; she awakes, dying, claiming innocence; Ysabel is heard under the bed, confesses her guilt; Fernán laments his ill deed and sentences Ysabel to death.
2713-2730	sueltos	Alfonso, having conquered Abdelmón's forces, orders him to return to Africa; Fernán's arrival is announced.
2731-2808	romance	Fernán relates to Alfonso how he killed Estefanía and asks that he be punished. Alfonso leaves his sentencing to his judges.

From the foregoing it will be noted that *redondillas* comprise the dominant verse form of the seven meters used, which is characteristic of Lope's work in the period 1601-04. Except for vv. 826-989, *redondilla* passages comply with Lope's *Arte nuevo* in that they concern "cosas de amor." [36] Other elements, of course, are present, but the basic situation depends on a love motivation.

Ysabel's sonnet (vv. 2389-2402) shows the characteristics noted by Lucile K. Delano: first, that "Lope shows a marked fondness for the adaptation of biblical and mythological allusions to a particular situation;" [37] secondly, that "... the octave states the

---

[36] *Arte nuevo*, p. 26.
[37] Lucile K. Delano, "An Analysis of the Sonnets in Lope de Vega's *Comedias*," *H*, XII (1929), p. 119.

situation and the sestet sums it up more succinctly.... in both types the octaves are more generalizing, while the sestets seem to constitute the personal element." [38] The sonnet follows the precepts of the *Arte Nuevo*.

Tercetos, for "cosas graves," are used in only one passage, which involves a plot to murder a king. As Hoge remarks: "It is clear that regicide was a dangerous topic in Lope's time.... When the plot ... seems to contain dangerous overtones, Lope removes the scene to an exotic locale...." [39] Such is the case in *La desdichada Estefanía*, for the plans involve an African king, and the plotters are later indirectly punished when Abdelmón's forces are defeated by Alfonso.

The *romance* passages mainly concern "relaciones," though as with the *redondilla* sections, various other elements are present, especially in the longer *romance* parts (e.g., vv. 1462-1587, where dialogue pertaining to the situation at hand is involved).

Octavas, in which "lucen las relaciones," conform to the expected type of situation. In the three occurrences of this meter, elements basic to the plot are presented (i.e., Ysabel's love for Fortunio, Estefanía's fall, her death at the hands of Fernán).

The common denominator of the *quintillas* concerns desire of various types: 1-275, Luis wants the truth as to the legitimacy of Costanza; 685-779, Albumasar and Abdelmón want power; 1020-1179, Fortunio wants Estefanía; 1588-1717, Ysabel wants Fortunio.

The *sueltos* form a "catch-all" category. In one case *romance* or *octavas* could have been used (276-320). It would seem that in several instances *suelto* passages afforded Lope a mode of transition in preparation for a more clearly defined mood (1838-1860, 2713-2730).

In all but three cases, verse-form changes occur in conjunction with the entrance or exit of characters or a change of scene. Those three cases are: in v. 276 Alfonso begins a *relación* after a dialogue in *quintillas*; at v. 1284, Fernán begins a *romance* passage after the shock of learning that Estefanía has left the convent to

---

[38] *Ibid.*, p. 120.
[39] Hoge, *op. cit.*, p. 836.

marry Fortunio; at v. 1861, Sancho begins a *relación* in *romance* of the *almohade* invasion of Spain.

In a number of instances Lope has indulged in identical rhyme, [40] not an uncommon practice with Golden Age dramatists. Following is a listing of these occurrences:

206 lengua	253 él	362 conçierto	506 Sancha	529 engaño
208 deslengua	254 él	363 çierto	507 ensancha	532 desengaño
726 hazes	1150 cassa	1176 tienpo	1277 llama	1434 tengo
728 desazes	1151 casa	1178 tienpo	1278 llama	1437 tengo
2014 justa	2190 abrazos		2210 mudo	
2015 injusta	2191 brazos		2211 mudo	

J. H. Arjona has made mention of the only appearance in the play of assonance for exact rhyme ("copas-pocas," which displays, in addition, the use of chiasmus), and the use of exact rhymes in succession. [41] "The repetition of the refrain ['mas si he subido y caydo, / yo he hecho lo que he podido, / fortuna lo que ha querido.'], which is a quotation from one of Quevedo's *letrillas,* accounts for three consonantal rhymes in succession without intervening blank verses. This is not a careless imperfection as much as an intentional departure from standard practice for poetic effect. The other consonantal rhymes are found shortly before: *sentido-podido-querido* [vv. 1523-27]. They appear in the same situation with intervening blank verses this time." [42] Another refrain is used in this *romance* section three times (vv. 1308, 1364, 1394):

> ... ...
> que ver la amada prenda
> gozar al enemigo es grande afrenta.

The refrain "y se queda Ysabel con mis entrañas" is used three times in a passage of *octavas* (vv. 612, 620 and 628).

---

[40] See J. H. Arjona, "The Use of Autorhymes in the XVIIth-Century *Comedia,*" *HR,* XXI (1953), pp. 273-301.

[41] Arjona, "Defective Rhymes," *op. cit.,* p. 113.

[42] J. H. Arjona, "Improper Use of Consonantal Rhyme in Lope de Vega and its Significance Concerning the Authorship of Doubtful Plays," *Separata de Hispanófila,* No. 16, p. 9. See pp. 248-49.

An Evaluation of the Play

I. *Tragedy*

La desdichada Estefanía figures incidentally in various studies, but except for Menéndez y Pelayo's *Observaciones Preliminares*, the play has never been the main subject of a work. [43] This situation has been the fate of many of Lope's plays, to be sure, but is the more noteworthy in this case since the autograph has been available for a number of years. In addition, there are several aspects of the play which one would expect to interest *lopistas*: the play's tragical-historical character, the fact that Vélez de Guevara has a play following the same plot, its concern with conjugal honor, etc. [44]

Lope has called *La desdichada Estefanía* a "Tragedia Primera," the "Tragedia Segunda" being *El pleito por la honra o el valor de Fernandico*. However, as indicated by H. Rennert, *Servir con mala estrella* also figures in the series, since it involves directly Estefanía's mother. [45] Morley and Bruerton, in determining composition dates for the three plays (*La desdichada Estefanía* the only certain one), show 1604-08, probably 1604-06 for *Servir con mala estrella*, [46] and for *El pleito por la honra* state that: "The *quintillas* are strong evidence that the play was originally written before 1604, which would agree with the natural course of legend in drama and epic." [47] They add that: "One might

---

[43] See J. Fitzmaurice Kelly, *Lope de Vega and the Spanish Drama* (Glasgow-London, 1902), p. 49; Arturo Farinelli, *Lope de Vega en Alemania*, p. 139, n.; E. H. Templin, "The Mother in the *Comedia* of Lope de Vega," *HR*, III (1935), pp. 226 and 236; E. Allison Peers, "Lope de Vega: Prólogo al Tercer Centenario de su muerte," *Bulletin of Spanish Studies*, XII (1935), p. 177.

[44] See W. L. Fichter (ed.), *El castigo del discreto* (New York, 1925), pp. 28-47 for an analysis of conjugal honor plays and a listing of all of Lope's plays on the theme.

[45] Hugo Rennert, "Bibliography of the Dramatic Works of Lope de Vega," extrait of *RHi*, XXXIII (1915), p. 165.

[46] C. E. Anibal, "Observations on *La estrella de Sevilla*," *HR*, II (1934), p. 17, n. 40, says that a reference to Granada "suggests that *Servir [con mala estrella]* may have been written at about the time of Lope's visit to Granada," summer, 1603, or spring, 1604.

[47] Morley-Bruerton, *Chronology*, p. 326.

expect that interest aroused by Estefanía's story would call forth a play about her antecedents. [48] It must be remembered, however, that Menéndez y Pelayo and others strongly doubt the authenticity of *El pleito por la honra* as we know it. [49]

Following are the key passages from *Servir con mala estrella* (as found in *Ac.*, XIV) referring to Estefanía:

ZELIMA	Que me engañe podrá ser;
	Mas ser mujer no era nada,
	Sino que he venido a hallar
	Que España la ha de llamar
	La mujer más desdichada.
DOÑA SANCHA	¡Válgame el cielo! ¡Qué pena!
	Pues de un Rey del mayor nombre,
	¿Saldrá cosa dese nombre?
	¿Será mala o será buena?
	El alma tengo turbada.
	¿Eso dices que ha de ser?
	¿No le basta ser mujer,
	Sino la más desdichada?
ZELIMA	¿Cómo tenías pensado
	Llamar al varón?
DOÑA SANCHA	Pensé
	Llamarle Alfonso; mas fue
	Mi pensamiento engañado.
	Pero si es hembra, la quiero
	Llamar...
ZELIMA	¿Cómo?
DOÑA SANCHA	Estefanía.
ZELIMA	Bien puedes desde este día,
	Aunque lo contrario espero,
	Tener por cierto que España
	La llamará Estefanía
	La desdichada. (pp. 548-49)

The last two lines of the above passage present the title of the play as Lope wrote it on the autograph. It appears in almost the same form, spoken by Fernán in our play: "Estefanía, al fin, la desdichada" (v. 2682).

---

[48] *Ibid.*, p. 241.
[49] *Ibid.*, p. 326.

In conversation with her brother, Don Tello, Doña Sancha
says:

> No te espantes
> Que esto intente quien es tan desdichada,
> Que en sus mismas entrañas este día
> Lleva a la desdichada Estefanía. (p. 550)

Later we see:

> Si Zelima a Estefanía
> Predijo fortuna airada,
> De madre tan desdichada,
> ¿Qué dicha tener podía? (p. 560)

As might be expected, Estefanía figures more prominently in
El pleito por la honra, even if it is only in the memory of the
characters (from *Ac.,* VIII); the King and Fernandico's *ayo* speak:

> REY   ¿Sabe quién es su padre?
> RAMÓN   Sí, ha sabido;
> Mas no el suceso triste y lastimoso,
> Que de su madre tan llorado ha sido,
> Y de Fernán Ruiz, tan valeroso.
> REY   Que ninguno le informe mando y pido. (p. 368)

Costanza, a young lady of the court, speaks to Fernandico:

> Mucho estimo vuestra fe,
> Y de veros me holgaré
> Siendo de vos estimada;
> Mas temo ser desdichada,
> Como vuestra madre fue. (pp. 370-1)

Alvaro, a relative of Fortunio Ximénez, comments on Fernán
Ruiz's imminent release from prison:

> Dichoso es Castro, a fe mía:
> De la muerte de Estefanía,
> No mujer baja y común,
> Y al desdichado Fortún,
> Noble hidalgo y sangre mía;
> ... ...
> Tan bien premia las traiciones
> Como si fueran servicios. (p. 372)

This particular passage is notable for the echo of a sentiment expressed by Fernán Ruiz (vv. 444-452) to the King in reference to Fortunio Ximénez's apparently preferential treatment by the King. Later, Ramón is in conversation with Fernandico as he says:

> No es tiempo, joven ilustre,
> Que entre temores tan varios,
> Te encubra la gran tragedia
> De que resulta tu agravio.
> Sabrás que el Rey tiene preso
> A tu noble padre, Castro,
> Porque dio muerte a tu madre,
> Que era de prudencia un vaso,
> Por falso testimonio,
> Fernando, que levantaron
> A su virtud inocente.
> ... ...
> Prendiéronle habrá veinte años.   (p. 376)

In effect, then, Lope has an Estefanía trilogy, making use of the legendary material for all three, but of course, most prominently in the tragedy *La desdichada Estefanía.*

Due to his prominence in the Spanish theater and his enormous production, Lope has been the object of attack and praise, scorn and adulation. A whole range of critical reaction can be seen in articles and books on Lope and his writings. On the one hand, adverse critics point out that his drama does not follow Aristotelian rules and is therefore defective. Others hasten to show that Lope did not follow them because he was involved in the creation of a form of drama which was to reach a high point in Spanish letters due to his influence. His defenders argue that he intentionally ignored such "rules" since they did not suit the needs of the emerging form as he envisioned it. This presents the problem of determining a sub-genre for *La desdichada Estefanía.* To be sure, it is an historical play, but Lope designated it a *tragedia,* the variant editions (MSA) call it a *tragicomedia,* or (B) a *comedia famosa,* and in v. 2805 Lope refers to it as a *comedia.* Added to the already conflicting views on what tragedy and comedy may consist of, this confusion of terms further obscures the issue. However, a great degree of clarity is restored

by Edwin S. Morby, who points out that a reading of *play* for
comedia eliminates one problem. Secondly, "such clichés as *comedia famosa* are generally, if not always, devices of printers
rather than authors." [50] In the same way, MSA's reference to
tragicomedia does not reflect Lope's terminology. We are again,
then, left with a play which Lope has termed a tragedy, and
according to the precepts which he has outlined in the *Arte nuevo*
for tragic plays, *La desdichada Estefanía* is a tragedy. It has
history as its *argumento*, [51] "trata las acciones reales y altas," [52]
and it has "lo trágico y lo cómico mezclado." [53] The difficulty,
however, lies in the fact that one individual's definition of tragedy
is not necessarily accepted by another. As Morby explains, "the
tragic artist is not interested in the whole truth, a small portion
only concerns him. . . . Now when Lope had gathered into a play
all the elements of tragedy as he conceived them, he entitled his
play *tragedia*. But he put too much else besides. . . . His *tragedia
al estilo español* is too rarely a tragedy, though its merits may be
enormous." [54] This represents the traditional, conventional view
of tragedy. Morby had previously stated that:

> In Lope's *tragedia*, where clowns and frivolities abound,
> one already finds "mezclados, contra el arte, las personas
> y los estilos," presumably with no sense that *tragedia* is
> a misnomer. And it is not one, as Lope viewed the matter,
> because in spite of its garnish of comedy, it retains the
> essentials of tragedy: its serious, non-fictional theme, its
> lofty characters, and its lamentable end. *Tragicomedia*,
> on the other hand, replaces at least one of these elements:
> lofty actors with base, dismal ending with happy. Thus
> in a true sense *tragicomedia* is a blending of tragic and
> comic ingredients, while tragedy merely superimposes
> the latter on the former, of which all must remain
> intact. [55]

The key words in the foregoing are "and it is not one [a misno-
mer], as Lope viewed the matter, because in spite of its garnish

---

[50] Morby, *op. cit.*, p. 190.
[51] *Arte nuevo*, p. 19.
[52] *Ibid.*, p. 17.
[53] *Ibid.*, p. 21.
[54] Morby, *op. cit.*, pp. 204-05.
[55] *Ibid.*, p. 200.

of comedy, it retains the essentials of tragedy." Lope's view of the matter was:

> Lo trágico y lo cómico mezclado,
> ... ...
> Que aquesta variedad deleita mucho.
> Buen ejemplo nos da naturaleza,
> Que por tal variedad tiene belleza.   (*Arte nuevo*, p. 21)

Supporting Lope's view, S. C. Boorman, discussing comedy as it appears in Shakesperae's tragedy *Othello*, accepts this mixture of elements in the following terms:

> In Scene I, quite oddly and even unnecessarily for a modern audience, there is the "comic" episode between the Clown and the musician. The "comedy," such as it is, is a mixture of the coarse and the naïve; I doubt whether it has much laughter for us to-day. This is an example of something purely Elizabethan in its appeal, to be accepted from the Elizabethan standpoint.... But Shakespeare always adds some laughter to his tragedies; usually the laughter has a bitter note of comment upon the tragic theme, and *Othello* is unique among the four great tragedies in using comic relief that is quite unrelated to the serious subject; ... However, such a mingling of comedy with tragedy is at least justified by the example of real life, where comedy and tragedy do exist side by side, and certainly the contrast here throws the tragic mood into greater relief.... We may not find such "comedy" very funny, but for Shakespeare's audience it would be a moment of necessary relaxation and amusement, and perhaps may be so for us. [56]

Lope and Shakespeare were not original in their use of comic qualities in tragedy, nor necessarily the first dramatists to be conscious of its presence and value in their works. Marvin T. Herrick points out that the moral reformation of Roman comedy in the sixteenth century contributed to tragicomedy, and asks: "Were the Biblical stories that were put into the Terentian framework suitable for tragicomic treatment? The answer.... is yes." [57] He adds:

---

[56] S. C. Boormn (ed.), *Othello* (London, 1962), pp. 37-38.
[57] Marvin T, Herrick, *Tragicomedy* (Urbana, 1962), p. 24.

The Christian Terence, in working out a reformed
kind of Terentian drama, actually arrived in most instances at tragicomedy. Probably all the writers of sacred
comedies and tragedies were conscious of this development; at all events, some of them provide convincing
testimony that they fully realized the tragicomic qualities
in the plays. [58]

What continues to surprise is the reluctance of Hispanists to
accept and admit what Boorman has readily accepted concerning
Shakespeare's work, that such comedy in tragedy "is at least
justified by the example of real life," and to view the work on
its terms, not on superimposed requirements. Essentially, the
detractors of Lope's tragedy subscribe to a definition of it which
does not recognize that his is valid. In this respect they do not
differ from the neo-classicists of the eighteenth century who
rejected Lope's production as irreconcilable with their concept of
drama. Equally true of Lope's tragedy is William J. Grupp's
statement that:

> The *comedia* itself ... is free of any traces that would
> display the effectiveness of classicist efforts to compress
> the Spanish genius into the form of regularity.... Lope
> took ... vague, formless ideas and blended them, infusing
> them with the color and beauty of which only he was
> capable. With a gesture of finality he banished classical
> precepts from the Spanish stage and proclaimed the
> freedom of the Spanish artist to create a native, appro-
> priate medium of dramatic expression. [59]

Charles D. Ley, in examining Lope's use of tragedy, decides that:

> Lope es el más alegre de los grandes escritores mundia-
> les, acaso humanamente el más sencillo. Era, efectiva-
> mente, incapaz de concebir una tragedia como tal. ... Lo
> que admiramos en Lope son otras cosas: su enorme ener-
> gía, que se revela en todo lo que escribe, y la gran va-
> riedad de su mundo. [60]

---

[58] *Ibid.*, p. 27.

[59] William J. Grupp, "Dramatic Theory and Criticism in Spain During
the Sixteenth, Seventeenth, and Eighteenth Centuries" (unpublished Ph. D.
dissertation, Cornell, 1949), p. 30.

[60] Charles D. Ley, "Lope de Vega y la tragedia," *Clavileño*, IV (1950),
p. 12.

Ley also declares that:

> Las pocas veces que Lope escribe una tragedia resulta, por así decir, casi doméstica. ... Hemos visto que es difícil que exista una acción trágica dentro de la obra de Lope. Sus personajes perversos se salvan, o, cuando menos, el bien acaba por triunfar rotundamente. Tal no es el asunto de las tragedias griegas, que nos presentan el fracaso de los que han ofendido a los dioses, pero que, habiendo seguido ciegamente en esto un destino ya trillado, son dignos de compasión más bien que culpables. En la tragedia shakespeareana, según el poeta Auden, 'el héroe trágico es un hombre que se condena,' punto de vista quizá arbitrario, pero merecedor de ser tenido en cuenta. La verdad es que el bien triunfa al final de las tragedias de Shakespeare, pero siempre de una manera muy callada, muy discreta; de no ser así la tragedia no sería posible. [61]

By applying the positive statements in the previous paragraph to *La desdichada Estefanía,* we find that Ley has described the ending of the play. To continue to live for a tragic hero is not necessarily a form of salvation, nor is this play an example of an ending where "el bien acaba por triunfar rotundamente."

For conventional critics, Lope's work is "nice," but it does not sufficiently reflect the more commonly held ideas of what tragedy consists of to be really accepted as tragedy. Lope is still being condemned by those who fail to realize the extent of their dependence on the precepts of Aristotle and Horace, as interpreted by Italian Renaissance theorists, from which Lope long ago declared his independence. A. A. Parker, discussing dramatic theory as it relates to Calderón de la Barca, calls for an examination of his dramatic practice in order to arrive at the theory behind his production. [62] This call for a reexamination also applies to Lope's work, for all too often his tragic theater has been evaluated by using standards which simply do not apply. As Reichenberger has pointed out: "Those who adhere to the classical and French ideal of form are disappointed by what

---

[61] *Ibid.,* p. 11.
[62] A. A. Parker, "Towards a Definition of Calderonian Tragedy," *BHS,* XXXIX (1962), p. 225.

seems to them a lack of unity and harmony, of polish and of sustained characterization." [63] This is only natural, since they are attempting to impose upon the work a set of ideas and restrictions which are not valid for Spanish drama. Parker has done much to clarify the evaluative process by formulating five principles, derived from the plays themselves, which govern (and explain) the structure of the Spanish drama of the Golden Age. These principles, illustrated by Parker with Lope's tragedy *El castigo sin venganza* and Calderón's *comedia El mágico prodigioso*, etc., are:

     1. The primacy of action over character drawing.
     2. The primacy of theme over action, with the consequent irrelevance of realistic verisimilitude.
     3. Dramatic unity in the theme and not in the action.
     4. The subordination of the theme to a moral purpose, through the principle of poetic justice, which is not exemplified only by the death of the wrongdoer.
     5. The elucidation of the moral purpose by means of dramatic causality. [64]

If we accept these principles and the idea that Spanish tragedy, seen on its own terms, is indeed tragedy, we find that Lope (as well as Calderón) has contributed greatly to the form.

A further point should be emphasized. Mr. Ley refers to "las tragedias griegas, que nos presentan el fracaso de los que han ofendido a los dioses, pero que, habiendo seguido ciegamente en esto un destino ya trillado, son dignos de compasión más bien que culpables." And Reichenberger says:

> The Greek theater is tragic. It shows man, not as the child of God, but essentially alone on earth, pitted against inexorable forces stronger than himself, supernatural (Oedipus), political and social (Antigone), or emotional (Phaedra), and eventually doomed, but compensating for human powerlessness by the dignity with which he bears his fate. [65]

---

[63] Arnold G. Reichenberger, "The Uniqueness of the *Comedia*," *HR*, XXVII (1959), p. 304.

[64] A. A. Parker, *The Approach to the Spanish Drama of the Golden Age,* "Diamante," No. 6 (London, 1959), p. 27.

[65] Reichenberger, *loc. cit.,* p. 306.

Parker dismisses this requirement of destiny's control, for: "Spanish dramatists present no victims of destiny or mischance, but only of wrongdoing — their own, or someone else's." [66] The basic difference, of course, is that Parker is refraining from making up the rules — he is observing them as they operate, and concludes that general dramatic theory is not only incomplete but unsubtle. Even Reichenberger recognizes that "it is methodically wrong to ask the *comedia* to give what it can not be expected to give in terms of its own ideological and esthetic system." [67] Replacing conventional Greek tragedy is a type of drama which envisions man as a responsible person, whose tragic fate is in part due to his own actions. Such a figure is infinitely more tragic than one which must be seen only as a plaything of an inimical destiny. The system of poetic justice elaborated by Parker is:

> By poetic justice I myself mean no more — and no less — than the fact that there is no moral guilt without suffering of some kind, and no suffering without some degree of moral guilt (except in the case of the innocent victim of another's wrongdoing). [68]

This is certainly more devastating and meaningful for a modern audience than the spectacle of a puppet being moved by the "superior, incomprehensible forces over which man has no control," which Reichenberger calls for. Parker has seen the greater profundity of the tragedy of man:

> Caught in the tangled net of interrelated human actions and imprisoned in his own limited vision ... not at odds with fate in the ordinary sense of the term — he is the victim of something more profound and more tragic, the victim of the sad irony of human life itself, in which each man is compelled to construct, and act upon, his own individuality in a world where the human individual, *qua* individual, cannot exist. [69]

---

[66] Parker, *loc. cit.*, p. 9.

[67] Reichenberger, *loc. cit.*, p. 315.

[68] Parker, "Towards a Definition," *op. cit.*, pp. 225-26, n. 1. This note corrects also his statement that poetic justice required that there be no innocent victim as appears in our play (*Spanish Drama*, pp. 9-10).

[69] *Ibid.*, p. 237.

The world has repeatedly been forced to widen its horizons as man acquired more knowledge of himself and his surroundings. Lope and his contemporaries have widened the scope of the portrayal of man in his modern situation; now criticism must raise its eyes from the static demands imposed on drama (demands derived from the limited idea that tragedy and what constitutes tragedy have been in stasis) in order to perceive that the world has moved to a different position.

The editor does not claim discovery of a "great" Spanish tragedy, but in the light of the above discussion, it is felt that *La desdichada Estefanía is* a tragedy. The following sections will attempt to bear out this assertion.

II. *Honor*

Departing from Menéndez y Pelayo's statement that the play is not "una obra de análisis," but rather a "novela dramática," let us consider aspects of it which are highlighted and form its major motivations: love and honor. The major force in the life of Lope's nobles is the Golden Age concept of honor, that fragile state which is conferred upon one by birth, which cannot be acquired, only maintained. It is the vulnerability of one's honor which gives rise to the infinite variations of situations available to the Golden Age dramatist. It is an ever-new topic, invested with an almost hypnotic fascination for its ritual action-reaction complex movement. Américo Castro, terming honor one of the fundamental motives of Spanish drama, also indicates that its presence as such was not a product of Lope's inventive genius, for it appeared first in Torres Naharro's *Himenea.* [70] Its rapid rise in popularity is attested to by the large number of plays which utilize it as a principal motive, reaching its highly stylized form in the plays of Calderón de la Barca. But as Fichter cautions, the popularity of the dramatized ideal of honor should not be construed as a realistic representation of life in that age. [71] C. A. Jones, investigating the relationship, feels that:

---

[70] Américo Castro, "Algunas observaciones acerca del concepto del honor en los siglos xvi y xvii," *RFE*, III (1916), pp. 15-17.

[71] Fichter, *loc. cit.*, p. 28.

There is no doubt that the theme of honour in the plays is not a complete fiction, and that there were cases in real life similar to those which occurred in the theatre, where we know them as cases of honour. But it is perhaps worth noting that the feature which the cases found in the records had in common was that they were sensational, and that they were sensational because, although perhaps not very rare, they were at least not normal. It is, moreover, not always clear how far the motive in these cases was regard for lost honour, and how far it was passion, jealous or otherwise. Honour was used as a theme in literary types other than the drama, and the fact that honour was frequently condemned by moralists and didactic writers is evidence that it must have had some importance in real life as well as in the drama. [72]

Keeping in mind the distinction between drama's reality and the reality of life, Alfonso García Valdecasas writes of generic honor in life:

El sentimiento del honor no solamente aparece como propio y característico de la vida de comunidad, sino que parece desempeñar un papel esencial en ella. El honor era un valor incondicionado y básico en la moral social, como si en él se cifrara la virtud y la cohesión de la comunidad. El honor era como savia del organismo, como sangre del cuerpo social.

... El honor que liga a cada miembro con el cuerpo social y dirige toda su conducta es, a un tiempo, un ánimo e inspiración del individuo y una tradición y una exigencia de la comunidad. [73]

And concerning honor in Europe and Spain, in particular, he says:

Al preguntar por lo que los españoles entendían por honor, contamos, desde luego, con que la significación de éste se cumple de manera adecuada a la circunstancia histórica a que va referido. Sin duda, en la medida en que el sentimiento del honor pueda tener raíces que sean propias del hombre como tal, o como ser social, aquel

[72] C. A. Jones, "*Honor* in Spanish Golden-Age Drama: Its Relation to Real Life and Morals," *BHS*, XXXV (1958), p. 200.

[73] Alfonso García Valdecasas, *El hidalgo y el honor* (2d ed.; Madrid, 1958), pp. 143-144).

sentimiento tendrá una base humana genérica. Y desde luego, el entendimiento español del honor tendrá, como la cultura española, fuentes comunes y analogías con otros pueblos de Europa. Pero si es cierta la significación excepcional asumida por el honor en nuestro pasado, ello de por sí agrega al honor español un sentido propio y singular. [74]

Honor, then, is not an isolated Spanish element of life, but it is the intensification of its force, especially in Spanish drama, which calls attention to it as a national characteristic of Spain.

Gustavo Correa discusses horizontal and vertical honor in drama, that is, relationships between individuals on the same level, and the degree of honor an individual has with regard to his relative proximity to the king, respectively. [75] The former is the category which generates the typical honor situation, for unlike vertical honor, which is automatically the patrimony of the highborn, this horizontal honor is in the hands of others. It is the action of forces beyond the control of the individual, hence one must use special care and exercise constant vigilance to prevent even the slightest whisper of scandal which might be harmful to one's honor. The Achilles' heel of man's honor is woman, "daughters, wives or sisters — should they overstep in any way the restrictions imposed upon them in their relations with the other sex." [76]

It is at this point that love assumes great importance as it is linked to honor. A single man, without family responsibility, is liable only for his own actions. Even as he is courting he does not assume liability for his sweetheart's actions. [77] But once married, the situation is radically changed and "celos de honra" come into play. Valdecasas distinguishes it from "celos de pasión amorosa" in the following way: "Los celos de honra son, en primer término, como resultado de una obligación, no como fruto de una pasión. El marido tenía el deber de velar por la intangibilidad de la honra familiar y el de vindicarla si era

---

[74] *Ibid.*, pp. 116-117.
[75] Gustavo Correa, "El doble aspecto de la honra en el teatro del siglo XVII," *HR*, XXVI (1958), pp. 99-107.
[76] Fichter, *loc. cit.*, p. 31.
[77] *Ibid.*, pp. 31-32, n. 42.

manchada." [78] Any wrong, real or suspected, must be avenged immediately, and in secret if feasible, for publicizing dishonor only increases its damage. Conjugal honor is valued so highly because it is closest to man's existence, his wife is "el otro yo."

Another aspect of honor which appears in the system is that of one person honoring another:

> El honor manifiesta virtud y que hacer honor es recono-
> cer virtud, sin que inicialmente sea precisa ni siquiera la
> nota de superioridad o excelencia. Sólo es precisa la de
> alteridad, esto es, de relación de uno a otro. En el hacer
> honor lo mismo se puede partir de una igualdad que de
> una desigualdad, aunque lo normal sea lo segundo, y en
> este segundo caso lo mismo puede hacer honor el supe-
> rior, que lo dispensa, o el inferior, que lo rinde. [79]

Alfonso, in the opening scene of *La desdichada Estefanía*, tells Luis:

> Sólo he mostrado contento
> de verme de vos onrrado.   (vv. 58-59)

Here are two equals, one being honored by the other. In a later passage, Fernán Ruiz de Castro says to Fortunio Ximénez, "tú a ningún rey has onrrado" (v. 147), showing that a subject can honor a king. Fernán Ruiz, speaking of Estefanía's planned marriage to Fortunio, says:

> Afrentar quiero a Fortunio
> si es posible que ya pueda,
> onrrado de Estefanía
> y yo sin onrra y sin ella.   (vv. 1390-93)

Here we see not only Fernán's "celos de pasión amorosa," but one person honoring another, which results in dishonor for a third.

The play rapidly establishes honor as the force which paces its forward movement. Fernán Ruiz is initially involved with Fortunio over a question of the latter's honor (or rather his lack

---

[78] García Valdecasas, *op. cit.*, pp. 170-71.
[79] *Ibid.*, p. 134.

of it). [80] Both show concern for their honor to Alfonso, Fernán first saying, "señor, bolued por mi onor" (v. 222), then Fortunio echoes, "señor, mi onor considera" (v. 245).

Love and its complications soon appear as the audience sees Estefanía with Fernán, who tells her that "[onrra] vençió al amor esta vez" (v. 324), and he must go to Fez for his duel with Fortunio. The statement is completely in keeping with the honor code, but receives its fuller significance at the end of the play. The motives of love and honor are developed on parallel lines until Fernán discovers that Estefanía is to wed Fortunio, but after that point has been reached, Fernán's quarrel with Fortunio achieves new depth as the two motives are combined. It is after the lovers (Fernán and Estefanía) are married that the greatest demands of honor are made, those requirements for the maintaining of conjugal honor. Fernán quickly passes from the stage of disbelief to that of tentative acceptance of his servants' information that Estefanía is secretly meeting a man in the garden. The intensity of his feeling of dishonor is reflected in his questioning of the value of objects which previously were symbols of his honor and station:

> ¿Qué sirben esos roeles,
> de los Castros sienpre honrrados,
> ya de la infamia manchados
> de aquellas manos crueles.
> Arcos honrrosos, ¡pluguiera
> a Dios que aquel mismo día,
> sobre mí y Estefanía

---

[80] The cause of Fernán's opinion is stated in vague terms, and is answered with equal vagueness by Fortunio; but public opinion has evidently been at work (or informers, as in the case of the Cid), to the detriment of Fortunio's honor:

> FERNÁN   Tú a ningún rey has onrrado,
> ni al de España antes que fuesses
> a Françia por ynteresses
> de tu mal tenido estado.   (vv. 147-150)

In reply to this accusation, Fortunio says:

> No me fui por ser traydor,
> sino porque la malicia
> de algún poderoso error,
> derribando mi justiçia,
> escureçió mi balor.   (vv. 181-85)

> v[uest]ra máquina cayera!
> ¿Para qué os aderezé?
> ¿Para qué con v[uest]ro escudo
> puse el de Castilla?   (vv. 2289-2299) [81]

Even the fountains and trees,

> Murmurarán, Bermudo, de mi afrenta
> y de que se detiene la venganza.   (vv. 2492-93)

But when concrete action is required to avenge his sense of honor, he says:

> Sobrándome corazón
> para solo acometer
> mil moros, le vengo a ver
> cobarde en esta ocasión.   (vv. 2545-48)

This passage supports Valdecasas in his assertion that viewing vengeance simply as a kind of cold, unfeeling calculation is inaccurate:

---

[81] Compare with Peribáñez, fearful that Casilda may have dishonored him with the Comendador:

> Si tan hermosa no fueras,
> Claro está que no le dieras
> Al señor Comendador
> Causa de tan loco amor.
> Estos son mi trigo y eras.
> ¡Con qué diversa alegría,
> Oh campos, pensé miraros
> Cuando contento vivía!
> Porque viniendo a sembraros,
> Otra esperanza tenía.
> Con alegre corazón
> Pensé de vuestras espigas
> Henchir mis trojes, que son
> Agora eternas fatigas
> De mi perdida opinión.   (Ac., X, p. 131b)

> Alojé mi compañía,
> Y con ligereza extraña
> He dado la vuelta a Ocaña.
> ¡Oh cuán bien decir podría:
> Oh caña, la del honor!
> Pues no hay tan débil caña
> Como el honor, a quien daña
> De cualquier viento el rigor.
> Caña de honor quebradiza,
> Caña hueca y sin sustancia.   (Ac., X, p. 140b)

En muchos casos, el protagonista, por muy resuelto
que esté a la venganza, que acepta como inevitable, antes querría morir que tenerla que realizar. ... La venganza no sólo se puede realizar sin odio, sino que puede ir
acompañada de amor a la esposa.

En los dramas de honor, la conducta celosa del marido, más que a su carácter personal, responde a la fuerza social del sentimiento del honor. El honor era el bien
más precioso, que al marido tocaba defender, no ya por
interés propio, sino como bien que estaba por encima de
él. ...

En los dramas de honor ningún personaje importa,
sino el honor mismo, misterioso en su poder, inexorable
en su imposición a la que todo se sacrifica. [82]

This characteristic of blind devotion to a rigid code of honor is
all the more impressive for its inevitability as Fernán discovers
Estefanía's innocence. At that point "celos de honra" cease to
function as a motive for action. It is the noble's innate sense of
right that then prompts Fernán to go to Alfonso and confess his
guilt. As Valdecasas indicates, Fernán did not stop loving Estefanía, he was answering to a higher duty, as "[onrra] vençió al
amor esta vez" (v. 324).

C. A. Jones writes convincingly of the probability that Lope
and other dramatists did not use the convention of the honor
code without reservations. He points out that "even in the plays
there is in fact more than a hint from time of Lope's dissatisfaction
with honour vengeances," [83] justifying its use on its success as a
motive. In the Arte nuevo (p. 27), Lope writes: "Los casos de la
honra son mejores, / porque mueven con fuerça a toda gente";
Sandoval's use of caso in describing the pardon which Alfonso
gives Fernán Ruiz may well refer to the implications of honor, as
expressed above by Lope, who was well noted for his sensitivity
to the desires of his public. But regardless of its popularity as a
motive, Jones feels that "one may attack or defend the drama on
moral grounds, as many have done and still do, but it seems to

---

[82] García Valdecasas, op. cit., pp. 172-73.
[83] Jones, op. cit., p. 206. See also A. Irvine Watson, "El pintor de su
deshonra and the Neo-Aristotelian Theory of Tragedy," BHS, XL (1963),
p. 17, and P. N. Dunn, "Honour and the Christian Background in Calderón,"
BHS, XL (1963), pp. 76-77, for concurring opinions.

me to be irrelevant to take the honour theme out of its context and to attack or to defend that, with reference to contemporary customs or moral ideas outside the drama." [84] Dunn sees in the characteristics of *honor* "the feeling of a compulsion towards death," [85] and:

> Calderonian men of honour embody common human characteristics carried to their logical end, because this enables the action to acquire tragic certainty, false gods to show their true nature, and the travesty of vital spiritual realities to be made clear. The presence of the divine realities then has an additional significance — the audience cannot sit in judgement . . . . without judging themselves. [86]

Though he is directing his remarks specifically to Calderón's use of honor, the applicability of his words to Lope is readily seen.

III. *Characters*

Due in part to the novelistic quality of the play, most of the characters are those stock personalities which people the typical drama of the period. With the exception of Ysabel and Mudarra, who hold special positions, the servants and nobles offer no appreciable variation from the mold. They appear and react within their limited areas due to exigencies of the situation, not because of any quality of internal motivation which might distinguish them from counterparts in other works.

The Moors are seen generically, not as individuals, though the representation of the two rival factions in Fez provides Lope with an opportunity to illustrate Dora Bacaicoa Arnáiz's generalization: "Son enemigos [los moros] de los cristianos en función de la política, no del corazón, por eso están dispuestos a alabar a los enemigos y a tratar con ellos razonablemente, si las circunstancias lo permiten, del mismo modo que a luchar denodada-

---

[84] Jones, "Honor in Spanish Golden-Age Drama," *ibid.*, p. 209.
[85] Dunn, *op. cit.*, p. 87. See above, n. 83.
[86] *Ibid.*, p. 88.

mente, si las necesidades de la situación lo exigen." [87] Thus the Miramamolín and his *alcayde* Learín liberally praise Fernán Ruiz de Castro, and in like manner Abdelmón praises Alfonso after the *almohade* forces in Spain have been defeated. But Abdelmón was also reported as being cruel, and he was determined to drive the Spaniards back to the mountains of Asturias. Other notable characteristics of the Moors concern the element of fanaticism, personified by Almohadí, and the strong faith in the predictions of the astrologer Albumasar. Lope did not use the name of the astrologer as it appears in the *Crónica general* (Abentumet), possibly because of the wider recognition of the name Albumasar and his connection with astrology (indicated also by the name of the protagonist of Giambattista della Porta's play *Lo astrologo* (Venice, 1606), and Thomas Tomkis's reworking of it as *Albumazar* in 1615). [88]

Alfonso and Luis display the dignity and authority expected of their rank, while by the nature of their meeting they reflect the "matiz especialísimo de *carácter personal* ... [del] institucionalismo de la Monarquía ... sin desvirtuar la eficacia real de la persona," [89] which José Pemartín notes. The potentially explosive nature of Luis's inquiry does give rise to a violent reaction, but not by Alfonso. The image of his supreme authority as King is maintained by Fernán Ruiz and Fortunio even in moments of extreme stress. The former, hearing of his loss of Estefanía to Fortunio, says:

> De ti no me quexo, Alfonso;
> plega a Dios que Rey te veas
> de toda el Andaluzía,
> de Çaragoza y Valenzia.
> Llamáronte Enperador
> por tus hazañas y fuerzas
> y mexor por tus uirtudes,
> que entonzes los reyes reynan.   (vv. 1296-1303)

---

[87] Dora Bacaicoa Arnáiz, *Notas hispano-marroquíes en dos comedias del Siglo de Oro* (Tetuán, 1955), pp. 41-42.

[88] Hugh G. Dick (ed.), *Albumazar: A Comedy* (Berkeley, 1944), p. 12.

[89] José Pemartín, "La idea monárquica en Lope de Vega," *Acción española,* XIV (1935), p. 449.

This speech is an echo of the sentiment expressed by Luis in the opening scene of the play:

> Dios os dexe, Alfonso, ver
> Rei absoluto de España.   (vv. 33-34)

Fortunio, rejected by Estefanía, says:

> Basta que me dixo el Rey,
> "yo he [e]cho lo que he podido."
> No puedo del Rey quexarme;
> quexaréme de mí mismo.   (vv. 1552-55)

It is at the end of the play that a curious note is touched upon by Alfonso, previously seen as a strong figure of central authority. The spectator rather expects a stern sentence for his daughter's murderer, or at least some pronouncement regarding his fate. Instead, the King expresses his grief and delegates his role as dispenser of justice to his judges. Several possible explanations for this move present themselves. The King's grief and shock and his actions while experiencing them underline his humanity and susceptibility to the same emotions and disappointments which his subjects experience. The audience is partially prepared for this by Alfonso's affirmation of his esteem for Estefanía after her fainting spell upon leaving the church:

> Ni Costanza, Fernando y don Garçía
> ygualan a tu amor, Estefanía.
> Quiérote más que a todos.   (vv. 1740-42)

But this expression of love is not sufficient to counterbalance the character of Alfonso as seen in the rest of the play. On the other hand, in a tragic sense, Fernán is punishing himself in a way which no man could equal by invention. In reverse logic, Alfonso would be helping him expiate his act by punishing him. By not doing so he is actually meting out an infinitely more painful punishment, which further intensifies the tragic quality of Fernán Ruiz as a figure trapped by himself and his circumstances. A third possible solution lies in the question of the sequence of writing of the three plays which compose the Estefanía trilogy. Assuming that *La desdichada Estefanía* was written after *El pleito por la honra,* Lope was faced with a situation he had revealed to his public via the first play: the imprisonment of Fernán Ruiz and his subsequent release. In order to maintain the dramatic reality he had already created, and to avoid the righteous wrath of the King-father, he chose to have Alfonso remove himself from the situation, avoiding the position of the Duque de Ferrara of *El castigo sin venganza,* who, though having a personal interest in the problem presented by his wife's adultery, still believed himself capable of dispensing justice. [90]

Estefanía herself is portrayed as a passive figure in the play, variously as an object of love or pity, but hardly more than that. Even in death she remains the sweet, accepting woman, not consumed by the burning passions of, for example, Ysabel. As she vows, "yo diré sí, el alma, no" (v. 1179), when forced to accept Fortunio as her husband, her words are only words, lacking drive and force. Her moment of real spirit and determination occurs when she demands that Fortunio meet Fernán in Fez to comply with the code of honor before she will accept him as her husband. E. H. Templin says of her that she "must be ranged beside, and not among, the paragons of *paciencia,* for hers is not the affirmative quality, but rather an effortless and negative *paciencia* . . ." [91]

In contrast with Estefanía, Ysabel is a much more effective character, her love for Fortunio making her a moving force in shaping the destiny of the other major characters. As a self-recognized force of evil she exerts a strong fascination. There is no doubt as to her designs on Fortunio and their probable result as she finishes her speech in Act I:

> Yo moriré, pero alabarme puedo,
> que vitoriosa de mis penas quedo.   (vv. 603-604)

Ysabel's duplicity is heightened by her relationship with Mudarra, her *amante.* Her conversations with him lean heavily on comic elements, but on occasion her words reveal a double significance, betraying the deadly earnestness with which she pursues her secret goal:

---

[90] C. B. Morris, "Lope de Vega's *El castigo sin venganza* and Poetic Tradition," *BHS,* XL (1963), pp. 77-78, points out the immorality of the Duke, who is acting as a *juez apasionado.*

[91] Templin, *op. cit.,* p. 236. See n. 43.

> Pues ten de mí segura confïanza
> de que obligada a lo que deuo acuda.   (vv. 649-50)

In context she is affirming her love for Mudarra, but in a wider view it is her plan of seduction to which she is pledging herself. This second level of meaning appears also in conversation with Fortunio as she is arranging for him to meet secretly with Estefanía:

> Tú verás lo que procuro,
> venzida de vn loco amor.   (vv. 1701-1702)

She is referring here to Estefanía, but the words are more closely descriptive of herself. As her plans advance, she gloats:

> ¡Dichosa
> mi suerte, oy mi pena acaua!   (vv. 1157-58)

> Fortunio, oy gozo de ti.   (v. 1717)

As they seem thwarted she laments:

> ¡Ay de mí!
> Perdióse el remedio mío
> a vista de mi esperanza.   (vv. 1528-30)

It is not without design that the play's sonnet is spoken by Ysabel. Its content gives further dramatic dimension to her character through its "unique capacity to reveal character, motives, tensions of all kinds within the speaker and also between him and other characters with whom he is involved." [92] Although she has achieved her goal, the nature of her relationship with Fortunio makes it a hollow victory:

> ¡O, quién de amor con libertad gozara!
> ¡O, quién llegara a verle sin disgusto,
> que no gozar el gusto cara a cara
> es ynfamia de amor, trayçión del gusto!   (vv. 2399-2402)

Ysabel's confession of guilt and her punishment are in keeping with Lope's ideals of justice. The shift from schemer to penitent

---

[92] P. N. Dunn, "Some Uses of Sonnets in the Plays of Lope de Vega," *BHS*, XXXIV (1957), p. 214.

is completed as she condemns herself when Mudarra asks what evil women deserve, and she answers: "Muerte y fuego" (v. 2704).

Fortunio, as Fernán's adversary, is less an active force of evil than a victim of circumstances. This characteristic is established early in the play when Fernán's disdain for him is replied to by reference to "algún poderoso error" (v. 183), which placed him in an unfortunate position.[93] As Fernán's competitor for Estefanía, Fortunio does not function as a result of inner motivation until Ysabel provides him with an opportunity to avenge himself by cuckolding Fernán, and as Olfos tells him:

> Y luego pasarte a Françia
> a publicar la desonrra
> de Rui de Castro.   (vv. 2447-49)

It is when Fortunio takes his fate into his own hands that he acquires proportion. Well aware of the dangers involved, but willing to take the risks, he soliloquizes in the presence of Olfos:

> Estefanía querida,
> ni quiero sin ti la uida,
> ni temo por ti la muerte.   (vv. 2484-86)

Fortunio's death, of course, is traceable directly to the honor code — in killing him, Fernán Ruiz acted as an instrument of that code, for he (Fernán) was as yet unaware that Ysabel was the woman with whom Fortunio was involved. It is indeed ironic that Fortunio should be killed without ever knowing that his death was for being involved with a slave, not with Estefanía (a lack of knowledge shared by Olfos).

Mudarra, as the play's *gracioso*,[94] provides the vehicle of expression for Lope's comical scenes. Through his witty remarks, plays on words (notably the scene in Fez where *mona* is used to suggest a drinking spree), misunderstandings, he furnishes the counterpoint to the developing tragedy. The usual *gracioso* philosophy of life and love are expounded (see vv. 1328-1347), and

---

[93] See n. 80.

[94] See José F. Montesinos, *Estudios sobre Lope* (México, 1951), pp. 13-70, for a discussion of the *gracioso*'s comic value and his "función constructiva."

his master's experiences are reflected in his own (vv. 1396-1417), mimicking the loftier ideals of Fernán, not without a certain lyricism in erudite amorous complaint (see vv. 605-35). Mudarra as a character is given a special dignity as his loyalty to Estefanía and belief in her innocence are shown when he learns that she has been mortally wounded by Fernán:

> El daño es çierto.
> ¡Señora de mi alma, alma bendita!
> ¿Cómo has echo, señor, tal desconçierto?   (vv. 2635-37)

Though typified as a coward more interested in wine than in fighting, Mudarra then tells Fernán:

> Luego, señor, desde la punta al pomo
> me atrauiesa el azero de esa espada.   (vv. 2643-44)

It is notable that of all the characters who were given notice of the involvement of Estefanía and Fortunio, only Mudarra refused to believe that she was capable of such action.

Fernán Ruiz de Castro is the most prominent of the characters. His actions are those which receive the most attention and are critical to the play. He embodies the concepts and expresses the sentiments of love, honor and vengeance. His contentious nature has been noted previously. It is his intense jealousy of reputation and sense of personal worth, established in his first appearance, which lead to the ultimate, inescapable tragic act of murdering his wife. Each affront elicits a flow of verse well tailored to the man and to the situation. He is similar to Ysabel as a character in that both pursue goals with a single-mindedness and purpose not present in other characters. Yet, Fernán has those qualities of human frailty which prevent his being depicted as a super-strong, idealized figure. These qualities are best seen when he has been denied what he feels is rightfully his, and he speaks out in either anger (vv. 1490-1505) or bewildered despair (vv. 1281-1311 and 2282-2308). It is when Fernán is with Mudarra, or is speaking to himself, that he gives full expression to his doubts, fears, hopes and joys, those inner feelings which serve as the key in revealing and understanding a character. Considering the importance of honor and nobility in Fernán's life, his exclamation,

¡O, nunca tuuiera onor!
¡O, nunca noble naçiera
para que este desafío
ocasionara mi ausençia!   (vv. 1366-69)

serves as a good index of his inner feelings of loss, anguish and
dismay, caused by Estefanía's presumed marriage to Fortunio.
In Act III Lope presents Fernán in a full range of character. We
first see the proud father, anxious to see his son and beloved wife.
His joyful return is clouded by the meeting with Bermudo and
Ximeno, but he still is master of himself and aware of his worth:

Porque tengo vn corazón
cubierto de más cabellos
que la cabeza, y con ellos,
fuerza, edad y discrezión.   (vv. 2205-08)

His next change is subtle, but the exchange between Bermudo
and Fernán shows clearly that the poison of suspicion has started
to work:

BERMUDO   ¿Y si vieses con los ojos
            alguna noche?
FERNÁN   ¡Ay de mí!
BERMUDO   Dos personas juntas, di,
            ¿juzgaras que son antojos?
FERNÁN   ¿Con los ojos?
BERMUDO   Sí, señor.   (vv. 2241-45)

Suspicion becomes certainty as Fernán believes his eyes when
presented the sight of the two figures in the garden, so his only
course of action becomes obvious. The peak of Fernán's emotion
is reached as he stabs his sleeping wife:

FERNÁN   ¡Muere, muere, cruel!
ESTEFANÍA   ¡Dios mío, Dios mío!
           ¿Qué es esto? ¿Quién me ha muerto?
FERNÁN   Yo, traydora.   (vv. 2609-10)

As the now tragic figure presents himself before the King for
punishment, well aware of the enormity of his act and the
crushing knowledge of his own self-destruction, the full horror
of the situation and its inevitability are underlined by Fernán's

résumé of the events of Act III. This recapitulation, after Fernán's eulogy of his dead wife's virtues, gives sharp focus to the point of the play as it ties together the acts of the players who contributed to the tragedy. Since the principals involved are dead, it devolves on Fernán to give the summation to the court, amazed at his appearance with the "soga al cuello." Though different in some respects from the recapitulation of Friar Laurence in Shakespeare's *Romeo and Juliet*, [95] both serve to give "the audience, which until then has borne alone and inexpressibly the mounting agony of knowing all, ... relief." [96] That Fernán is to be pitied, guilty as he is, is indicated by Ordoño and Ramiro, who in turn exclaim: "¡Gran dolor! ¡Gran desbentura!" (v. 2801), applicable to Fernán as well as to Estefanía.

IV. *Plot*

The first scene of *La desdichada Estefanía* affords an opportunity to establish Fernán's and Fortunio's animosity, and then to present Estefanía. The first act, and part of the second, develop more fully the rivalry between the two nobles, interweaving the parallel love interest of Mudarra and Ysabel, plus the scenes involving the Moors. As Menéndez y Pelayo has pointed out, "la acción camina con bastante lentitud en los dos primeros actos... pero empieza a animarse en las últimas escenas del segundo, desde que forman nefanda e invisible alianza el despecho de Fortún y la liviandad de Isabel." [97] There is, of course, no lack of action *per se*, but it is a peripheral movement, which alternates Mudarra's comedy with the other characters' serious, more somber pursuits, gives a wide view of the historial material, provides veiled hints that fleetingly indicate that below the surface larger issues await exposure, and ties the characters closer to one another. The pressure of circumstances and suspense build up to a point previous to that indicated by Menéndez y Pelayo

---

[95] In this instance it highlights Fernán's personal tragedy as he recounts the steps which led to his own destruction. This awareness is his suffering.

[96] Bertrand Evans, "The Brevity of Friar Laurence," *PMLA*, LXV (1950), p. 864.

[97] Menéndez y Pelayo, *op. cit.*, p. 33.

(he refers to the alliance of Fortunio and Ysabel at the end of Act II), for issues receive a more distinct shape when Ysabel, in an *aparte* (vv. 1528-34), makes known her intentions. So intense is her concentration that Mudarra must speak to her several times in order to get her attention. Indicating her preoccupation, she says to him: "No me puedo detener" (v. 1540). Then indeed does the plot focus more narrowly on future evil events, as in quick succession Estefanía falls at the church, four of Fernán's servants are killed in the collapse of his house when the wedding party is about to enter, and another servant is accidentally killed by a *cochero*.

Sancho Laynez's report of the invasion of the Moors sets the stage for Fortunio's relatively easy access to Estefanía while Fernán Ruiz is absent, involved in the defense of Spain. This second absence renders significant his first, and is an echo of it. In both cases he returns to discover that Estefanía has apparently been unfaithful. His reaction in the second instance varies in intensity and in nature, for now it is a question of his wife, "las espaldas del hombre" (see vv. 2765-68), who has been untrue. The range of his mood and reaction to this information, described above, lead Act III to its horrifying scene of the death of Estefanía, and its tragic climax with Fernán's realization of her innocence. Lope then uses a mere 118 lines to bring the play to a close. In this last section there is a unity in the nature of the situations which are resolved, for first Ysabel, through the principle of poetic justice as defined by Parker (see above), is given her just deserts, then the defeated Abdelmón is sent back to Africa, and Fernán enters to receive his punishment.

Two traditional elements of the play, brilliantly developed in *La Celestina* and subsequently presented in Spanish literature, are the fall of Fortune and the *saltaparedes* motifs (see Stephan Gilman's *The Art of "La Celestina"* [Madison, 1956], pp. 127-30, and his article "The Fall of Fortune: From Allegory to Fiction," *Filologia Romanza*, IV [1957], pp. 337-354. Juan Bautista Avalle Arce also discusses the fall in "Poesía, historia, imperialismo: *La Numancia*," *Anuario de Letras*, II [1962], pp. 70-72). Both of these elements refer to happenings which have to do with Fortunio and Estefanía, or Ysabel in her role as Estefanía, the three major characters who die in the work.

It is Fortunio who first expresses the allegorical fall from Fortune's high position (the combination Fortunio-*fortuna* is clearly not accidental), related to the mythological framework of Phaeton's fall through space. After Estefanía has rejected him he says:

> Si enprendí llegar al sol,
> si de sus rayos diuinos
> me tube asido en el ayre
> y de su çielo he caydo,
> yo he hecho lo que he podido,
> fortuna lo que ha querido.   (vv, 1560-65)

The relationship between the spatial fall and the influence of Fortune is further emphasized as Fortunio continues:

> Abrasóme tanto sol,
> dexé riendas, perdí estribos,
> la tierra abrasé y cay.
> Mas si he subido y caydo,
> yo he hecho lo que [e] podido,
> fortuna lo que ha querido.   (vv. 1582-87)

In order to fall, Fortunio must first have ascended; this is accomplished as he tells Alfonso:

> No la merezco, señor,
> mas si deste baxo suelo
> a tal grandeza me subes,
> ... ...   (vv. 1089-91)

Ironically, Fortunio is speaking the truth when he says to Alfonso that he does not deserve Estefanía, an irony which is carried a step further when he loses her because of the workings of Fortune. Just as he was not responsible for winning her, he had nothing to do with losing her.

After this initial reference to his fall, Fortunio speaks of another fall, that of Lucifer, whose expulsion from Heaven is considered a fall (see A. Valbuena Briones, "El simbolismo en el teatro de Calderón," *Romanische Forschungen*, LXXIV [1962], p. 72: "Oy caerás, Luzbel hermoso, del çielo..." vv. 1683-84). Already equated with evil, contrasting with Fernán's representation of good, Fortunio names his symbolic identity in the play and in so doing he predicts his own fate. His second fall is foreshadowed as Ysabel tells him in Act III: "Pues por el jardín subid" (v. 1991); from the example of his previous ascent and fall, plus his allusion to that of Luzbel, the audience expects that Fortunio is about to experience another fall — in this case fatal. A. Valbuena Briones has indicated that: "El emblema en conjunto [de la caída] indica un mal agüero, puesto que los instintos van a arrastrar a la destrucción en el caso de la tragedia..." (see the above work, p. 61).

The other two examples of falls involve actual physical falling. Both specifically are related to the idea of *malos agüeros* and identified as such. The first occurs when Estefanía falls upon leaving the church. Interspersed with expressions of solicitude appear the following remarks:

DAMA 2ª   ¡Con qué extraños azares ha salido!   (v. 1721)

RAMIRO   El ha sido, por Dios, estraño caso.
DAMA 2ª   Es propio de vna fiesta mui solene.
               Vn mal suçeso, vn lastimoso paso.   (vv. 1729-31)

The next occurrence comes immediately after the above, when the wedding party, approaching Ruiz's house, hears a noise, "como que la casa se hunde" (stage directions before v. 1766). The first reaction to this noise is rendered by the Dama 1ª: "Agüeros son estraños" (v. 1765). Nuño voices his opinion that: "Sin duda que la casa se ha caydo" (v. 1767). Alfonso and Ordoño emphasize the seriousness of the situation in vv. 1796-97, while Fernán and Estefanía predict:

FERNÁN   Algo me ha de suçeder.
ESTEFANÍA   Algún daño se me açerca.   (vv. 1816-17)

After a subsequent incident (the *cochero* causes the death of one of Fernán's *escuderos*), Alfonso, as if to frighten away evil spirits by denying their existence, states that:

Si contra n[uest]ra fee santa no fuera
creher agüeros, diera a tantos crédito,
mas estas cosas son mui naturales.   (vv. 1852-54)

The system of *agüeros* and predictions (see vv. 2471-75 for another example of a forecast), the symbolism of the fall, are all linked to produce a mood of ominous foreboding, foreshadowing the tragedy which is to occur.

The second traditional element of the play which is reminiscent of *La Celestina* is the mode of entry into the *jardín* (called a *huerto* in *La Celestina*) used by Fortunio to meet Estefanía, and the use of the expression *saltar paredes* in vv. 2066, 2497, 2588. (See María Rosa Lida de Malkiel, *La originalidad artística de "La Celestina"* [Buenos Aires, 1962], pp. 200-205). The symbolism of the *escala* does not escape Ximeno, who in answer to Bermudo's statement about what he sees: "Al jardín la escala pone," responds: "Al honor de Castro di" (vv. 2073-74). The walls of the garden do not protect Fernán's home nor his honor against Fortunio's assault, aided as he is by the *escala*. The ladder's importance for both Fortunio and Ysabel is indicated as each inquires: "¿Traes la escala?" (v. 1973 and 1989). He directs his question to Olfos, while she asks it of Fortunio.

Just as the use of the *escala* resulted in death for Calixto and Melibea, so too do Ysabel and Fortunio perish. Calixto's servants met with death for their part in their master's plan, and Olfos suffers a like fate.

A conventional view of the play might suggest that due to the title and her unfortunate death, Estefanía is the principal figure, but this is definitely not the case. In this respect the structure of *La desdichada Estefanía* is paralleled by that of *El castigo sin venganza,* whose principal character has correctly been shown to be the Duque, not Casandra. [98] Estefanía's death, to be sure, is pathetic, but it is Fernán who is the central character. If one reviews his actions in relation to the whole, it becomes clear that his is the real tragedy of the play. Parker's principle of causality, working backward from Fernán's act of murdering his innocent wife, will show that though he is not completely to blame for his sin, his total dependence on his

---

[98] See Parker, *loc. cit.,* pp. 14-16, and T. E. May, "Lope de Vega's *El castigo sin venganza:* The Idolatry of the Duke of Ferrara," *BHS,* XXXVII (1960), pp. 177-78. Reichenberger, *loc. cit.,* p. 316, n. 19, still fails to grasp this point. He feels that the title of the play contradicts such an analysis.

sense of honor is what made the tragedy possible. It is the real
departure point of the trajectory which, with the help of circumstances and the other characters, constitutes the vein of irony
which runs through the play. Over-zealous in protecting his honor,
Fernán ends by killing the one person whom he loved most, and
whose existence gave meaning and substance to his very honor.
It should be noted in passing that the principle of poetic justice
(except in the case of Fernán's servants) operating in the play
dealt death to those who contributed to Fernán's commission of
murder. As for his punishment, Fernán is echoed by the Duque
of *El castigo sin venganza,* who suffers what Parker calls punishment by frustration. Death would be a reward and a release for
Fernán from the hell, torment and torture which must be his
for as long as he lives.

P. N. Dunn, in his article on honor, begins by quoting a passage from Fray Diego de Estella, which is crucial to an understanding of Fernán and the moral implications attendant on
his act of murder:

> Tres cosas reservó Dios para sí, y no quiso que nadie se
> las tomase. La primera es juzgar la intención y pensa-
> miento de nuestros prójimos, según aquello que él mes-
> mo dice: "No queráis juzgar, y no seréis juzgados"... La
> segunda, la honra y gloria, conforme a aquello que dice
> el mesmo Dios: "No daré a nadie mi gloria". La tercera
> cosa que reservó para sí es la venganza. Guárdate de
> hurtar a Dios ninguna de estas cosas. [99]

Fernán usurps God's vengeance, indicating that he conceives
of himself as His agent, as he prepares to kill Estefanía:

> No disimules el delito fiero,
> que del çielo el castigo te ha venido.   (vv. 2603-04)

In a similar situation in *El castigo sin venganza,* the Duke declares:

> Çielos,
> oy se ha de ver en mi casa
> no más de vuestro castigo.   (vv. 2834-36)

---

[99] Dunn, "Honour and the Christian Background in Calderón," *op. cit.,*
p. 75.

Both protagonists delude themselves when they declare that their acts constitute a *castigo*, for both are attempting to "reconcile themselves to their code through bloodshed, instead of to human nature through mercy." [100] T. E. May says of *castigo* and *venganza*:

> The first is a punishment decreed by a lawful authority, natural or public (parent, judge), while the second is a personal affair, a punishment decreed and inflicted by the injured party. *Venganza* is properly self-regarding, while *castigo* envisages the good of the community and, so far as is practicable, of the culprit.... *Castigo* cannot of its nature exclude the possibility or even the duty of mercy. [101]

In neither case is mercy shown. Both assume the double functions of prosecutor and judge, while Fernán is also the executioner. But where Casandra and Federico were guilty of crimes, Fernán only *believed* that Estefanía was guilty of adultery. In numerous scenes Lope has portrayed Fernán's inability to *see* in matters concerning Estefanía. As she is dying she asks:

> ¿Quién te ha engañado?   (v. 2618)

> ¿Cómo que dieses crédito tan presto
> a quien te puso en tan notable engaño?
>   (vv. 2662-63)

She could well have used the same reproach when he so quickly accepted, without substantiation, that she had rejected him in favor of Fortunio, when he was ready to believe the worst. Gilman says:

> Where previously seeing had been certain and believing confused, now seeing was confused and believing certain.... Each author or artist acts as a miniature divinity and imparts his own providence to the structure of his creation.... The illusions, the mistaken identities, etc. of the later *comedias* were derived from human blindness and ignorance rather than from external mystery.... The

---

[100] *Ibid.*, p. 84.
[101] *May, op. cit.*, p. 163.

inequalities and deceits of the world (and in style) were purposeful and not haphazard. [102]

Lope emphasizes the limited perception of Fernán by repeated use of *ver* and *ojos* (see vv. 2217, 2226, 2233, etc.), investing them with special significance. He tells Bermudo and Ximeno, who have "seen" Estefanía in the garden with another man:

> Mirad que habláis de vna cosa
> que la he de ver y tocar,
> que yo no he de castigar
> vna muger virtüosa
> por siniestra ynformaçión.   (vv. 2225-29)

In effect, this is precisely what happens. Fernán "sees," but since he is not God, he cannot evaluate properly what his eyes show him. Parker refers to the human predicament of man:

> ... caught in circumstances that are the responsibility of all, whose ramifications the individual cannot see, prisoner as he is of the partial perspectives of a limited time and space, yet both the sufferer of acts that come in from outside the partial perspectives and the agent of acts that have their repercussions beyond them. [103]

Bermudo and Ximeno share the same inability to see and contribute to Fernán's partial vision:

> BERMUDO Será lo que yo temí:
> rebuelta en aquel manteo
> que suele traher de día,
> en la güerta Estefanía,
> en la ventana la veo.
> XIMENO ¿Sin luz le ves?
> BERMUDO   Luz me dan,
> Ximeno, los pasamanos,
> que lo que tocan las manos
> los más çiegos lo verán.   (vv. 2036-44)

---

[102] Stephen Gilman, "An Introduction to the Ideology of the Baroque in Spain," *Symposium*, I (1946), pp. 103-04.

[103] Parker, *loc. cit.*, p. 236.

But the *luz* which all three need is the *entendimiento* of God; all are in reality blinded by what each brings to the situation. [104] Fernán warns the servants:

> ... abrí muy bien los ojos.
> No seáis, con çiençia vana,
> los dos viejos de Susana,
> çiegos de locos antojos.
> ... ...
> porque seré Daniel
> y os haré matar con piedras.   (vv. 2217-24)

As events transpire, it is he who becomes blinded like *los dos viejos,* blinded by the source of his *engaño, los ojos.* After Estefanía dies he exclaims:

> ¡Ay, dulçe suerte,
> si mis ojos çerrara assí la muerte!   (vv. 2679-80)

As has been seen, he is not to gain the release of death so easily. Although he does not die, order is restored after what Mudarra calls Fernán's *desconçierto* (v. 2637), as the latter appears before the figure of supreme terrestrial justice, the King. Reichenberger refers to the saying that "all's well that ends well," and in drama "everything ends well when *honra* has been restored to everyone who as lost it." [105] In the sense that order is regained, this play follows that pattern. But it must be remembered that Fernán is guilty of a sin other than just the murder of Estefanía; he is also guilty of the idolatry in which the Duque of Ferrara indulged. So all does *not* end well. Fernán's life is not worth living, but he must continue to contemplate the shambles of a once happy existence. Again, this is the real tragedy of the play.

Menéndez y Pelayo has compared *La desdichada Estefanía* favorably with Shakespeare's *Othello,* stating that "cuando el horror trágico llega a su colmo, cuando no depende ya del carácter, sino de la situación, Lope y Shakespeare se encuentran como espíritus gemelos." [106] He admits frankly: "Cierto que en la obra

---

[104] Morris, *op. cit.,* pp. 69-78, shows the great influence of *los ojos* in *El castigo sin venganza* and the consequences of such blindness.

[105] Reichenberger, *loc. cit.,* p. 307.

[106] Menéndez y Pelayo, *op. cit.,* p. 34.

de Lope, medio improvisada y completamente legendaria en su estructura, se echan de menos la profundidad de observación moral, la anatomía desgarradora de la pasión celosa.... La comedia de Lope es una novela dramática, no es una obra de análisis." [107] But it would appear that Menéndez y Pelayo's statement that the play lacks profundity of moral observation and is *medio improvisada* is without foundation. On the contrary, Lope has delved more deeply into the question of Fernán's morality than Menéndez y Pelayo realized, possibly because he failed to see that Fernán is the protagonist, not Estefanía. Insofar as improvisation is concerned, one need only point to the complexity and interrelationship of elements such as the legend itself, the motif of the fall, the *engaño*, honor and Fernán's ultimate tragedy. It is not by chance alone that they not only appear in the work, but function at various levels via suspense and dramatic presentation to form the whole — a tragedy.

"LA DESDICHADA ESTEFANÍA" THEME IN SPANISH LITERATURE

Los zelos hasta los cielos y desdichada Estefanía, by Luis Vélez de Guevara, [108] follows the same general outlines of Lope's play, but it is patently inferior to it. Characters are assigned different names (Fortún-Don Vela, Ysabel-Fortuna, Mudarra-Lebrel, Bermudo-Ordoño, etc.), and two new figures are introduced, Don Sancho, who is Estefanía's brother, and Blanca, his bride. The Moors do not appear, nor does King Luis of France. Vélez dispenses with the *desafío* material, thereby effecting only one absence for Fernán. He and Don Vela compete for Estefanía, but only on a verbal level — there is none of the open, longstanding animosity between the men, initially presented by Lope as a matter of honor. If anything, *Los zelos* underlines that they are friends. Estefanía is married "por cierta razón de estado," with a series of evil omens accompanying the ceremony. [109] This

[107] *Ibid.,* p. 33.

[108] Luis Vélez de Guevara, *Los zelos hasta los cielos y desdichada Estefanía* (Madrid, 1747).

[109] Forrest E. Spencer and Rudolph Schevill, *The Dramatic Works of Luis Vélez de Guevara* (Berkeley, 1937), pp. 160-163, give a résumé of the

causes Alfonso to want her to return to the palace, which she refuses to do. These facts are given to Don Vela by Lebrel; they are not dramatized. The device of having Fortuna give Don Vela a ring belonging to Estefanía is introduced. Fernán, recognizing the ring in Don Vela's possession at a later point, is thus primed to accept readily the report of his wife's adultery and is certain of the identity of her partner.

Lebrel is not involved with Fortuna in a parallel love situation — indeed, he is seen more as a figure *away* from his master than with him. It is he who accompanies Fernán in the garden vigil of Act III as Don Vela and Fortuna meet. Lebrel's comic value is almost non-existent.

The couple's son is born at the beginning of Act II, a fact which eliminates the contrast between Fernán's urgency to return home and his despair upon learning of Estefanía's infidelity, as Lope presents it. Don Vela openly declares his love to Estefanía *after* her marriage; her rejection of his suit is arrogant:

> ¿Cómo, Conde, una muger
> como yo, al fin, que el poder
> de un imperio la venera,
> muger de quien soy, primera
> en Castilla, y en León,
> y muger de mi opinión,
> aspiras a alzar los ojos,
> sin temor que mis enojos,
> rayos dellos mismos son?

When Fortuna informs Don Vela that Estefanía secretly loves him, there is none of the doubt and fear that Fortunio expresses. Don Vela accepts the ring which Fortuna has stolen (see above), congratulating himself on his good fortune. He gains access to Estefanía, having been assigned by Alfonso to stay with Don Sancho to guard the realm against a possible attack by one Aben-Ragel, Rui de Cuenca, while the main body of the army is away

---

play with action in the first act which does not appear in the *suelta*: "The emperor Alfonso VII (called Alonso VIII by Vélez) enters to inquire the cause of the recent disturbance, and is shocked to discover that the picture is a likeness of his daughter, Estefanía. He resolves to keep the affair quiet. . . ." (pp. 160-61).

in battle with the Miramamolín and Almanzor. Fernán, charging
Don Vela with the care of Estefanía, sees the ring on his finger.
This situation deprives Don Vela of the atmosphere of secrecy
and stealth with which Fortunio's return is surrounded, as well
as the self-awareness of the trap which his love for Estefanía has
forged.

When the servants inform Fernán that he is without honor
it is accomplished abruptly, without the building of dramatic tension that Lope creates via the insistent use of the visual *engaño*
discussed previously. In its place Vélez has the three ramble
through some 100 lines before Fernán and the audience are told
exactly why Fernán's "honra ha muerto:"

> ... hemos visto
> entrar con mucho silencio
> un hombre no conocido
> por la puerta del jardín ...

Even the *saltaparedes* value has been removed, for Don Vela
enters with comfort via a convenient door. Fernán asks for no
proof of Estefanía's alleged acts — instead, he verbally denigrates
her, then treats her coldly when she greets him. He has already
accepted her guilt as fact. His only doubt is brushed away immediately:

> ¿Es posible que esto puede
> ser engaño, ser fingido,
> y aquestas lágrimas falsas?
> Sí, que un filósofo dijo
> que era la muger tyrana
> dueño de nuestros sentidos,
> fiera de muchos dobleces,
> y animal de muchos visos.

Lope has Fernán wait in the garden to obtain proof of Estefanía's
infidelity; Vélez has him wait to catch the lovers and punish them.

In order to demonstrate the almost total lack of perception
as to the real tragedy of the play and its dramatic craftsmanship,
the following comparison of the two plays by Menéndez y Pelayo is offered:

No hay en la refundición de Vélez de Guevara tanta frescura y naturalidad de dicción como en el original de Lope, y, por el contrario, abundan los rasgos enfáticos y culteranos, pero hay más artificio teatral y algunas innovaciones felices. Si alguien intentara poner de nuevo en escena tan patética fábula, haría bien en aprovechar juntamente el drama de Lope y el de Luis Vélez. Este ha graduado mejor los tormentos celosos por que pasa el alma de Fernán Ruiz en la escena con los escuderos, sus angustias, sus dudas, el esfuerzo que hace sobre sí mismo para disimular con su esposa, cuando ésta sale a recibirle, su desesperación, sus proyectos de venganza. La escena del jardín está conducida con más arte. En la muerte de Estefanía, el genio de Lope lleva la ventaja; pero el talento de Luis Vélez se manifiesta en dar a Fernán Ruiz un momento de indecisión antes de herir, contemplando a su mujer dormida; ... Otra modificación de muy buen efecto consiste en prolongar la agonía de la esposa, para que muera con el consuelo de ver reconocida su inocencia. [110]

He had previously mentioned that Vélez concentrates the tragic action more, whose interest consists of the person of Estefanía, and limits the accessory elements which Lope's work contains. [111] That Estefanía is not the protagonist has already been demonstrated. True, Vélez creates an Estefanía with more lines in the play, but she never becomes what could be considered a tragic heroine. Menéndez y Pelayo correctly states that Lope's play has more natural action, a smooth quality, etc. Vélez, on the other hand, by lengthening speeches (to replace the *elementos accesorios?*) to the point where they lose themselves in a high-flown, artificial rhetoric which misses the point, in effect has created a parody, not a *refundición* of Lope's work. If by *innovaciones felices* (other than those he mentions), Menéndez y Pelayo refers to such devices as the use of the opening scene in which Fernán and Don Vela quarrel over a picture of Estefanía until they are about to duel (a rather puerile representation of the more serious aspects of the honor code), the use of the ring, the reduction of Lope's dramatic presentation of action to a chronicle of events

---

[110] Menéndez y Pelayo, *op. cit.*, pp. 38-39.
[111] *Ibid.*, p. 38.

which happen off the stage (eliminating the force of suspense and tension), then they should be called *infelices*. Vélez has not "graduado mejor los tormentos celosos," nor are Fernán's efforts to "disimular con su esposa . . ." of particular note, except to demonstrate a singular insensitivity. The following passages are offered for comparison:

Vélez de Guevara

FERNÁN
¡Mal habláis!
Por arrancaros estoy
las lenguas; y si pudiera,
lo mismo pienso que hiciera
de los pensamientos oy.

Lope de Vega

FERNÁN
¡Dios me guarde!
No me habléys, no digáis más.
¡Jesús, qué ynfierno, qué rabia,
qué desdicha! Estefanía,
hija del Rey, muger mía,
cuerda, onesta, santa y sabia,
no es posible. ¡Hombres del diablo,
vosotros mentís!
XIMENO
¡Señor!
FERNÁN
¿Háoslo dicho algún traydor
de los que en Burgos no hablo?
¿Quánto os dan por este enrredo?
(vv. 2259-69)

FERNÁN
¿Una muger tan heroyca
(de aquesto me maravillo)
corrido aya débilmente
a tan locos precipicios?
Mas, ¿qué me espanto, si todos
vienen de un origen mismo?
¡Para ver anticipados
mis agravios he corrido
tantas postas! ¡Para ver
los ojos de un basilisco,
hermosos, pero tyranos,
que me han muerto los sentidos!

FERNÁN
Arcos honrrosos, ¡pluguiera
a Dios que aquel mismo día,
sobre mí y Estefanía
v[vuest]ra máquina cayera!
¿Para qué os aderezé?
¿Para qué con v[uest]ro escudo
puse el de Castilla? Dudo,
temo; no ha sido, no fue.
¿Cómo me pudo ofender
muger de tan alto nombre?
Pero díxome aquel ombre:
"que dudes lo que es muger."
Muger es; si quiso pudo.
Pudo, pues ausente fui.
Fui onrrado, ynfame boluí;
pues si es ansí, ¿qué lo dudo?
(vv. 2293-2308)

ESTEFANÍA
¿Cómo venís, dueño amado?
FERNÁN
De Alfonso favorecido,
y del moro vencedor:
[*ap.*] ¡Assí de tus desatinos
no estuviera, monstruo ingrato,
tantas veces ofendido!

ESTEFANÍA
Déxame, mi solo bien,
descansar en esos brazos.
FERNÁN
[*ap.*] ¡Quién los hiziera pedazos
y a quién se los dio tanbién!
Dulçíssima Estefanía.
... ...
Luz mía.
[*ap.*] Luz fue, pero ya eclipsada
de infamia, tinebla es.
... ...
Querráme ver la çiudad.
[*ap.*] Çielos, ¿si será verdad?
Tened lástima de mí.

(vv. 2313-60)

Menéndez y Pelayo errs in his intimation that Estefanía dies
before having her innocence recognized in Lope's play. Ysabel
reveals her guilt in vv. 2653-2658, and Estefanía is still speaking
in v. 2675. He correctly assesses Lope's death scene as superior
to that of Vélez (the latter's extends 19 lines from Fernán's entrance to the discovery of Fortuna, versus 45 lines in Lope's
version). Regardless of Fernán's allegedly more dramatic moment
of hesitation in Vélez's play, he is without the moral conviction of
the evidence furnished Lope's protagonist, who doubted until he
saw "con los ojos," and believing his eyes, claimed that Estefanía's
murder was a "castigo del cielo." Vélez's Fernán is without the
doubts which became certainty for his counterpart via the *engaño
que engaña;* the former's act is reduced to the performance of a
brutal act. It then takes over 200 lines to have Fernán lament
Estefanía's death and recapitulate the events to Alfonso and the
courtiers who accompany him to Fernán's house.

Don Alberto Lista calls *Los zelos* "el drama de Vélez de
Guevara en que sintió mejor la inspiración trájica..."[112] Since
he does not mention Lope's *La desdichada Estefanía,* one can
only conjecture that he was not aware of its existence.[113] What

---

[112] Alberto Lista y Aragón, *Ensayos literarios y críticos* (Sevilla, 1844),
I, p. 146.
[113] Menéndez y Pelayo reaches the same conclusion for Schack, who
"ensalza demasiado la de Luis Vélez...", *op. cit.*, p. 39, n. 1.

Vélez de Guevara's play represents is an attempt by "otro drama-turgo, insigne entre los de segundo orden," [114] to copy, without success, the magic that was Lope's. This was the fate of so many who, by imitation, hoped to capitalize on Lope's genius, but succeeded only in displaying their own inferior talent.

As indicated by Menéndez y Pelayo, Padre Arolas and Don Ramón de Campoamor have written poems based on the trag-edy. [115] Lope's play was evidently the source for neither. The former follows the general story as it appears in Sandoval's account, while the latter reflects elements from Vélez's work.

---

[114] *Ibid*, p. 38.
[115] *Ibid.*, p. 39. Later editions than those cited Menéndez y Pelayo are: Ramón de Campoamor, *Obras poéticas completas* (Barcelona, 1903), III, pp. 132-34; J. R. Lomba y Pedraja (ed.), *Poesías del P. Arolas* (Madrid, 1928), pp. 109-120.

ESTEPHANIA LA DESDICHA DA

TRAGEDIA PRIMERA

1604 · Passa en

(rúbrica) Burgos

MSA list the title as TRAGICOMEDIA FAMOSA DE LA DESDICHA-DA ESTEFANIA. B shows LA DESDICHADA ESTEFANIA, COMEDIA FAMOSA DE LOPE DE VEGA CARPIO. G reads PRIMERA TRAGEDIA DE ESTEPHANIA LA DESDICHADA, Año de 1604 Passa en Burgos *(rúbrica)*. J omits the *rúbrica,* and renders *Pasa.**

The punctuation and accentuation given in the footnotes are those of M. Minor differences are not noted.

An asterisk indicates that a word, passage, etc., is treated in the notes.

Los que hablan en el Acto Primero

Rey Luis de Françia
Rey Alfonso de España
Fernán Ruiz de Castro
Fortunio Ximénez
Estephanía, hija del Rey
Ysabel, esclaua
Mudarra, escudero o lacayo
Almohadí
Zerbino
Lisardo
Albumasar
Learín
Abdelmón
Miramamolín

(rúbrica)

MSBA list all the characters of the play on the title page. Each has the same order, but A lists only one character per line, showing two groupings of *moros,* indicated by a side bracket. Following is the *reparto* as it appears in MSB:

Hablan en ella las personas siguientes.

El Rey Alfonso.	Rey Miramamolin Moro.
El Rey Luys.	Zayde Moro.
Fernan Ruyz de Castro.	Audelmon Moro.
Fortun Ximenez.	Ximeno. Ceydan Moro.
Estefania. Ysabel.	Albumasar Moro.
Mudarra lacayo.	Almohadi Moro.
Olfos criado.	Ordoño. Ramiro.
Bermudo.	El Conde don Nuño.

G reads "Personas que..." and *Luis Rey de francia, Alfonso Rey de españa, Estefania...*

M omits the *s* of Ysabel, B spells the name with an *I*. A groups the listing in three columns, changing Audelmon to Andelmón, reduces *don* to *D*. before Nuño, changes Ceydan to Zeydán, modernizes Ximenez to Jiménez, Luys to Luis, etc. When the variants are identical except for the modernized spelling of A, MS are reproduced.*

ACTO P[RIMER]O

Rey Luis de Françia, Rey Alfonso de España,
Fernán Ruiz de Castro, Fortunio Ximénez.

LUIS	Contento en estremo voy	
	de la merzed reçiuida.	
ALFONSO	En obligaçión estoy	
	mientras que tuuiere uida.	
LUIS	Señor, v[uest]ro hijo soy,	5
	que con aquesto confieso	
	la obedienzia y sujeçión.	
ALFONSO	Aunque ser padre profeso	
	por sangre, a esta obligaçión	
	quedo por mil causas preso.	10
	En esta breue distanzia,	
	aunque es grande la gananzia	
	que fuesse, no es marauilla	*
	corta huéspeda Castilla,	
	Luis, para un Rey de Franzia.	15
	Mal sin regalo os detengo,	
	pues sólo en esta ocasión	

St. dir. before v. 1. MSBA, Salen el Rey Luys, y el Rey Alfonso, Fernan
Ruyz de Castro, y Fortun Ximenez.*
    1. *
    4. MSBA, Dios me diere vida.
    5. *
    9. *
    11-15. MSBA, omit.
    17. MSBA, aunque en aquesta.

en que a reçiuiros vengo,
he ensanchado el corazón,
donde como a hijo os tengo.   20

Luis   Quando el huésped que reçiue *[fol. 1 v.]*
es pobre, cunple mostrando
la voluntad con que uiue;
quando es rico, sólo obrando
las grandezas que aperçiue.   25
      Déstas, tantas ha mostrado
Castilla, que voy, señor,
de v[uest]ro reyno admirado.
Justamente Emperador
de España fuistes llamado.   30*
      No crehí que tal poder,
teníades. ¡Cosa estraña!
Dios os dexe, Alfonso, ver
Rei absoluto de España.
Dios y vos lo hauéis de hazer: 35
      Dios, con ayudar el çelo
de v[uest]ra fee contra el moro;   *
vos, en derribar al suelo
su imperio, y deste tesoro
ofreziendo el quinto al çielo.   40
      Que tenéis de ilustre gente,
que en las fiestas han mostrado
tal balor, que no consiente   *
ygualdad con el pasado
ni fama con el presente.   45

---

18. MSBA, ya que.
21. M, q̄ os recibe.*
23. MSBA, la obligacion en que viue.
26. *
27. B, vos.*
28. MSBA, nombre.*
33. MSBA, ser.
36. MSBA, en ensanchar.
40. MSBA, ofrecerle.
41. MSBA, omit *de.**
42. MSBA, ha.

¡Qué gallardos caballeros!   *[fol.] 2 [r.]*
Conquistar pueden mil mundos,
naciendo entre moros fieros;
en la edad, al Cid segundos,
pero en el balor primeros.   50
　　Yo llebo bien que contar
a mis nobles en París.

ALFONSO   No tenéis vos qué embidiar,
porque v[uest]ra flor de lis
cubre el suelo, ocupa el mar.   55
　　No he mostrado cunplimiento:
como a hijo os he tratado;
sólo he mostrado contento
de verme de vos onrrado,
aunque en este fabor, siento   60
que no mostráis alegría.

LUIS   Voi, qual veis, en romería
a Santiago, y es razón   ✳
yr con igual debozión,
y es tanbién condición mía.   65

ALFONSO   　　No, por Dios, algo tenéis,
que quando a alegraros vais,
aquel plazer suspendéis
y en la suspensión mostráis
que del gusto os ofendéis.   70
　　¿Cánsaos Castilla, o quedó
algo en París que os lastima?   *[fol. 2 v.]*
Suegro y amigo soy yo.
Quien esto postrero estima,
mi voluntad agrauió.   75

---

46. MSBA, Que de ilustres.✳
47. MSBA, gouernar.
50. M, en el Balbi.
51. ✳
52. MSBA, a Paris.
56. ✳
59. MSBA, en verme.
68. B, aquel valor.
75. MSBA, la voluntad.

	¿Qué tenéis? ¿De qué estáis triste?	
LUIS	Yo os dixera en qué consiste	
	a estar solos.	
ALFONSO	Aquí están	
	dos hombres que os seruirán.	
	Sangre y nobleza los uiste.	80

El vno, aunque es español,
se passó a Françia a seruiros.
Su pecho es oro en crisol,
y sólo puedo deçiros
que es sombra de v[uest]ro sol.   85
                                                    *
    Con vos priba, y la pribanza
es sólo hazer confianza
de la verdad del que priua,
para que seguro uiua
quien noble priuado alcanza.   90
    El otro, y de cuya mano,
espada y roxo pabés,
tiembla el morisco africano,
Fernán Ruiz de Castro es,
que llaman el Castellano.   95
    Este, como allá con vos
Fortuno Ximénez priua,   [fol.] 3 [r.]
es mi priuanza, por Dios.
Si en los dos tal fuerza estriua,
delante hablad de los dos,   100
    o entranbos se salgan fuera.

LUIS	Pues agora puedo hablar.
	No es bien que, callando, quiera

---

77. MSBA, omit *os*.
78. *
81. *
82. *
83. *
84. *
86. *
91. MSBA, omit *y*.
100. MSBA, habla.*
102. *

	con el silenzio aumentar	
	causas a mi pena fiera.	105
	Tu hija, Alfonso, me diste	
	en casamiento.	
ALFONSO	Es verdad.	
LUIS	Ser legítima dixiste,	
	y ygual a la magestad	✿
	que en Françia y sus reyes uiste.	110
ALFONSO	¿Quién lo duda?	
LUIS	Yo, que he sido	
	de lo contrario ynformado,	
	y que bastarda ha naçido,	
	Alfonso, y que has engañado	
	quien no te lo ha mereçido.	115
	¿Costanza, bastarda tuya,	
	me das a mí?	
ALFONSO	¿Que a esto vienes	
	de Françia?	
LUIS	La graçia suya	
	y mil naturales bienes	
	quieren que su sangre arguya,	120*
	mas yo tengo información	
	de que es bastarda Costanza, *[fol. 3 v.]*	
	y entre reyes no es razón	
	engañar la confïanza	
	y ofender la estimaçión.	125
	Con esta pena fingí	
	la romería a Santiago	

----

104. MSBA, mi silencio.*
105. MSBA, mi pasion desta manera.
106. ✿
109. MSBA, omit *y*.
111. ✿
114. MSBA, Rey.
115. MSBA, a quien no lo.
116. ✿
117. MSBA, esso; J, a mi?
121. J, informaçion.
122. ✿
125. MSBA, ni ofender.
126-130. MSBA, omit.*

	por informarme de ti,	
	para no darle mal pago	
	a quien quiero más que a mí.	130
	Dime, Alfonso, la verdad.	
ALFONSO	Costanza, Luis, sin cautela,	✽
	que no cabe en amistad,	
	es hija de Berenguela,	
	mi muger.	
FERNÁN	¡Qué gran maldad!	135
	Viue Dios, que si supiera	
	de çierto quién ynformó	
	a tu magestad, que hiziera ...	✽
FORTUNIO	¿Tú hablas donde estoy yo,	
	Fernán Ruiz, desa manera?	140
FERNÁN	Pues, ¿cómo tengo de hablar?	
FORTUNIO	Sin mirarme, porque es dar	
	ocasión que piense el Rey	
	que dexé la noble ley	
	quando le dexé de onrrar,	145
	y que en esto soy culpado.	
FERNÁN	Tú a ningún rey has onrrado,	
	ni al de España antes que fuesses *[fol.] 4 [r.]*	
	a Françia por ynteresses	
	de tu mal tenido estado,	150
	ni al de Françia, pues allá	
	le has dicho lo que le ha hecho	
	venir con despecho acá,	
	en que muestras que tu pecho	
	en ninguna parte está.	155

---

131. ✽
132. MSBA, Rey.
133. MSBA, en mi amistad.
134. ✽
135. MSBA, Ay tal maldad.
136. MSBA, entendiera.
137. MSBA, quien de essa suerte informò.
138. ✽
139. MSBA, Como hablas.
145. MSBA, la dexè.
153. A, desprecio.
154. MSBA, se vee que.

Tu mudable condizión
y el desseo de venganza
ha hecho aquesta inuenzión,
porque tienes esperanza
de tu injusta posesión. 160

Y mouiendo los que están
en paz a perpetua guerra,
quando las manos se dan,
ser el rayo de tu tierra, ❋
como otro Conde Julián. 165❋

Pero antes que seas rayo,
y buelba a tan vil desmayo
tu patria España, infamada,
pondrá Dios en esta espada
la ventura de Pelayo. 170❋

FORTUNIO Rui de Castro, yo naçí
noble en Castilla, y al Rey
que está presente, seruí
en defensa de la ley
que en la crisma reçiuí. 175

Antes que de España fuera *[fol. 4 v.]*
a Françia, con la venera
que la cruz roxa acompaña ❋
ayudé a ganar a España,
y lebanté su vandera. 180

No me fui por ser traydor,
sino porque la maliçia
de algún poderoso error,
derribando mi justiçia,
escureçió mi balor. 185

157. B, mudança; MSBA, omit *el.*
158. MSBA, han.
159. B, confiança.
160. MSBA, de la injusta.
162. ❋
163. MSBA, tus malos intentos van.
164. MSBA, a ser rayo.
166. MSBA, Mas antes.
176. ❋
180. MSBA, y a leuantar.

Busqué rey a quien seruir
y halléle de ygual poder,
y esto no puede ympedir
que aquí no pueda boluer,
pues no salí por hüir.   190
   Si es mal echo, y si esto ofende,
el Rey de Alfonso deziende,   *
que siruió en Toledo a un moro,
y esto no inporta al decoro
que la nobleza pretende.   195
   Que tanbién Guzmán el Bueno   *
fue en Marruecos capitán,
mas no dexó, de onor lleno,
de ser bueno y ser Guzmán
por seruir a rey ageno.   200
   En lo que toca a que he sido *[fol.] 5 [r.]*
quien al de Françia ha ynformado
que la Reyna no ha naçido
de reyna, si lo has pensado,
tu pensamiento ha mentido.   205
   Y si lo dize tu lengua,
Castro, por la barba mientes.

FERNÁN   La tuya vil se deslengua,
porque, dos Reyes presentes,
no se conozca tu mengua.   210
   Pero toma aquese guante,
y al Rey de Castilla pido
campo.

---

187. *
192. *
194. MSBA, ofende el.*
196. *
198. MSBA, y no.
199. *
200. MSBA, al Rey.
201. MSBA, Y en lo que toca que.*
203. *
210. *
211. B, Y si eres Fortun valiente; MSA, reçibe esse.*
212. B, yo al Rey.

ALFONSO   En causa semejante
no os puede ser conçedido,
y estando otro Rey delante—   215
    y, Rui de Castro, aduertid
que no me enojo con vos.
Agradezido a la lid
que vençí, después de Dios,
por ser vos el adalid.   220
        Que si otro que vos no fuera . . .

FERNÁN   Señor, bolued por mi onor,
porque si de vos no espera
remedio, podré, señor,
cobrarle de otra manera,   225
    y así al Rey de Françia pido
campo en su tierra.

LUIS   No puede
ser en París conçedido
lo que en Burgos no conçede
Rey a quien hauéis seruido.   *[fol. 5 v.]*   230

FERNÁN   Pues, Fortunio, en Fez te espero.
Ni a España ni a Françia quiero,
ni a Nauarra ni a Aragón.
Muestra tú en esta ocasión
que eres noble y caballero.   235
        Que si no muestras balor
en yr a Africa esta vez
para defender tu onor,
pondré carteles en Fez   *
y quedarás por traydor.   240

FORTUNIO   Bámonos juntos, espera.

FERNÁN   Nunca voy con mi enemigo.

✠ *Váyase Fernán Ruiz.*

---

227. *
233. MS, omit *a* before Aragón.
234. MSBA, omit *tú;* aquesta.
235. MSBA, si eres noble Cauallero.*
236. MSBA, tienes; G, y si no.
237. MSBA, y vas a.
238. MSBA, boluer por tu.

ALFONSO	Teneos, no salgáis fuera.
FORTUNIO	Gran señor ...
ALFONSO	Teneos, digo.
FORTUNIO	Señor, mi onor considera. 245
LUIS	Vos no quedáis agrauiado,
	Fortunio, pues no habéis sido
	el que desto me ha informado.
	Ni él pudo ser desmentido
	por sólo haberlo pensado. 250
	Açierta su magestad
	en no daros libertad
	para que salgáis con él.
	Enbïad, señor, tras él,
	no salga de la çiudad. 255
FORTUNIO	Pues, ¿quedo yo bien ansí?
ALFONSO	Basta, Fortunio, que el Rey
	lo diga.
LUIS	Hiziérala aquí ✿
	si en esto no hubiera ley.
	Corra el agrauio por mí. 260
ALFONSO	Vos quedáis bien satisfecho, *[fol.] 6 [r.]*
	y para que el Rey lo quede
	de la verdad de mi pecho,
	que a quien soy faltar no puede
	en éste ni en otro echo, 265
	quiero que este caso entienda,
	y en lo que estriua el engaño.
LUIS	No ay cosa que yo pretenda

St. dir. before v. 243. MSBA, Vase; G, Vayase Fernan.
247. MSBA, que no.
248. MSBA, quien del caso.
249. S, desmenrido.✿
251. ✿
254. MSBA, por el.✿
260. ✿
261. B, quedas.
262. ✿
267. MSBA, y la verdad del engaño.
268. B, Dame Luys atento oydo; repeated in its correct position six lines later.

| | como el çierto desengaño | |
| | de mi amada y dulçe prenda. | 270 |

        Señor, dadme este contento,
porque sepa yo que ha sido
legítimo el casamiento.

ALFONSO   Dadme, Luis, atento oydo.

LUIS   Ya os escucho.

ALFONSO   Estadme atento.   275
        De Berenguela, mi muger primera,
tube tres hijos y una hija sola:
Sancho, el mayor, Fernando, y don Garçía,   *
y Costanza Ysabel, que todo es vno.
Por dicha, equiuocándose en los nonbres,   280
piensan que os engañé, Rey cristianísimo,
y que por daros a Ysabel, mi hija,
os he dado a Costanza. O por ventura,
piensan que os he cassado con la bella
y hermosa Estefanía, a quien agora   285
veréys para más prueba deste engaño.

LUIS   Pues, ¿quién es essa bella Estefanía?

ALFONSO   Vna hija que tuue de vna dama
tan buena como yo, porque fue nieta
del Conde Albar Fernández, el de Castro,   290
                    [fol. 6 v.]
Sobrino de aquel Çid, honor del mundo,
y de doña Menzía Ansures, hija
del baleroso Conde Pedro Ansures.
Fue hija doña Sancha, que este nombre   *
tubo esta dama, de Fernán Garzía,   295
hijo del Rey Garzía de Nauarra.

---

271. *
275. *
280. MSBA, omit *en*; J, nombres.
287. MSBA, esta.
288. MSBA, en.
290. *
291. J, Cid.
292. *
294-296. MSBA, omit.*

Así que Estefanía se pudiera
cassar con qualquier prínçipe del mundo,
por ser de tantos reyes sangre ilustre.
Que lo que le faltó de ser legítima,   300
suple su gran belleza y alto ingenio,
aconpañado de virtudes raras.
Esta es la hija que bastarda tengo,
y no Costanza, Rey, que si os la diera,
¿no encubriera el engaño que os descubro   305
por ynterés humano?

LUIS   Echarme quiero
a v[uest]ros pies.

ALFONSO   Jesús, señor, teneos,
que habéis de ver con v[uest]ros mismos ojos
a Estefanía. Partid vos delante,
Fortunio, y a la puerta del conuento   310
deçid que esté esperándonos.

LUIS   Pues, ¿cómo?
¿Es religiosa ya?

ALFONSO   No ha profesado,
ni tengo pensamiento que lo sea,
mas pretendo escusar con aquel háuito
pretensiones de nobles de mi reyno   315
que me la piden, ya por ser mis deudos,
ya por seruiçios que me han echo en guerras.

                                            [fol.] 7 [r.]

LUIS   Bámosla a ver, que me olgaré en estremo.

ALFONSO   Eslo de discrezión y de hermosura.   ✿

LUIS   ¡Quiera Dios que le yguale en la ventura!   320

---

297. MSBA, bien pudiera.
299. MSBA, omit.
300. ✿
305. MSBA, omit os.
307. MSBA, Teneos señor, que es esto?
308. MSBA, no mas, que aueys de ver por vuestros ojos.
309. MSBA, partid Fortun delante.
310. MSBA, y a la puerta seglar de aquel Conuento.
312. ✿
313. MSBA, ni aun tengo.
318. B, Vamola.
320. MSBA, imite.

✠ *Estefanía entre con vn háuito blanco de la Conçepçión*
y Fernán Ruiz y Ysabel, criada de Estefanía.

ESTEFANÍA	En fin, ¿te partes a Fez?
FERNÁN	¿Qué quieres? Ya es onrra mía.
ESTEFANÍA	¿Onrra?
FERNÁN	Bella Estefanía,

venzió al amor esta vez.
Pasiones son naturales   325*
yra y amor, y el onor
ynçita mucho el furor
en ocasiones yguales.
Como es rayo açelerado,
del amor no me acordé,   330
que después que lo pensé,
¡Dios sabe si me ha pesado!
Pártome a Fez a esperar
este cobarde traydor.

ESTEFANÍA	Quien ha estimado tu amor 335

sabrá tu onor estimar.
Parte animoso, Fernando,
mi fee será la que fue.
Pero mira en Fez la fee
con que te quedo esperando,   340
que no quiero detenerte,
porque te conozco ya.

FERNÁN	Pienso que el çielo querrá,

señora, que buelba a verte.

St. dir. before v. 321. MSB, Vanse, y salen Fernan Ruyz de Castro,
y Estefania de Monja, y Ysabel esclaua; G, Estephania sale con hauito...
criado de...; A, same as MSB, but omits first y, uses lower case for *monja*,
changes last y to *é*.*
321. MSBA, Al fin.*
324. MSBA, el honor.*
326. MSBA, iras; G, omits y after *yra*.
327. G, ymita.
328. MSBA, en las personas Reales.*
329. *
331. MSBA, mas despues que en mi tornè.*
334. MSBA, a esse.

Y tengo a dicha mi afrenta,   *[fol. 7 v.]*   345
pues por ella he merezido
haber de tu boca oydo
que mi amor corre a tu cuenta.
  Sólo pido, si es que tiene
fuerza en muerte y en partida   350
la palabra prometida,
que mientras tu esclabo viene
  del cautiberio de Fez,
no sea el Rey, ni otro, parte
para desta fee mudarte.   355

ESTEFANÍA   A Dios pongo por juez,
  Fernando, de la fee mía.
Parte seguro y aduierte
que no ay poder en la muerte,
ni tienen los tiempos día   360
  en que desta fee me oluide,
ni del tratado conçierto.
Porque el amor, quando es çierto,
con ningún tiempo se mide.

✠ *Fortún entre.*

FORTUNIO   El Rey me manda auisarte   365
que el de Françia viene a verte.
Rui de Castro, ¿desta suerte
con la Infanta vengo [a] hallarte?
  ¿Tú aquí? ¿De dónde o por qué?
¿Es ésta la balentía?   370

FERNÁN   ¡Ay, tan gran desdicha mía!
Respeto y Amor, ¿qué haré?

---

346. MSB, para ella.
348. MSBA, honor; B, borre.*
350. MSBA, o.
354. MSBA, ni el Rey ni otro no sea parte.
362. MSBA, passado.
363. MSBA, vn amor; J, cuando.
St. dir. before v. 365. MSBA, Sale Fortun Ximenez; G, Sale Fortunio.
368. MSBAG, vengo a hallarte?
369. *
372. MSBA, honor.

Honrra, ¿qué me aconsejáis?
¿Mataré aqueste traydor?
¿Que no respondéis? Amor,   [fol.] 8 [r.]   375
si lo soys, cobarde estáis.
    Di, Fortunio mal naçido,
¿sabes que soy aquel ombre
cuyo çelebrado nombre
es del Africa temido?   380
    ¿Sabes que en toda Castilla ...?

ESTEFANÍA   Fernando, ¡estando yo aquí!
FERNÁN   Pues por esso tengo así
en la vayna la cuchilla.
    Que, ¡viue el çielo! que has sido,   385
quando tal causa me dan,
como el ángel de Abrahán,   *
que la mano me has tenido.
    Porque si no, ya no hubiera,
aunque el mismo Rei llegara,   390
cabello en aquella cara
que por el ayre no fuera.
    A Fernán Ruiz, a un onbre
que llaman el Castellano,
¿osas desmentir, villano?   395

FORTUNIO   Ya sabes que ése es tu nombre
y que estando desmentido
y el desafío aplazado,
ni quedas desagrauiado
ni de ti quedo ofendido.   400
    El cabello de mi cara
que hiziera en tu mano fío,

---

374. G, a aqueste.
375. MSBA, honor.
376. MSBA, andays.
377. MSBA, Dime.
379. MSBA, valeroso.
381. *
388. MSBA, ha.
395. MSBA, ofender.
396. B, saber.
402. *

        lo que el Çid con el judío   ❋
        que aun muerto resuçitara.

FERNÁN   ¿Qué dizes, Fortún? ¿No miras *[fol. 8 v.]* 405
        que está aquí el sol ya partido,
        y que si canpo te pido
        y como vil te retiras,
           pediré liçençia al sol,
        y que con su rayo eterno   410
        te seguiré hasta el infierno
        con este brazo español?
        Si es porque está en medio el çielo
        y las estrellas hermosas,
        a conuertir poderosas   415
        la esfera del fuego en yelo,
           mira que podrás hazer
        que pierda al çielo el respeto.
        Que no ay agrauio discreto
        ni firme çielo en muger.   420
          Y te asiré, por Dios, viuo,
        no en túmulo de alabastro,
        ni como el Çid, que soy Castro,
        y entre mil reyes me escriuo,
           sino como Hércules fiero   425❋
        a Licas, rebuelto al brazo.
        Y abrá del tuyo pedazo,
        que passe el çielo primero.

FORTUNIO   Si esse çielo que respetas
        no estuuiera entre los dos,   430

---

404. MSBA, omit *aun*.
405. MSA, Que es esto Fortun?; B, Que es esto Fortuno?
407. G, si el campo.
411. MSBA, arrojarè.
412. B, rayo.❋
415. ❋
419. ❋
423. MSBA, ni con.❋
425. MSBA, qual Hercules.
426. MSBA, que la piel rebuelta al braço.
427. MSBA, harè que el menor pedaço.
428. MSBA, estrelle el cielo primero.
430. ❋

trocada vieras, por Dios,
la fábula que ynterpretas.   *
Que al Hércules arrogante
yo le arrojara de modo
que pasara el çielo todo.   435
Si ay lugar más adelante ...

ESTEFANÍA   Quedo, Fortún; poco a poco,   *[fol.] 9 [r.]*
Fernando.

YSABEL   Los Reyes uienen.

✠ *Alfonso y Luis.*

ALFONSO   Los dos son.
LUIS   Espadas tienen.
ALFONSO   ¿Qué es esto, Castro, estás loco?   440
            ¿Aquí tu furia paró?
            ¿Esta es la Fez a que fuiste?
            ¿Campo el monesterio hiziste?   *
FERNÁN   ¡Siempre soy culpado yo!
            Por Dios, que pagas mui bien   445
            los seruiçios reçiuidos
            a mis maiores deuidos,
            y a mis hazañas tanbién.
            Pues a fe que en causas tales
            no heredas de tus mayores   450
            el defender los traydores
            y el ofender los leales.
            Delante del Rey Lüís,
            Alfonso, deçirte puedo
            que de León a Toledo,
            que es lo más en que viuís,   455
            debéis, reyes castellanos,
            a mis nobles asçendientes

---

434. *
St. dir. before v. 436. MSBA, Mete mano a la espada, y Castro empuña
la suya.
St. dir. before v. 439. MSBA, Salen los Reyes; G, omits.
443. MSBA, al.
449. MSBA, casos.*

coronando v[uest]ras frentes
por el balor de sus manos.   460
   Los Castros, sangre del Çid,
¿tratas desta suerte ya?
Quando ganaste a Alcalá,
a Atienza y a Almonaçid,   *
   ¿no dixiste en vozes altas: *[fol. 9 v.]*   465
"Castro, pariente y amigo,
todo lo venzo contigo,
todo lo pierdo si faltas"?
Pues, ¿cómo así me despreçias?
Pero Fortunio es mexor,   470
que deçiende de vn traydor,
y tú a los traydores preçias.
   Sangre tiene de Bellido.   *
¿Qué miras? Verdad te hablo.
Guárdate de otro venablo,   475
que es cobarde y atreuido,
   que si aquí saqué la espada
fue porque se vino aquí
después que vn ángel que ui   *
la tuuo vn rato enbaynada,   480
   cuyo respeto me ha hecho
faltar a mi condiçión.
Mas pues ya las tuyas son
fiar de yguales tu pecho,
   en el Africa le espero,   485
y me parto a Gibraltar;

---

459. MSBA, el coronar.
460. MSBA, con el laurel.*
462 MSA, de essa.
464. MSBA, Atiença y Almonacid.
468. B, todo rdlo pieo si faltas.
472. B, precia.
473. A, tienes.*
476. MSBA, y mal nacido.
477. MSBA, empuñè.
478. MSBA, fue porque el la sacò aqui.*
480. MSBA, un poco.
482. MSBA, salir de mi.
486. MSBA, que oy me.

que por Çeuta quiero entrar,   *
y en Fez ver si es caballero;
   que a estas puertas les ofrezco
la lengua con que amenaza   490
como cabeza de caza,   *
si la vitoria merezco,
   que con esta misma daga   *[fol.] 10 [r.]*
la he de clauar y escriuir:
"Así el hablar y el mentir,   495
traydor Fortunio, se paga."

        [Váyase]

ALFONSO   ¡Prendelde!
FORTUNIO   Déxale vn poco,
en tanto que le castigo.
LUIS   Detente, Fortunio amigo.
FORTUNIO   Voy a castigar a un loco.   500
LUIS   Es mi gusto que te esperes.
ALFONSO   ¿Qué es aquesto, Estefanía?
ESTEFANÍA   A despedirse venía.
Desto, señor, no te alteres,
   que es deudo, como tú sabes,   505
de mi madre doña Sancha.
ALFONSO   Rey, el corazón ensancha,
salgan las sospechas grabes,
   que ésta es aquélla de quien
te dixeron en París.   510
ESTEFANÍA   Cristianísimo Lüís,

---

487. MSBA, que pienso por Zeuta entrar.
489. A, le ofrezco.
St. dir. before v. 497. MSBA, Vase.*
497. MSBAG, Prẽdedle; MS, Dexalde; BA, Dexadle.*
500. MSBA, omit *a* before *loco*.
504. MSBA, señor desto.
507. *
509. MSBA, omit *que*.
510. *
511. S, Christianisimo Rey Luis.

	que el çielo prospere en bien,	
	dadme esos pies generosos.	
LUIS	Cuñada, el pecho y los brazos,	
	lazos que desazen lazos	515
	de cuidados temerosos.	
	Mucho me huelgo de veros.	
	La fama venzéis, por Dios.	
ESTEFANÍA	Rey sois, reçiuo de vos	
	merzedes.	
LUIS	No ay que ofrezeros,	520
	que como el alma llebáys,	
	no dexáis que daros pueda	
	quien tan pobre y solo queda [fol. 10 v.]	
	después que vos le miráis.	
	Aunque Costanza, mi esposa,	525
	Rey, tenga más calidad,	
	oxalá tu magestad	
	me diera esta prenda hermosa,	
	que yo olgara del engaño.	
	Mas pues ya no puede ser,	530
	vna m[e]r[ce]d me has de hazer	
	por fin deste desengaño,	
	que es dársela en casamiento	
	a Fortún, que me ha obligado,	
	seruido y aconpañado,	535
	pues tiene merezimiento.	
ALFONSO	Fortún es gran caballero,	
	mas responda Estefanía.	
ESTEFANÍA	Señor, la ventura es mía,	

513. MSBA, Dame.
515. *
517. MSBA, alegro; J, güelgo.*
521. *
523. MSBA, solo y pobre.*
525. *
530. *
531. G, omits de after has.*
532. MSBA, por vltimo desengaño.
536. MSBA, y tiene.
539. G, la Fortuna.

	mas venza Fortún primero	540
	de Fernando el desafío,	
	que no me he de hallar mañana	
	sin marido.	
Luis	Cosa es llana,	
	que a cuenta del onor mío	
	puede Fortunio quedarse	545
	en Castilla con su onor.	
Estefanía	Si le retó de traydor,	
	¿de qué puede asegurarse?	
	Sepa v[uest]ra magestad	
	que los castellanos fueros	550
	son los que a los caballeros	
	dan onrra y autoridad.	

Arias Gonzalo ofreçió   [fol.] 11 [r.]   *
tres hijos a tantos daños,
y él se armó de setenta años   555
y a la canpaña salió.
     Los Condes de Carrïón
murieron en estacado;   *
y Rui Velázquez retado,   *
pagó su infame trayçión.   560
     Ningún retado en Castilla
tiene onor. Fortunio salga
con aquella espada hidalga,
del Africa marauilla,
     que quando le aya vençido   565
aquí para suya estoy.

Fortunio	Bien dize; al Africa voy.	
	Que me deis lizenzia os pido,	
	que pues dixo que yo hauía	
	ynformado al Rey tan mal,	570
	y en mi Reyna natural	

---

552. MSBA, dan honor.
553. *
556. *
568. MSBA, des; omit *os.**
570. B, tan mar.
571. MSBA, su Reyna.

	presumido bastardía,	
	no cunpliré con mi onor	
	sin hazer el desafío.	
ALFONSO	Pues si ya es con gusto mío, .	575
	en Burgos será mexor.	
	Llamen a Fernando luego.	
LUIS	Hablar quiero a mi cuñada.	
FORTUNIO	Por verme ya en la estacada,	
	me voy consumiendo en fuego.	580

✠ *Todos se van, Ysabel quede.*

YSABEL   Si merezen los altos pensamientos
          y las enpresas dignas de memoria
          honrroso nombre, penetrad los vientos,
          atreuidos prinçipios de mi gloria.

                                                [fol. 11 v.]

          No conpiten así los elementos,   585
          como para llebar de amor vitoria
          mis ymaginaçiones. Mas no bastan,
          que los desseos su rigor contrastan.

              ¿Quién dirá que vna esclaua a Fortún quiera,
          caballero de sangre tan altiua,   590
          y por tan altos ymposibles muera,
          que ausente dél con esperanza viua?
          Cautiua fui del Rey en la frontera,
          y de Fortunio en Burgos soy cautiua.
          Tres años ha que le miré, y tres años   595
          que viue mi esperanza en sus engaños.

              Fuese a Françia y pensé que la distanzia
          mudara la firmeza de mi pecho,
          pero después que aquí boluió de Françia,

---

575. MSBA, Pues que ya.
578. MSBA, Quiero hablar a.
580. MSBA, me estoy.
St. dir. before v. 581. MSBA, Vanse todos, y queda Ysabel sola.*
582. B, impressas.
589. B, omits *a.**
595. MSBA, diez años ... y diez años.*
597-604. *

maior estrago en mi sentido ha hecho.   600
Mi perdiçión estimo por ganançia,
que en los daños de amor está el probecho.
Yo moriré, pero alabarme puedo,
que vitoriosa de mis penas quedo.

✠ *Mudarra, lacayo de Fernán Ruiz, entre.*

MUDARRA   Túrbense los discordes elementos,   605
desencáxese el çielo de sus quizios,
suelten sus alas por el mar los vientos,
rómpanse los çelestes frontispiçios,
a mi desdicha, a mi dolor, atentos.
Dexen todas las cosas sus ofiçios,   610
pues que me parto a tierras tan estrañas,
                    [fol.] 12 [r.]
y se queda Ysabel con mis entrañas.   *

Arrebózesse el sol por quatro messes,
póngase luto la redonda luna,
ráxense Marte y muerte los arnesses   615
por quien se meta monja la fortuna.
Cómanse de langosta n[uest]ras miesses,
dáñese el vino en su primera cuna,
pues me lleban a Fez a jugar cañas,
y se queda Ysabel con mis entrañas.   620
Entren los ríos a so[r]ber las troxes,   *
baxen rayos de amor, haziendo rajas   *
lomos de puercos, lenguas de reloxes,

St. dir. before v. 605. MSBA, Sale Mudarra lacayo; G, ... sale.
606. *
607. MSBA, tiendan las alas.*
608. *
609. MSBA, y mi dolor.*
610. *
611. MSBA, pues me lleuan.
612. *
613-620. MSBA, place after v. 628, with *rasguense* and *sus arnesses* the
only variations, in v. 615.
621. MSBAG, sorber.
622. MSBA, baxen jaras.*
623. MSBA, lenguas de puerco, y manos de reloxes.

	y canillas de piernas, de tinajas.	
	Tírenme balas, bolas, bolos, boxes,	625
	ballestas, bancos, baras y barajas,	
	pues me voy donde no ay vino y castañas,	*
	y se queda Ysabel con mis entrañas.	
YSABEL	Mudarra.	
MUDARRA	¿Qué es aquesto? ¿Quién me nonbra?	
	¿Quién me consuela en tanta desbentura?	630
YSABEL	Tu Ysabel, prenda mía.	
MUDARRA	¡O, bella alfonbra	*
	donde puso su estrado la hermosura!	
	¡O, bello sol con quien el sol es sombra,	
	primauera de amor, troncho y verdura	
	de mi abrasado espíritu!	
YSABEL	¿Qué tienes,	635
	que tan enamorado y tierno vienes?	
MUDARRA	¿No has sabido, Ysabel, como se parte	
	Fernán Ruiz de Castro a Fez agora,	
	y que se va con él tu Durandarte?	*
	¿Aún no sabe estas nuebas tu señora?	640
	[fol. 12 v.]	
YSABEL	Ya de su ausenzia él mismo le dio parte.	
MUDARRA	¿Quiérele bien?	
YSABEL	Presume que le adora,	
	y que ha de hazer notable sentimiento.	
MUDARRA	Y a ti, ¿cómo te va de pensamiento?	
YSABEL	Que temo desta ausençia tu mudanza.	645*
MUDARRA	Si fuera yo muger, no pongas duda,	

---

624. MSBA, y tinajas.
625. MSBA, tirenme balas, bolos, troncos, boxes.
626. MSBA, bancos, varas, ballestas, y barajas.
627. MSBA, pues voy donde no ay vino ni castañas.
629. MSBA, assign *que es aquesto?* to Ysabel.
630. B, aconsuela.
632. B, estado.
634. MSBA, de Abril, tronco.
635. MSBA, afligido espiritu.
639. B, a Durandarte.*
642. MSA, Presumo.
644. B, sentimiento?

que quien firmeza espera, viento alcanza,
porque a qualquiera vendaual se muda.

YSABEL   Pues, ten de mí segura confianza
de que obligada a lo que deuo acuda.   650

MUDARRA   ¿Quiéresme bien, por vida de esos ojos?

YSABEL   Tú sólo eres la paz de mis enojos.

No quiere la amorosa madre tanto
al hijo que le cuelga de los pechos,
ni al agua el triste enfermo, al gozo el llanto, 655
ni a la llubia los ásperos barbechos,
al puro sol el temeroso manto,
las aues a los nidos en los techos,
amor la paz, las yerbas al roçío,
quanto te quiero yo, Mudarra mío.   660

MUDARRA   Ni quiere tanto el auariento el oro,
ni a sus mismos donaires los discretos,
al Alcorán de su Mahoma el moro,
el poeta sus versos y sonetos,
el botón al oxal, la baca al toro,   665
el agüelo caduco tiernos nietos,
la guardosa donzella su alcanzía,
quanto te quiero yo, perrona mía.

YSABEL   ¿Quándo se va Fernán Rüíz de Castro?

MUDARRA   Las postas dexo en cassa, y puestas botas   670*
a aquel Fernán González de alabastro.   *

[fol.] 13 [r.]

---

647. MSA, busca firmeza el; B, omits.
651. MSBA, de tus ojos?
653. *
655. MSBA, al agua el triste enfermo, el gozo al llanto.
657. MSB, el puro sol el tenebroso.
658. MSBA, sus techos.
660. MSBA, lacayo mio.
661. MSBA, No quiere tanto al auariento al oro.
662. MSBA, place after v. 665, omitting *ni.*
663. MSBA, el Alcoran.
664. MSBA, place after v. 661, reading *los diuinos poetas sus conceptos.*
666. MSBA, appears after v. 663, reading *a tiernos nietos.*
667. MSBA, la donzella guardosa.
669. J, ¿Cuándo...?
671. MSBA, omit *a.*

	¿Qué mandas para Fez, reyna de sotas?
	Haz cuenta que çinquenta nabes lastro
	de alfonbras, alquizeles y marlotas.
	Acá te traygo media Berbería, 675
	y todo es poco, perrigalga mía. *
YSABEL	Vete con Dios, y abrázame.
MUDARRA	Vna prenda
	te quiero dar.
YSABEL	Y yo a llorar comienzo.
MUDARRA	Este para la buelta se encomienda
	a tus manos. Xabóname ese lienzo. 680
YSABEL	¿Este angeo? *
MUDARRA	Mi fee quiero que entienda.
YSABEL	¡Jesús! Aun de tocarle me abergüenzo.
MUDARRA	Mis prendas son de dura, mi amor fuerte.
YSABEL	No te verán mis ojos hasta verte.

✠ *Entren Albumazar, moro astrólogo, y Abdelmón, con vnos calzones de lienzo largos y una almilla colorada, y bonete.* *

ABDELMÓN	¿No me dirás qué me quieres 685
	con tanta ymportunaçión?
	¿Sabes quién soy?
ALBUMASAR	Sé quien eres.
ABDELMÓN	De mi baxa condizión,
	noble Albumasar, ¿qué infieres?
ALBUMASAR	¿Sabes que astrólogo soy, 690
	no sólo en Fez y Marruecos
	conozido, donde estoy,

---

673. MSBA, a cincuenta.
675. MSBA, y que te.
676. MSA, y es poco para ti perrenga mia; B, as MSA, but *perrona.*
680. MSBA, este.
St. dir. before v. 681. MSBA, Dale vn pañuelo muy suzio.
681. MSBA, mi amor.
St. dir. before v. 685. MSBA, Vanse, y salen Albumasar Moro viejo, y delante Audelmon vestido de Moro pobre, como cautiuo; B, also reads *Moro vieja;* A, divides directions in two parts, omitting the first *y* (and will not be noted further); G, Salen . . .; J, Albumasar.*
689. MSBA, sabio.
692. B, conocidos.*

mas que a España con los ecos
de mi fama y nombre doy?

ABDELMÓN   Sé que si alguno ha naçido   695
que sepa esa inçierta çiençia,
tú solo en el mundo has sido,
porque la antigua esperiençia
has puesto en eterno oluido.

Sé que de qualquiera estrella   700
sabes de manera el curso,
lo que influye y cabe en ella,
que pareze en tu discurso   *[fol. 13 v.]*
que has caminado con ella.

Sé que de esferas, planetas,   705
çielos y otros mobimientos,
sabes las causas secretas,
y que n[uest]ros naçimientos
por su asçendente interpretas.

Mas si soy vn pobre ollero   710
que me sustento del barro,
¿de mí qué infieres?

ALBUMASAR   Infiero
el soldado más bizarro
y el más galán caballero.

Si entendieras el camino   715
de aquestas causas secretas,
vieras su curso diuino
y el fabor de los planetas
de aspecto dichoso y trino.   *

¡O, si del sol entendieras   720
y de Júpiter el bien
que por su respeto esperas!

_____

694. MSBA, de mi nombre fama doy?
698. MSBA, y que la.
700-704. MSBA, omit.*
706. G, astros mouimientos; omits *y*.*
710. *
712. *
715-719. MSBA, omit.*
720. S, de sol.

    ¡Tú has de ser Rey!

ABDELMÓN   ¿Rey tanbién?

    ¿Qué dizes? ¿Hablas de veras?

ABLUMASAR   Ven acá. Quando del barro   725
    que tratas, si quieres hazes
    vn grande o pequeño xarro,
    tal ensanchas, tal desazes,
    tal es pobre y tal bizarro.

    ¿No consideras que Alá   730
    así con el barro está,
    de que a todos nos fabrica?
    Pues vna materia aplica
    y dibersas formas da.

    Todos están de alma llenos, *[fol.] 14 [r.]* 735
    ya en concauidad angosta,
    ya en más estendidos senos,
    que no le tienen más costa
    que el barro, qual más, qual menos.

    A ti para Rey te ha hecho   740
    en la rueda de su mano,
    que aunque vaso vil y estrecho,
    ya su poder soberano
    puso gran alma en tu pecho.

(ABLUMASAR)   Rey del Africa serás.   745
    a España con gente yrás;
    tu frente espera vn laurel,
    que en todas las ojas dél
    vn reyno, Adbelmón, pondrás.

ABDELMÓN   Dame esos pies.

ABLUMASAR   Sólo a vno   750
    que es Alá, por justas leyes.

---

725. *
729. A, omits *y.*
733. *
735. MSBA, almas.*
737. S, ya mas escondidos; MBA, escondidos.
742. *
745. *
748. *
750. MSBA, tus pies.*

ABDELMÓN	Y a ti después, si ay alguno...
ALBUMASAR	Tente, Abdelmón, que los reyes

no han de humillarse a ninguno.
Vete a tu ofiçio, que viene   755
gente.

ABDELMÓN   Voyme, y ruego [a] Alá
açerque el bien que preuiene
por darte, si me le da,
todo lo mejor que tiene;
que sin duda será çierto,   760
porque quando de mis vasos
miraua el suelo cubierto,
yba yo con graues passos,
glorioso de aquel conçierto;
y deçía: "aquéstos son   *[fol. 14 v.]*   765
mis basallos, y han de ser
algún día vn esquadrón
que el Africa ha de poner,
y aun a España en sujeçión."
Al vaso que grande vía,   770*
"éste es general," deçía,
haziendo a los más pequeños
los capitanes y dueños
de la humilde ynfantería.
Sin esso, lo que me cuentas   775
muchas vezes he soñado.

ALBUMASAR	Parte, y sigue lo que yntentas.
ABDELMÓN	Póngame el çielo en mi estado.
ALBUMASAR	Lo que serás representas.

---

752. MSBA, omit *y*.
756. MSBAG, a Alá.
758. MSBA, la da.*
760. MSBA, acierto.*
762. B, cielo.*
763. A, grandes pasos.
765. *
768. MSBA, al Africa han.
774. B, infateria.
775. MSBA, esto.
776. MSBA, muchas noches lo.
St. dir. before v. 779. G, vase.*

✠ *Váyase Abdelmón, entren Almohadí, Zerbino y Lisardo.*

ALMOHADÍ	¿Quién puede ya sufrir tanta insolençia 780
	como la deste bárbaro cobarde?
ZERBINO	Villana, que no hidalga, es la pazienzia.
LISARDO	O claro Albumasar, Alá te guarde.
ALBUMASAR	¿Del Miramamolín venís quexosos? ✻
ALMOHADÍ	¿Cómo es posible que tu çiençia tarde? 785

Rebuelbe, Albumasar, los poderosos
effetos de tu çiençia, y di si es çierto
lo que intentan mis brazos belicosos.
¿Has hablado a Abdelmón?

ALBUMASAR   Hazed conçierto
sobre matar al Rey, que ya lo sabe.   790

ZERBINO   ¿Muestra balor?

ALBUMASAR   Balor tiene encubierto.
Admiréme de ver el rostro grabe
que me mostraua, siendo vn pobre ollero.
                                        [fol.] 15 [r.]
Aunque al agradezer blando y suabe,
no lo dudéys, tan fuerte caballero   795
no abrá tenido el Africa, o me engaña
el çielo todo en cuyo curso espero.
Este ha de ser el que, pasando a España,
de Córdoua renuebe la mezquita.

St. dir. before v. 780. MSBA, Vase Audelmon, y salen Zayde, Almohadi, y Zeydan. *Zayde* for *Zerbino*, *Zeydan* for *Lisardo*; G, Salen . . . ✻
783. A, que Alá.✻
784. MSBA, vendreys.
785. B, como es pasible.
787. ✻
788. ✻
789. ✻
790. MSBA, como matar al Rey, que ya el lo sabe.
791. MSBA, assign Zerbino's line to Almohadí.✻
792. MSBA, admirame.
794. MSBA, el agradecer.
795. S, no lo deueys.✻
796. MSBA, no ha de tener.
799. MSBA, en Cordoua.

	Pasando la çiudad que el Betis baña,	800
	éste ha de ser...	
ALMOHADÍ	Detente, que me inçita,	
	Albumasar, el odio y la venganza.	
	Dexa de hablar, las armas soliçita.	
ALBUMASAR	Baliente Almohadí, ten esperanza,	
	que de tu nonbre abrá por mil edades	805

Pasando la çiudad que el Betis baña,   800
éste ha de ser...

ALMOHADÍ   Detente, que me inçita,
Albumasar, el odio y la venganza.
Dexa de hablar, las armas soliçita.

ALBUMASAR   Baliente Almohadí, ten esperanza,
que de tu nonbre abrá por mil edades   805
memoria en quanto el sol del m[un]do alcanza.   *
Llamaránse los moros almohades
de tu ñonbre, los fuertes africanos
que a España ganarán tantas çiudades.
Tomad todos las armas en las manos,   810
hazed Rey a Abdelmón, y el de Fez muera.
Pasad el mar, hazed los montes llanos,
corónese de Çeuta la ribera
de nabes altas, con que tienble Europa,
que v[uest]ro yugo temerosa espera.   815

ALMOHADÍ   Pongámosle real corona y ropa
a n[uest]ro Rey primero, y bamos luego
donde, llebando la fortuna en popa,
al Miramamolín pongamos fuego.

LISARDO   ¿Qué señas llebaremos p[ar]a el día,   820
y porque no se acuda en tropel çiego?

ZERBINO   Sea la seña, por opinión mía,
si vna caxa de guerra se tocare.

ALMOHADÍ   Bámosle a hablar.   *[fol. 15 v.]*

ALBUMASAR   Almohadí, confía
si el çielo no se muda.

ALMOHADÍ   Alá me ampare.   825

---

800. MSBA, ganando.
803. B, lar armas.
806. MSBA, su curso alcança.*
811. MSBA, omit *y*.
812. MSB, cubri los montes canos; A, as MSB, but *cubrid*.*
815. M, temeroso.*
816. MSBA, Pongamos la Real; Almohadí's lines assigned to Zayde.*
821. MSBA, para que no; G, omits *y*.
822. MSBA, assign Zerbino's lines to Almohadí.*
824. B, vamosla.*

✠ *Fernán Ruiz de Castro y Mudarra, de camino.*   ❋

FERNÁN	Más he sentido la posta,
	Mudarra, hasta Gibraltar
	que los peligros del mar.
MUDARRA	Yo, hasta aquí desde la costa,

	tres leguas de mar que ençierra,	830

de Gibraltar el Estrecho,
no me han alterado el pecho
como esta fragosa tierra.
  ¡O, qué llebo que contar
de Tetüán!   ❋

FERNÁN   ¿De sus moros,   835
trages, caballos, tesoros,
fértil tierra, estrecho mar?

MUDARRA   ¡Que no, señor!

FERNÁN   Pues, ¿de qué?

MUDARRA   De la sierra de las monas
que andauan como personas,   840
qual trepando y qual en pie.

FERNÁN   Tras el agua que has pasado,
aún no está tenplado el vino.

MUDARRA   ¡A fee que es éste camino
para salir bien tenplado!   845
  No me llebaras a Françia
o a Flandes, donde le hiziera
brindis a España y bebiera
en bacanal consonanzia,
sino a esta mora campiña   850
que algún demonio gouierna,

St. dir. before v. 826. MSBA, Vanse, y salen Fernan Ruyz de Castro,
y Mudarra.
   829. ❋
   830. ❋
   832. MSBA, afligido.
   834. ❋
   839. MSBA, tierra.
   845. MSBA, quedar.
   846. S, Fracia.
   847. MSBA, omit *a.*
   850. MSBA, Y no a.

donde no ay vna taberna
ni se descubre vna viña.
¿Aquí quieres pelear?   *[fol.] 16 [r.]*
¿Con qué aliento has de salir?   855
¡Dixérasmelo al partir!
Enbarcara en Gibraltar
    quatro cueros de Xerez,
con que no sólo venzieras
a Fortunio, mas te hizieras   860
Rey de Marruecos y Fez.
    ¿Esta es Africa, ésta llaman
la sierra de Tetüán,
aquí por las monas van?   *
¡Viue Dios, que a España ynfaman!   865
    ¿No era mejor yr a Coca,   *
a San Martín, o [a] Alaejos   *
a cazar monazos uiejos,
y cueros hasta la boca,
    que no aquí donde se bebe   870
agua como mulas?

FERNÁN   Calla,
que si de aquesta batalla
sale mi onor como debe,
    y a España me buelbe Dios,
a este ayuno haremos fiesta.   875

MUDARRA   Desdichada tierra es ésta: *
toda es romadizo y tos,
    distilaçiones y flemas...

FERNÁN   El Rey sale; buelbe en ti,
que habemos de estar aquí...   880

MUDARRA   Con mil reumas y postemas.

---

855. MSBA, animo.
860. B, pero.
862. MSBA, a esta llaman.*
863. MSBA, tierra.
864. MSA, aqui por monas se van; B, aqui por ellas se van.
867. MSBA, y Alaejos; G, a Alaejos.
870. MSBA, y no.
877. MSBA, todo.
878. BAG, destilaciones.

FERNÁN   Con atenzión y respeto,
                 porque el Miramamolín
                 es Rey del Africa, en fin.
MUDARRA   Desde agora le prometo   885
                 vna mona a Estefanía,
                 y otra pequeña a Ysabel.
FERNÁN   Mira, que viene con él
                 lo mejor de Berbería.
MUDARRA   La mexor mona será   [fol. 16 v.]   890
                 que se aya jamás tomado.
FERNÁN   Parézese tu cuidado
                 al que Fortunio me da.

✠ *El Rey Miramamolín y aconpañamiento, Learín, alcayde.*

MIRAMAMOLÍN   Que es de gallarda persona.
LEARÍN   Grandeza se muestra en él.   895
MUDARRA   ¡Lo que se olgara Ysabel
                 de que yo tome esta mona!
FERNÁN   Dadme los pies, gran señor.
MIRAMAMOLÍN   Cristiano, seas bien venido.
                 ¿Qué es lo que me pides?
FERNÁN   Pido   900
                 a tu magestad fabor.
MIRAMAMOLÍN   ¿De dónde eres?
FERNÁN   De Castilla.
                 Tube con vn caballero
                 palabras, y aunque su fuero ...

---

882. MSBA, Con reuerencia.
885. *
891. *
St. dir. before v. 894. MSBA, Salen el Rey Miramamolin, y Almoadi,
y Zeydan, y Zayde, y Albumasar; J, omits *y.*
894. *
895. MSBA, Grandezas me quentan del; assign to Albumasar; J. assigns
to *Alc.**
897. MSBA, vna mona.
898. MSBA, Dame tus.
899. *
902. MS, de adõde.

MUDARRA	Con cadena y con euilla	905
	yrá lindamente atada.	
FERNÁN	A dar canpo al retador	
	obliga al Rey, mi señor,	
	y asegurar la estacada,	
	por pasión me le ha negado,	910
	y así te hago juez	
	de mi agrauio, porque a Fez	
	le traygo desafïado,	
	seguro de que darás	
	canpo a un Castro castellano.	915
MIRAMAMOLÍN	Ya te conozco, cristiano;	
	en alta opinión estás.	
	Los Castros soys deçendientes	
	de los reyes.	
MUDARRA	Vna mona	
	alegrará vna persona	920
	que tenga el alma en los dientes.	
	Viue Dios que he de tomalla	
	por donde pudiere asilla.	
MIRAMAMOLÍN	¿Y vendrá desde Castilla	
	ese hidalgo a la batalla?	925
FERNÁN	Vendrá si tiene balor. [fol.] 17 [r.]	
	Yo, según fuero de España	
	con salir a la canpaña	
	cunplo con mi honor. Señor,	
	dame lizencia que ponga	930
	carteles de desafío,	
	para que al agrauio mío	
	armas y fuerzas disponga,	
	que fío de mi contrario	

---

905. MSBA, y con traylla.
907. MSBA, reversed with v. 908.
910. MSBA, han; J, la.
912. *
920. MSBA, a vna.
925. MSBA, este.
926. J, valor.
930. MSBA, Dadme.
932. MSBA, porque assi.

	que está mui çerca de Fez.	935
MIRAMAMOLÍN	Si, fuera de ser jüez,	
	a tu intento es neçesario	
	guarda o seguro, aquí estoy.	
FERNÁN	Merzed espero de ti.	
	¿Voy con tu lizenzia?	
MIRAMAMOLÍN	Sí.	940
FERNÁN	Pues con tu liçençia voy.	
	Mudarra.	
MUDARRA	¿Señor?	
FERNÁN	Ya es echo,	
	liçençia dio a mi persona.	
MUDARRA	¿Para llebar esta mona?	
FERNÁN	Que estás borracho sospecho.	945
	Bestia, ¿sabes lo que enprendo?	
	Ven, y búscame vna caja.	
MUDARRA	De pesadunbres ataja,	
	que todo tu intento entiendo.	
	Sin caja la llebaré	950
	con vna cadena buena.	
FERNÁN	Mereçieras la cadena	
	como esclauo puesta al pie.	
	Caxa de guerra te digo.	
MUDARRA	Espantaráse de oylla.	955
FERNÁN	¡Que viniese de Castilla	
	aconpañado contigo!	
	Ven por aquí, maxadero.	
MUDARRA	Si no la llebare bien,	
	quéxate.	
FERNÁN	¡Miren a quien	960
	truxe a Fez por escudero!	

[Váyanse]

---

935. MSBA, que estarà dentro de; J, cerca.
942. MSBA, Ea Mudarra esto es hecho.
944. MSBA, vna.
946. MSBA, Necio.
947. MSBA, corre buscame.
960. G, Miran.
961. MSBAG, traxe.

MIRAMAMOLÍN	Gallardo es este cristiano.	*[fol. 17 v.]*
LEARÍN	Es Castro.	
MIRAMAMOLÍN	Gentil presençia.	
LEARÍN	En Burgos, por exçelençia	
	le llaman el Castellano.	965
MIRAMAMOLÍN	Deseo su buen suçeso.	
	¿Díxote a ti la razón	
	del desafío?	
LEARÍN	Allá son	
	por cosas de poco peso.	
MIRAMAMOLÍN	¿Es por conpetençia acaso	970
	de alguna dama?	
LEARÍN	No sé.	
	Sienpre este Fernando fue	
	de sus secretos escaso.	
	Allá le traté en España.	
	¡Desdichado del contrario!	975
	Gran balor le es neçesario	
	si ha de salir a canpaña,	
	porque Rui de Castro es onbre	
	con quien destetan allá	
	los niños.	
MIRAMAMOLÍN	Ya suena acá	980
	la exçelençia de su nombre.	
	¿Querráme seruir a mí	
	si le trata mal su Rey?	
LEARÍN	Defiende tanto su ley	

St. dir. before v. 962. MSBA, Vanse los dos; J, does not supply st. dir.*

963. MSBA, assign to Zeydan; J, identifies as *Alc.* through the passage.
964. MSBA, assign to Zayde.
967. MSBA, ocasion.
968. MSBA, assign to Zayde.
970. MSB, omit *por;* A, ¿Es competencias?
971. MSBA, assign to Zayde.
976. MSBA, omit *le;* G, omits.*
977. MSBA, para emprender esta hazaña.
980. B, Miramamolín's speech is continued as Zayde's.
984. MSBA, assign to Almohadí.

que dudo el pensar que sí,   985
mas yo le hablaré, que el sol
no ha uisto mexor soldado.

MIRAMAMOLÍN   Estimaré que a mi lado
asista vn Castro español.

✠ *Mudarra con vna caxa de guerra, y detrás, con vnos*
carteles, Fernán Ruiz de Castro, y un bastón.

FERNÁN   Aquí puedes echar, Mudarra, vn vando,   990
en tanto que yo pongo los carteles.

MUDARRA   Fixa en aquestas calles tres o quatro,
en tanto que comienzo.   *[fol.] 18 [r.]*

FERNÁN   Toca.

MUDARRA   Escucha:
"Fernán Ruiz de Castro, el Castellano,
a Fortunio Ximénez desafía,   995
el plazo de aquí a un mes de aqueste vando,
juez y fiador de que es seguro
el Miramamolín, señor del Africa."

✠ *Al tocar, sale vna tropa de moros, y con ellos*
Almohadí, Albumasar, Zerbín y Lisardo, trayendo a Ab-
delmón, vestido de rey. Cada vno viene por sí.

ALMOHADÍ   La caxa y la señal sin duda es ésta.

ZERBINO   ¿Si es ésta la señal que conçertamos?   1000

---

985. MSBA, que serà imposible el si.
986. MSBA, le he de hablar.
St. dir. before v. 990. MSB, Vanse, y sale Fernan Ruyz de Castro, y
Mudarra con vna caxa de guerra; A, Sale Fernán . . .*
990. MSBA, Mudarra echar el vando.
991. MSBA, fixo.
992. MSBA, aquessa calle; J, cuatro.*
994. MSBA, omit *el Castellano*. The announcement appears as a stage
direction in MSBA.*
995. MSBA, en campo de aqui a vn mes, desde este vando.*
998. MSBA, de Africa.*
St. dir. before v. 999. MSBA, Toca la caxa, y van saliendo cada vno
de por si, Albumasar, Almohadi, Zayde, y Zeydan; B, Tocan . . .
999. MSBA, assign to Albumasar.
1000. MSBA, assign to Zayde.*

LISARDO	Caxa, y en Fez. N[uest]ro conçierto llega.
ALBUMASAR	Al arma tocan, los amigos vienen.
ABDELMÓN	¿Qué es esto, amigos, es ya t[iem]po?
ALBUMASAR	El çielo,

Abdelmón generoso, te prospere.

ABDELMÓN	¿Qué caxa es ésta?
ALBUMASAR	Escucha, que vn cristiano 1005

la toca.

LISARDO	Di, español, ¿qué caxa es ésta?
FERNÁN	Vn desafío. No temáis, hidalgos,

que el Rey me dio lizenzia que pusiese
estos carteles.

ALBUMASAR	Todo ha sido engaño,

mas ya que nos juntamos, ¿qué haremos?   1010

ABDELMÓN	Que pues se a conozido n[uest]ro yntento,

y la conjuraçión contra el Rey echa,
no nos boluamos, generosos moros,
sin salir con la enpresa comenzada.

ZERBINO	Al arma pues, al arma.
LISARDO	Al arma, y muera 1015

el Miramamolín. ¿Quién viue?

ALBUMASAR	Viua

1001. MSBA, assign to Almohadí.*
1002. MSBA, assign to Zeydan.
St. dir. before v. 1003. MSBA, Sale Audelmon vestido de Rey.*
1005. MSBA, calla.*
1006. MSBA, assign Lisardo's line to Audelmon; G, continues as Albumasar's speech.*
1007. MSBA, Vn desafio es, no tengays miedo.*
1008. MSBA, fixasse.
1009. MSBA, vnos carteles; assign Albumasar's speech to Almohadí.
1010. MSBA, estamos juntos.
1011. MSBA, continue this speech as Almohadí's; J, se ha.
1012. A, A la conjuración.
1014. MSBA, sin acabar la.
1015. MSBA, Zayde — Al arma pues. Zeydan — Al arma, al arma, y muera; G assigns Lisardo's speech to Almohadí.*
1016. MSBA, Quien viue? assigned to Audelmon; Albumasar's lines assigned to Todos; G, el Miramamolin continues as Almohadí's speech.*

        n[uest]ro Rey Abdelmón.

FERNÁN   Estraño casso,

(FERNÁN)   Mudarra. Defendamos su persona.

MUDARRA   ¡Mas que me voy a España sin la mona!   ❊

    St. dir. before v. 1017. MSBA, Vanse todos metiendo mano.❊
    1018. ❊
    1019. G, following is *Fin de este Acto Primero (rúbrica).*❊

2º

ACTO

(rúbrica)

Los que hablan en el 2º Acto

Rei Alfonso
Fortún Ximénez
Estefanía
Ysabel
Ordoño
Fernán Ruiz de Castro
Mudarra
Nuño Osorio
Ramiro de Guzmán
Sancho Laynez
Vn Alguazil
Vn Cochero

(rúbrica)

MSBA do not repeat the list of characters here; G, Personas que hablan en el acto segundo.*

Rey Alfonso, Fortún Ximénez.

ALFONSO	Mucho me he holgado de verte.	1020
	Seas, Fortún, bienvenido.	
FORTUNIO	He tenido a buena suerte	
	haber con mi honor cunplido	
	sin dar a Castro la muerte.	
	Luego que el franzés se fue,	1025
	partí, señor, a Lisboa.	
	Della a Çeuta me enbarqué,	
	dando al mar la herrada proa	
	de vna tartana que hallé.	
	Quando de Çeuta salía,	1030
	supe como Fez se ardía	
	de vn rebelión y motín,	✿
	donde el Miramamolín	
	fue muerto a trayzión vn día.	
	Con dos mil guardas las puertas	1035
	çerradas y defendidas,	
	jamás me fueron abiertas,	
	y a costado tantas vidas	

MSBA do not repeat this act heading.
St. dir. before v. 1020. MSA, Salen el Rey Alfonso, y Fortun Ximenez, y acompañamiento; B, omits.
1032. MSBA, o motin.
1033. MSBA, en que el.
1035. ✿
1038. MSBA, han.

que ay seys mil personas muertas.
Vn çierto moro Almohadí   1040
fue autor deste rebelión,
según en Tánger hoy,
con otros de su naçión
que le ayudaron allí,
juntos, de varias çiudades,   1045
se llaman los almohades.
Vn astrólogo los guía,   *[fol. 1 v.]*
que estiende su monarquía
a las futuras edades.
Han hecho Rey a Abdelmón,   1050
hijo de vn humilde ollero,
aunque de gran corazón,
altiuo, gallardo y fiero,
dispuesto a qualquier trayçión.
Han echo, en fin, Rey de barro   1055
por hazerle más bizarro   *
contra el balor español,
porque ha jurado que el sol
no tiene seguro el carro.
Diez mil hombres en canpaña,   1060
y más de ocho mil caballos
quiere poner contra España.
Junta, Alfonso, tus basallos;
no salgan con esta hazaña,
que si pasan, y se alaua   1065
esta naçión almohadí,   *
que ésta, flecha es de su alxaua,
vendrá mayor mal por ti

1039. B, mnertas.
1041. S, desta.
1044. MSBA, ayudauan.
1046. MSBA, llamanse.
1047. *
1057. MSBA, contra tu carro.*
1058. *
1061. MSBA, omit *de.*
1063. *

que a Rodrigo por la Caua.   ⁕

ALFONSO   De tu venida y la suya,   1070
             Fortún, tengo ygual contento,
             y espero en Dios que destruya
             mi mano su atreuimiento,
             porque su poder se arguya.
             Venga el bárbaro, y con él   [fol.] 2 [r.]   1075
             los villanos almohades,
             que de su intento cruel
             quedará por mil edades
             memoria, y de mí por él.
             No será mui grande exçeso   1080
             quebrar ese Rey de barro,
             ni llebar, aunque vil peso,
             al que al sol le quita el carro,
             en el de mis triunphos preso.
             Tú cunpliste con tu honor;   1085
             traygan a mi hija luego,
             oy la enpleo en tu balor.

FORTUNIO   Quedaré de su sol çiego.
             No la merezco, señor,
                 mas si deste baxo suelo   1090
             a tal grandeza me subes,
             de mi humilde amor y çelo
             a sus rayos haré nubes,
             y miraréle con velo.

ALFONSO   Venga con real vestido,   1095

1069. J, Cava.
1071. MSBA, gran.
1074. MSBA, mi poder.
1075. ⁕
1078. MSBA, hallaràn.
1080. MSBA, Mas no serà grande.⁕
1081. MSBA, este.
1082. ⁕
1085. MSBA, has cumplido.
1086. MSBA, llamenme.
1087. J, hoy.⁕
1090. ⁕
1094. MSBA, mirarela.⁕

          dexe el háuito y entienda
          que desde oy tiene marido,
          y tú que llebas la prenda
          de más balor que he tenido.
          Jacob a Joseph quería,   1100*
          por ser hijo de Raquel,
          más que a los hijos de Lía,
          que amándola, amaua en él   *[fol. 2 v.]*
          lo que della en él se vía.
          Yo, de mi Sancha, contenplo   1105
          en Estefanía vn dechado,
          vn retrato, vn alto exenplo.
FORTUNIO   Haz cuenta que has fabricado
          para su ymagen vn tenplo:
          las puertas serán mis ojos,   1110
          el altar será mi pecho,
          ara el alma a los despojos
          más bellos que el çielo a echo
          para paz de mis enojos.
          No bolueré a Françia más;   1115
          conpras vn esclauo en mí.

✠ *Entre Estefanía, gallarda aunque triste, Ysabel y Ordoño.*

ORDOÑO   ¿Sabes que a casarte vas?
ESTEFANÍA   Ya sé, Ordoño, que naçí
          para no tener jamás
          sola vn ora de alegría.   1120*
ORDOÑO   Aquí viene Estefanía.

1100. A, José.*
1101. B, hija.
1103. MSBAJ, amandole.*
1110. *
1111. B, Alrar.
1112. MSB, harà.*
1115. *
St. dir. before v. 1117. MSB, Salen Estefania de dama, y Ordoño, y
Ysabel; G, omits *entre*, reverses *Ordoño* and *Ysabel;* A, Sale ... é Isabel.
1118. J, Ya sé el signo [en] q̄ nací.*
1120. G, una hora; omits *sola*.
1121. A, assigned to Fortún.

ALFONSO   Esta es mi hija, Fortún,
                  no de la plebe común,
                  sino toda sangre mía.
                  La torre de Mormojón,   1125*
                  Castromocho y Palençuela   *
                  con ella tu dote son.
                  Llamen luego, Ordoño Vela,   *
                  quien les dé la bendizión.
                  Pareze que triste vienes.   1130
ESTEFANÍA   Tengo ocasión.
ALFONSO   Tú, ¿de qué?
                  Responde, ¿en qué te detienes?
ESTEFANÍA   Señor, ¿qué responderé   [fol.] 3 [r.]
                  quando casada me tienes?
                  Eres padre y magestad,   1135
                  la fuerza y la voluntad
                  son tuyas.
ALFONSO   ¡Esto es vergüenza!
                  Todo quiero que lo venza
                  tu amor y mi autoridad.
                  Ven donde a tu esposo hables,   1140
                  que es vn grande caballero.
ESTEFANÍA   Mis desdichas son notables: [ap.]
                  tardó Rui de Castro; oy muero.
                  ¡O, tienpos sienpre mudables,
                  lo que adoro me quitáis,   1145
                  lo que aborrezco me dais.
YSABEL   Mis desseos se han cunplido, [ap.]
                  siendo Fortún su marido.
                  Oy, çielos, de graçia estáis;

_____

1123. *
1128. MSBA, a Ordoño.*
1129. MSBA, que les.
1130. MSBA, Para que tan triste vienes?
1132. B, te entretienes?
1140. MSBA, omit a.
1143. MSBA, tarde Ruyz de Castro muero.*
1147. *
1149. A, cielo.

	que en fin si con ella cassa,	1150
	tendré mi bien en mi casa,	
	y dándole yo ocasión,	
	merezerá su afiçión	
	este fuego que me abrassa;	
	que ay ombre que de su hermosa	1155
	muger cansado, en su esclaua	
	pone los ojos. ¡Dichosa	
	mi suerte, oy mi pena acaua!	
ESTEFANÍA	¡Que soy de vn bárbaro esposa! *[ap.]*	
	¡Que me pierde el más galán,	1160
	el más fuerte, el más baliente,	
	y que a un villano me dan!	
FORTUNIO	Aunque en la ocasión presente *[fol. 3 v.]*	
	çiegos mis ojos están,	
	bellísima Estefanía,	1165
	mira mis dichas contenta,	
	que el bien que el çielo me enbía	
	desde oy corre por su cuenta,	
	no por la tuya y la mía.	
	Del mundo quisiera ser	1170
	oy absoluto señor;	
	mas si suele merezer	
	qualquiera imposible amor	
	más que el humano poder,	
	con él te merezca yo.	1175
	¿No me hablas?	
ALFONSO	Aún no es tienpo.	
ESTEFANÍA	Ved lo que el çielo me dio *[ap.]*	
	por no venir Castro a tienpo.	
	Yo diré "sí", el alma "no".	

1150. MSBA, al fin.*
1151. A, omits.
1153. MSBA, merecerè el.
1154. MSBA, deste.
1161. MSBA, y mas valiente.
1170. *
1172. MSBA, puede.
1173. MSBA, qualquier.
1175. MSBA, merezco.

✠ *Váyanse y entren Fernán Ruiz de Castro y Mudarra con*
    vestidos de moros, y Mudarra a lo graçioso.

MUDARRA	¿Para qué me has puesto ansí?	1180
FERNÁN	Para engañar a mi bien,	
	y poder mexor tanbién	
	pedirle albrizias de mí.	
MUDARRA	Osaré en la portería	
	entrar de aquesta manera?	1185
FERNÁN	No, mas pregunta acá fuera	
	por la bella Estefanía,	
	y di que vn moro de Fez	
	trahe nuebas del de Castro.	
MUDARRA	Parezco moro del Rastro, *[fol.] 4 [r.]*	1190
	y voy temiendo la nuez;	✿
	que de tales inuenziones	
	suele venir con razón	
	el echar la bendiçión	✿
	al pueblo con los talones.	1195
	Ya que Dios nos escapó	✿
	de la sierra de las monas,	
	y salbas n[uest]ras personas	
	de tantos moros sacó,	
	que fue mucho en su motín	1200
	no dexar tanbién las vidas,	
	¿no fuera mexor . . . ?	
FERNÁN	No inpidas,	
	Mudarra, mi onesto fin.	
	Mira si ay a quién preguntes,	
	y déxate de razones;	1205

St. dir. before v. 1180. MSBA, Vanse y salen Fernan Ruyz de Castro, y
Mudarra de Moro gracioso; G, Vanse y sale Fernan Ruiz y Mudarra vestidos de Moros y Mudarra de gracioso. J, gracioso.✿
  1185. MSBA, hablar.
  1188. MSBA, Dile que.
  1191. MSBA, ya voy.
  1193. MSBA, salir.
  1197. A, tierra.
  1200. MSBA, tanto Moro.
  1203. MSBA, Mudarra amigo este fin.
  1205. MSBA, inuenciones.

	que no es bien que mis pasiones
	a tus disparates juntes.
MUDARRA	¡Moros en vn monesterio,
	y yo con tan mal adorno!
FERNÁN	Pregunta ya.
MUDARRA	Aquí está el torno. 1210
FERNÁN	Sí, estará, que no es misterio.
MUDARRA	O, torno, en que cada día
	se ylan tantos recados,
	se dizen tantos enfados
	y tanta filatería, 1215
	¿posible es que a veros torno?
	Tórnome loco de hablaros.
	Viue Dios, que he de besaros.
	¡Ay!
FERNÁN	¿Qué es eso?
MUDARRA	Andubo el torno,
	y ame dado vn bofetón 1220
	que estrellas me ha hecho ver. [fol. 4 v.]
FERNÁN	Abrazo debió de ser.
MUDARRA	¿Así los abrazos son?
	Mas bien es que así sacuda
	con fuerza tan cautelosa 1225
	al hombre que bessa cosa *
	que por momentos se muda.
	Deo graçias.
FERNÁN	Neçio, ¿qué dizes?

1206. MSBA, que a mis razones.
1207. MSBA, essos disparates.
1208. SBAG, monasterio.
1209. *
1210. MSBA, Cas. — Llega acaba.
1212. MSBA, en quien.*
1214. MSBA, texen; G, enfadados.
1218. MSBA, abraçaros.
St. dir. before v. 1219. MSBA, Va a abraçar el torno, y dan vn golpe dentro.
1221. BA, me hizo.*
1223. S, braços.
1224. G, le sacuda.
1225. S, caudalosa.

MUDARRA	Guardo a este torno el decoro.
FERNÁN	Pues, Deo gr[aci]as, ¿siendo moro? 1230
	¿No ves que te contradizes?
MUDARRA	Pues, ¿qué tengo de dezir,
	Mahoma?
FERNÁN	Quedo, que ya
	responden.
MUDARRA	¿Quién está acá?
FERNÁN	Por fuerza me hazes reír. 1235
MUDARRA	¿Están las monjas en casa?
FERNÁN	Bestia, ¿hauían de estar fuera?
(Dentro)	Deo gr[aci]as.
FERNÁN	Es la tornera.
MUDARRA	La tornera, o lo que amasa.
	Ello se abla por tramoya, 1240*
	ello es voz de çerbatana,
	sea Catalina o Juana,
	o el laberinto de Troya.
	Suplico a vuesa merzed,
	baya a la çelda o al coro 1245
	y diga que está aquí vn moro
	que quiere hablar por la red
	a la señora. ¿No entiende? [fol.] 5 [r.]
(Dentro)	¡Jesús! No le entiendo bien.
	¿Moros aquí? ¿Diga a quién? 1250
MUDARRA	Ves, que del nombre se ofende.
FERNÁN	Dile a quién.
MUDARRA	No son tan moros
	que si ay algún vino allá

1233. MSBA, Apartate allà.
1234. MSBA, Mud — Deo gracias, quiẽ està acà?
1235. MSB, haze.
1237. MSBA, Necio.
1238. *
1239. MSBAJ, la que.
1243. *
1244. MBA, vaya vusted; S, vaya vuested.*
1245. MSBA, a la celda, o vaya al coro.
1247. MSBA, en la.
1251. B, repeats v. 1239.
1253. B, por allá.

	y quiere passarlo acá,	
	no lo metan en sus poros;	1255
	y así la dé Dios salud,	
	que con algún panezillo	
	trayga, siquiera, vn quartillo;	*
	que está mui floxo el laúd.	*
(Dentro)	No se da limosna aquí.	1260
FERNÁN	¡Maldito seas, amén!	
	¿Vino pides que te den,	
	y vienes vestido ansí?	
MUDARRA	Señor, cada uno pide	*
	aquello que ha menester.	1265
FERNÁN	Oye, vn moro quiere ver	
	la infanta que aquí reside,	
	que trahe vnas cartas. Baya,	
	y llámela, por su vida.	
(Dentro)	Ya deste conuento es yda.	1270*
FERNÁN	¡Yda! La voz me desmaya.	
	¿Adónde, o cómo, señora?	
(Dentro)	Casóla el Rey.	
FERNÁN	¡Ay de mí!	
MUDARRA	¿Era malo el vino aquí	
	para esforzarnos agora?	1275
FERNÁN	¿Quién, señora, es su marido? *[fol. 5 v.]*	
(Dentro)	Fortún Ximénez se llama.	
FERNÁN	¡Qué uiento para mi llama	*
	de aquesta boca ha salido!	
MUDARRA	Ygual le pedía yo.	1280
FERNÁN	Agua traherá de mis ojos;	
	venzióme, pues los despojos	

1254. MSBA, quieren meterlo.
1256. MSBA, ansi Dios le dè.
1259. MSBA, flaco.
1261. MSBA, Maldigate Dios.*
1266. MSB, Oy; A, Hoy.
1273. B, Casala.
1276. S, tu marido?*
1279. MSBA, aquella.
1281. MSBA, traerè.

de mi vitoria llebó.

¿Qué menos pudo esperar
vn amante que se ausenta?   1285
Pues no ay luna tan mudable
como la fee del ausenzia.
Muerto soy; matóme el Rey.
Llorad, esperanzas muertas.
¡Bálame Dios, lo que puede   1290*
vna lengua lisongera!
Bien ayan pribanzas justas
que el bien general aumentan;
maldiga el çielo traydores
que a los reyes aconsejan.   1295
De ti no me quexo, Alfonso;
plega a Dios que Rey te veas
de toda el Andaluzía,   *
de Çaragoza y Valenzia.
Llamáronte Enperador   1300
por tus hazañas y fuerzas
y mexor por tus uirtudes,
que entonzes los reyes reynan.
Mas, ¿qué diré de la yngrata   *[fol.] 6 [r.]*
que por Fortunio me dexa?   1305
Pero, si no fue culpada...
¿Qué importa que no lo sea?
Que ver la amada prenda   *

1283. MSB, la vitoria; A, la victoria.*
1284. MSBA, Que mas bien puede alcançar.
1285. MSBA, villano.
1286. MSBA, si no.
1287. MSBA, como vna muger. Mud — ya empieça; J, ausençia.
1290-93. MSBA, omit; G, valgame.
1294. MSBA, maldiga Dios los traydores.
1297. MSB, se vea; A, te vea.
1300. A, llamárante.
1301. MSBA, y letras.
1305. MSBA, si por.
1306. MSBA, culpado.
1307. B, le sea.
1308. MSBA, Que es ver.

	gozar al enemigo es grande afrenta.	
	Mudarra, ¿sabes acaso	1310
	de mis sentidos?	
MUDARRA	Quisiera,	*
	mas preguntaré en el torno.	
	Podrá ser que allá lo sepan,	
	que lo que aquí no se sabe,	
	menos se sabe acá fuera.	1315
	Deo gr[aci]as, señoras mías.	
	¿Han visto allá por sus çeldas	
	los sentidos de mi amo,	
	en la noria o en la güerta?	
	Que si buscara los míos,	1320
	dixera que en la bodega,	
	que allí se me pierden sienpre.	
FERNÁN	¡Que esto los çielos consientan!	
	¡Que se cassó Estefanía,	
	que aquel villano la lleba,	1325
	que la tiene entre sus brazos,	
	que ella le regala y bessa!	
MUDARRA	¡Estraños soys los amantes,	
	filosophando quimeras!	
	¿Qué sirbe desmenuzar	1330
	las cosas con tanta fuerza?	
	¿No es mexor ymaginar *[fol. 6 v.]*	
	que ya se enfada de vella,	
	que le agrada otra muger,	
	que la posesión despreçia,	1335
	que a visto ya sus defetos;	

1309. MSBA, gozar del enemigo grande afrenta.
1312. MSB, preguntarele al torno; A, preguntarélo al torno.
1315. MSBA, allà.
1316. A, señora mía.
1320. MSA, buscaran; B, dixeran.
1324. MSBA, se case.
1326. MSBA, goze.
1330. *
1332. *
1333. MSBA, se enfada ya.*
1335. MSBA, appears as v. 1339.

que verla sienpre en la mesa
y en la cama le da enfado;
que alegran las cosas nuebas;
que no estar alanbicando   1340
el seso con tanta pena,
haçiendo mil notomías;   *
si la bessa, o no la bessa;
si la goza o no la goza,
si se llega o no se llega;   1345
si se junta o no se junta,
si se açerca o no se açerca?

FERNÁN   ¡Ay, Mudarra, que es amor
enbidia, y la enbidia çiega!
Por la fantasía mira   1350
lo que ymagina y sospecha.
Çeloso estoy y enbidioso.
Çelos, para que lo sepas,
son tablilla de pintor
de varios colores llena.   1355
Llega el pinzel del temor,
y pinta lo que sospecha
en el lienzo del sentido,
blanco de flechas de ofensas
de Angélica y de Medoro.   *[fol.] 7 [r.]*   1360*
Con la sangre de mis venas
pinté la historia, Mudarra.
Déxame que llore el verla,

1337. J, siempre.
1339. MSBA, appears as v. 1335; porque alegran cosas.
1341. MSBA, fuerça.
1342. *
1348. *
1349. MSB, es ciega.
1350. S, fantasia mia.
1351. SBA, y dessea.
1352-55. MSBA, omit.
1355. GJ, varias.*
1356. *
1359. MSBA, flechas diuersas.
1361. MSBA, omit.*
1362. MSBA, pinta la historia sin verla.
1363. MSBA, omit.

que es ver la amada prenda
gozar del enemigo grande afrenta.   1365
¡O, nunca tuuiera onor!
¡O, nunca noble naçiera
para que este desafío
ocasionara mi ausençia!
¡Ay, mudable Estefanía,   1370
por tus papeles quisiera
obligarte a mis seruizios,
pues has negado la deuda!
Pero tanbién negarás
las firmas, si ves en ellas   1375
más amores que razones,   *
y más mentiras que letras.
¡Con Fortunio, aquel cobarde
que se quedó en la frontera
de Fez, que apenas osó   1380
pasar los muros de Zeuta;
con vn ombre que esperé,
la lanza en el ristre puesta,
de sol a sol en canpaña,
con estar de vandos llena!   1385
A hablar voy al Rey, Mudarra.
Oy me pierdo.

MUDARRA   Tente, espera.

FERNÁN   Quitarme quiero este trage.
              ¡Ay, si pudiera la pena!   *[fol. 7 v.]*
              Afrentar quiero a Fortunio   1390*

1366. MSBA, amor.*
1369. MSBA, no ocasionara mi ofensa.
1372. MSBA, mi seruicio.
1373. MSB, ya que negaste las deudas; A, ya que negastes las deudas.
1375. MSA, la firma si ves en ella; B, la firma si ve en ella.*
1377. MSBA, mas falsedades que.
1378-85. MSBA, omit.*
1381. *
1387. MSA, aguarda, espera; B, Guarda, espera.
1388. MSBA, Quitarte quiero esse.*
1389. MSBA, ansi pudiera mi pena.*

si es posible que ya pueda,
onrrado de Estefanía
y yo sin onrra y sin ella;
que es ver la amada prenda
gozar del enemigo grande afrenta.   1395

✠ *Váyase.*

MUDARRA   ¿Si se abrá Ysabel casado
con aquella carta vieja   ✱
de Ramiro, mi enemigo?
¡Más mal ay en el aldea!   ✱
¡O perra, viue el dios Baco   1400
con sus parras y sus çepas,
que te he de arañar la cara
con vnas martas flamencas!   ✱
Para ti, por Tetüán
andube a caza vna siesta   1405
de la más alegre mona   ✱
que se ha tomado en su sierra.
Para ti vine vestido,
por agradar tus ojeras,   ✱
de aranbeles de Mahoma   1410✱
y tiritañas turquescas.   ✱
Para ti vine a la posta
en el caballo Babieca,   ✱
más colorado el envés   ✱
que salmón partido a ruedas.   1415
¡Muera Ysabel, que no es bien que vna perra
lama a Ramiro y a Mudarra muerda!

St. dir. before v. 1396. MSBAG, Vase.
1400. G, omits *el*.
1403. ✱
1406. MSBA, honrada.
1407. MSBA, caçado en su tierra.
1409. MSBA, para alegrar tus orejas; G, orejas.
1411. MSBA, y tiritaña Turquesca.✱
1412. MSBA, corri la posta.
1415. MSBA, en ruedas.
1416. MSBA, muera Isabel, no es justo.✱
1417. ✱

✠ *Rey Alfonso, Fortún Ximénez, Estefanía.   [fol.] 8 [r.]*

ALFONSO	Alça el rostro, que no es justo	
	que muestres tanta tristeza.	
FORTUNIO	¿Posible es que a tal belleza	1420
	da el çielo tanto disgusto?	
	Mas tenéis mucha razón	
	de sentir el baxo enpleo,	
	no viendo de mi desseo	
	quáles los méritos son;	1425
	que reparando en los míos,	
	no es mucho que triste estéys.	
ESTEFANÍA	Los que vos, señor, tenéis,	
	antes me pusieran bríos.	
	Es mi condizión ansí;	1430
	nunca más alegre estoy.	
FORTUNIO	Culpa a mis desdichas doy.	
ESTEFANÍA	De éssas ay artas en mí.	
	¿Posible es que agora tengo *[ap.]*	
	de dar la mano a este ombre,	1435
	quando de sólo su nombre	
	tal miedo y enojo tengo?	
	¿Cómo que podré quebrar	
	la palabra a mi Fernando?	

✠ *Ordoño entre.*

ORDOÑO	A la puerta está llamando	1440
	Fernán Ruiz.	
ESTEFANÍA	Déxale entrar.	
ALFONSO	¿Qué [e]s lo que dizes?	
ESTEFANÍA	Señor,	

St. dir. before v. 1418. MSBA, Vase y salen el Rey Alfonso, y Estefania, y Fortun, y Ordoño, y acompañamiento de boda, y Ýsabel; A, Salen el ...
1420. MSBA, omit *a.*
1421. MSBA, a tanto.
1429. MSBA, pusieron.*
St. dir. before v. 1440. MSBA, Sale Ramiro de Guzman; G, Sale Ordoño.
1440. MSBA, aguardando; assigned to Ramiro.
1442. MSBA, Quedo, que dezis? G, Que le dizes? J, ¿Qué es lo ...?*

Fernán Ruiz, el Castellano,
dizen que es mi primo hermano,
y es de tu reyno el mejor.   1445
   En día que yo me caso,
hónrreme vn Castro tan bueno.   *[fol. 8 v.]*

ALFONSO   Estoy de saber ageno
la deçisión de aquel casso.

FORTUNIO   ¿Qué ay que saber? Yo partí   1450
a Fez, y si en Fez no entré,
culpa de las guerras fue;
ya con el reto cunplí.
   Entre Fernando, pues gusta
mi esposa, y dé su razón.   1455

ESTEFANÍA   Tu esposa no, ni lo son
aquellas que amor no ajusta.
   Entre Fernando, señor,
no me casses sin oyr.

ALFONSO   Entre.

ORDOÑO   Vóyselo a dezir.   1460

FORTUNIO   Yo voy de mal en peor.   *[ap.]*

    ✠ *Fernán Ruiz, enojado.*

FERNÁN   Del Rey abaxo, qualquiera
que dixere que ha cunplido
Fortún Ximénez el reto,
ni las palabras que dixo   1465
delante del Rey franzés,
quando de Santiago vino,

1444. ✻
1445. MSBA, omit *es.*
1447. ✻
1449. MSBA, dissension.
1452. MSBA, guardas.
1453. MSBA, mi voto.
1457. MSBAJ, aquellos.✻
1459. MSBA, case.
1460. MSBA, assign Ordoño's speech to Ramiro.
  St. dir. before v. 1462. MSB, Sale Fernan Ruyz de Castro, y Mudarra; A, Salen . . .; G, Sale Fernan Ruiz de Castro.
1465. MSBA, y las.

	miente por la barba; miente	
	desde vna vez hasta çinco.	
	Yo esperé, desde que el sol	1470
	sobre los muros moriscos	
	de Tarudante y Marruecos	✿
	tendió sus rayos diuinos,	
	hasta que en los suyos pobres	
	le vieron los indios ricos,	1475
	vn día a Fortún Ximénez [fol.] 9 [r.]
	en Fez, pero a Fez no vino.	
	Traygo de su nuebo Rey,	
	de sus alcaydes y amigos,	
	diez firmas que lo confirman,	1480
	y a Mudarra por testigo.	
	Y si contra la verdad	✿
	que digo, y que sienpre he dicho...	
FORTUNIO	Fernán Ruiz, poco a poco.	
	Con mi onor tengo cunplido.	1485
	Llegué a Fez, no pude entrar;	
	testigos ay fidedinos,	
	quanto más que a t[iem]po estamos...	✿
ALFONSO	No prosigas.	
FORTUNIO	Perdón pido.	
FERNÁN	Basta, Alfonso, que no sólo	1490
	me ynpides que en desafío	
	cobre el onor que mis padres,	
	difuntos en tu seruiçio,	
	para seruirte me dieron;	
	ni muchos que has reçiuido	1495✿
	desta mano y desta espada	
	me pagas, siendo tú el mismo	
	que en las guerras y en las pazes	
	tantas vezes los has uisto;	

1469. J, cinco.
1471. ✿
1479. ✿
1483. MSBA, siempre digo.
1486. S, puede.
1489. ✿

	pero que gustas de dar	1500
	a mis propios enemigos	
	lo que es raçón que me dieras,	
	pues lo tengo merezido	
	por quien soy, que soy tu deudo, *[fol. 9 v.]*	
	por mis echos, que son míos.	1505
ALFONSO	¿Qué dizes?	
FERNÁN	Que a Estefanía	
	abrá seys años que sirbo,	
	y se la das a Fortún	
	porque el de Françia lo quiso.	
	¿Es mejor Fortún que yo?	1510
	¿Quándo Fortunio ha tenido	
	pensamiento de agradalla?	
ALFONSO	Castro, hubiérasmelo dicho.	
	Hija, yo pongo en tu gusto,	
	por fin deste desafío,	1515
	la elecçión destos dos nobles.	
	Escoje al tuyo marido,	
	no te quexes de mi fuerza.	
ESTEFANÍA	Señor, si queda a mi arbitrio,	
	confieso mi obligaçión;	1520
	que quiero a Fernando digo.	
ALFONSO	Pues alto; dale la mano.	
FORTUNIO	¡A Castro! Pierdo el sentido. *[ap.]*	
ALFONSO	Aduierte, Fortún Ximénez,	
	que he hecho lo que he podido,	1525*
	mas como suelen dezir:	
	"fortuna lo que ha querido."	
	Vamos, hijos.	

✠ *Váyanse el Rey y los nobios.*

1500. MSBA, sino.
1504. MSBA, su dueño.*
1512. MSBA, pensamientos de agradarte.*
1517. MSBA, al tuyo escoge marido.*
1523. A, ¡Ah, Castro!*
1528. MSBA, hijo.
St. dir. before v. 1528. MSBA, Vanse, y quedan Fortun, y Ysabel, y Mudarra; G, Vase el Rey y los nouios.

YSABEL   ¡Ay de mí! *[ap.]*
                        Perdióse el remedio mío   ❋
                        a vista de mi esperanza;   1530
                        ya no es Fortún su marido,
                        mas yo haré tales enrredos   *[fol.] 10 [r.]*
                        que goze el bien que ymagino.
                        ¡Muger soy!
MUDARRA   ¿A mí señora,
                        no me escucha? ¿Qué la digo?   1535
YSABEL   ¿Es Mudarra?
MUDARRA   ¿No me ve
                        con mis botas de camino?
                        Pues a fee que más de vn çiego   ❋
                        olgara de haberme visto.
YSABEL   No me puedo detener.   1540
                        ¿Bienes bueno?   ❋
MUDARRA   A tu seruiçio.
YSABEL   ¿Qué me has traydo de allá?
MUDARRA   Todo es monas; truxe vn mico.
YSABEL   Sería entre carne y cuero.
MUDARRA   No, sino vn perrito lindo.   1545
YSABEL   Esta noche quiero ablarte.
MUDARRA   ¿Qué ora?
YSABEL   Entre quatro y çinco.
MUDARRA   Ladraré por señas.
YSABEL   No.
MUDARRA   ¿Por qué?
YSABEL   No ladran los ximios.
MUDARRA   ¿Qué seña haré?
YSABEL   Rebuznar.   1550
MUDARRA   Ya lo entiendo; daré vn silbo.

1533. MSBA, que goze lo que he querido.
1535. A, ¡Ah, mi señora!
1536. ❋
1537. ❋
1541. B, viene.
1543. MSBA, traygo; G, traxe.
1544. MSBA, Serà entre la carne.
1547. MSBA, a q̄ hora?
1551. MBA, Ya te entiendo; S, Ya te endiendo.

✠ *Váyanse los dos.*

FORTUNIO   Basta que me dixo el Rey,
           "yo he [e]cho lo que he podido."
           No puedo del Rey quexarme;
           quexaréme de mí mismo;   1555
           ni de mí será razón,
           onrrado mi yntento ha sido;
           del çielo me han derribado
           mis desdichas al abismo.
           Si enprendí llegar al sol,   *[fol. 10 v.]* 1560
           si de sus rayos diuinos
           me tube asido en el ayre
           y de su çielo he caydo,
           yo he hecho lo que he podido,
           fortuna lo que ha querido.   1565
           La conquista era ynposible
           de quien fui Faetón altiuo;   ❋
           el carro de oro pedí,
           del sol me llamaron hijo.
           Salí, quando el alba hermosa   1570
           vierte azuzenas y lirios,
           con quatro caballos blancos
           al dorado carro hasidos;
           huyeron de mí las nubes,
           espantáronse los signos,   1575
           retroçedieron los astros,
           la eclíptica se desizo.
           Por los cristales del çielo
           abrieron çanja y camino

St. dir. before v. 1552. MS, Vase, y queda Fortun solo; G, Vanse; BA,
as in MS, but *Vanse.*
    1558. MSBA, al cielo lleguè y subi.❋
    1559. MSBA, mas si he llegado, y caydo.
    1560-63. MSBA, omit.
    1566. MSBA, fue.❋
    1567. ❋
    1568-75. MSBA, omit, but 1569 appears after v. 1578.
    1577. MSBA, y la eleccion.
    1578. MSBA, en lo mas alto me vi.❋

con el gran peso las ruedas   1580
del estrellado edifiçio.
Abrasóme tanto sol,
dexé riendas, perdí estribos,
la tierra abrasé y cay.
Mas si he subido y caydo,   1585
yo he hecho lo que [e] podido,
fortuna lo que ha querido.

✠ *Entre Ysabel.*

YSABEL   Mi señora, arrepentida,   *[fol.] 11 [r.]*
Fortún, de haberse casado,
ya de Fernando ofendida,   1590
me enbía a hablarte.

FORTUNIO   Oy has dado
nueba esperanza a mi vida.
¿Más cómo podrá boluer
su palabra atrás?

YSABEL   No buelbe,
porque ya no puede ser,   1595
pero a querer se resuelbe
a quien es razón querer.
El casarse es ya forzoso,
mas dize que si tú quieres,
en dulçe trato amoroso   1600
gozarás de los plazeres
de amor que oy rinde a su esposo;
que no faltará lugar,
y ella buscará ocasión

1579-84. MSBA, omit.
1583. *
1585. MSBA, pero llegado y caydo.*
1586. JG, he podido.*
St. dir. before v. 1587. MSBAG, Sale Ysabel.
1592. MSBA, luz al alma, al pecho vida.
1593. MSBA, puede.*
1596. MSBA, mas en.
1597. MSBA, no es.
1598. MSBA, ya es.
1599. MSBAG, si la quieres.

	como la puedas hablar.	1605
FORTUNIO	¿Esto es verdad o es trayzión?	
	¿Castro me quiere matar?	
	Ven acá, Ysabel, por Dios.	
	¿Habéis hablado las dos,	
	o es enrredo de Fernando?	1610
YSABEL	¿Tu esperanza está dudando?	
	¡Ay de quien la pone en vos!	
	Si eres noble, contradize	
	a la nobleza el temor.	
	Yo con esto satisfize;	1615

como la puedas hablar. 1605

FORTUNIO ¿Esto es verdad o es trayzión?
¿Castro me quiere matar?
Ven acá, Ysabel, por Dios.
¿Habéis hablado las dos,
o es enrredo de Fernando? 1610

YSABEL ¿Tu esperanza está dudando?
¡Ay de quien la pone en vos!
Si eres noble, contradize
a la nobleza el temor.
Yo con esto satisfize; 1615
no lo dize mi señor,
que mi señora lo dize.
Que si él matarte quisiera,
cara a cara lo emprendiera,   *[fol. 11 v.]*
sin querer interponer 1620
la infamia de su muger.
Queda para neçio.

FORTUNIO   Espera,
espera, Ysabel. Aduierte
que quererse asegurar
no es el temor de la muerte. 1625

YSABEL ¿Qué disculpa puedes dar
que a satisfazerme açierte?
Pensé que me hubieras dado
vn diamante que baliera,
Fortunio, más que tu estado, 1630
¿y eso respondes?

FORTUNIO   Espera.

YSABEL Ni eres amante ni onrrado.

1605. MSBA, en que la puedas gozar.
1606. G, omits *es*.
1607. B, quieres.
1608. *
1609. MSBA, los dos.*
1611. MSBA, estas.
1613. *
1624. MSBA, que el querer assegurarme.
1626. MSBA, darme.
1632. MSBA, No eres.

Yo le diré a mi señora
que no te quiera, cobarde.   *

FORTUNIO   ¿Pues es mucho, escucha agora,   1635
que en darte crédito tarde,
si tú dizes que me adora
    vna muger que me dexa
por quien la goza?

YSABEL   ¿No sabes
que estiman lo que se alexa   1640
y sólo se muestran grabes
a quien de su amor se quexa?
    Si supieras qué es muger,
supieras que no ay mudanza
ygual a su proçeder.   1645
Despreçian quien las alcanza.

FORTUNIO   Pues, ¿tan presto puede ser?
    ¿Aún no le ha dado la mano *[fol.] 12 [r.]*
y ya le despreçia assí?

YSABEL   Es su pecho tan liuiano   1650
que ya se muere por ti.

FORTUNIO   ¡O, monstros del bien humano!
    ¿Pero de qué tengo miedo?
Pues asegurarme puedo,
que si alcanzo lo que sigo,   1655
de mi mayor enemigo
vengado en su infamia quedo.
    Ysabel, bien puede ser
que Estefanía me quiera,
que Estefanía es muger,   1660
oja a los uientos ligera

1633. MA, lo.
1635. MSBA, Pues es mucho amiga agora.
1641. MSBA, y siempre.
1642. MSBA, con quien.
1645. MSBA, que yguale su.
1648. *
1652. MSBA, O mõstro de viento vano.
1653-72. MSBA, omit.*
1661. *

en querer y aborrezer.
Pero lo que es humildad,
no lo juzg[u]es a temor,
que fuera temeridad   1665
atreuerse a tal balor
mi abrasada voluntad.
Dame señas, por tu vida,
en que yo conozca y crea
que está a quererme rendida.   1670

YSABEL   Aunque cossa injusta sea,
y esté de tu fee ofendida,
pide, Fortún, qualquier cosa
de su vestido o tocado,
de poco preçio o preçiosa.   1675

FORTUNIO   Su liuiandad me ha espantado,
pensión de muger hermosa.   *
¡O, sienpre loca hermosura,   [fol. 12 v.]
aquí apenas me despreçia
quando gozarme procura!   1680
En muger hermosa y neçia,
¿quál onrra estuuo segura?
Oy caerás, Luzbel hermoso,
del çielo de tu balor.

YSABEL   Fortunio está sospechoso,   [ap.]   1685
pero ya pierde el temor.
¡Vitoria, amor cauteloso!
Sácame bien deste enrredo,
porque si gozarle puedo
y este engaño effeto alcanza,   1690
confesaré en tu alabanza

1668. *
1670. *
1673-77. MSBA, see v. 1693 below; 1675. MSBA, o costosa.
1678. *
1680. MSBA, y ya gozarme.
1683. *
1684. MSBA, fauor.
1687. AG, victoria.*
1689. MSBA, que si assegurarme.
1691. B, confeslarè.

	lo que obligada te quedo.	
FORTUNIO	Pídele, por cortesía,	
	de su cabello vn cordón,	
	y di que señale vn día	1695
	en que goze la ocasión	
	y yo conozca si es mía;	
	que estas señas y fabor	
	serán carta de seguro	
	para mi justo temor.	1700
YSABEL	Tú verás lo que procuro,	
	venzida de vn loco amor;	
	conzertaré que la veas	
	para en pasando las bodas,	
	y que ese cordón poseas.	1705
FORTUNIO	Si estas uistas acomodas,	
	mi dueño quiero que seas.	
YSABEL	No dudes de que tendrás	
	la ocasión por los cabellos.	

FORTUNIO	Tendréla si me los das.	[fol. 13 r.]	1710

YSABEL	Veráste enlazado en ellos,	
	y libre en ellos, que es más.	
FORTUNIO	Viuirá tu nombre en mí	
	más que en bronçe y alabastro.	
YSABEL	Para seruirte naçí.	1715
FORTUNIO	Oy me vengo, Rui de Castro.	[ap.]
YSABEL	Fortunio, oy gozo de ti.	[ap.]

1693. MSBA, preceded by vv. 1673-77.*
1694. *
1695. MSB, el dia; A, señale día.*
1696. *
1697. MSBA, que es mia.*
1698. MSBA, Que con aqueste fauor.*
1699. MSBA, y estas cartas de seguro.
1700. MSBA, serà el remedio mejor.
1705. MSBA, este.
1706. *
1709. MSBA, el cabello.*
1710. MSBA, la das. *
1711. MSBA, ello.
1712. MSBA, ello.
1714. MSBA, ni alabastro.
1716. *

✠ *Dentro ruido, Alfonso, Fernán Ruiz, Ordoño y padrinos.*

FERNÁN	Desgr[aci]a estraña; tenla de essa mano. ❋
ALFONSO	¿Cómo cayó?
DAMA 1ª	No sé.
FERNÁN	Desmayo ha sido.
(FERNÁN)	Vn poco de agua.
ALFONSO	Llámala.
FERNÁN	Es en vano. 1720
DAMA 2ª	¡Con qué estraños azares ha salido!

✠ *Saquen en brazos a Estefanía.*

ALFONSO	¡Caer en lo más raso, en lo más llano!
FERNÁN	Siente, mi bien, si tienes ya sentido,
	que me tienes sin él.
ESTEFANÍA	¡Bálgame el çielo!
FERNÁN	La mano es niebe, y conuirtióse en yelo. 1725
ALFONSO	Al salir de la iglesia...

✠ *El Conde Nuño Osorio, Ramiro de Guzmán*
   con toalla al honbro y agua en salua.   ❋

DAMA 1ª	El agua viene.
FERNÁN	Muestra, Ramiro de Guzmán, el baso.
	Bebe, mi bien.
ALFONSO	Mexores pulsos tiene.
RAMIRO	El ha sido, por Dios, estraño caso.

St. dir. before v. 1718. MSB, Suena ruydo, sale Fernan Ruyz de Castro, y el Rey Alfonso sacan a Estefanía desmayada, entre los dos, sale Ramiro Guzman, y el Conde don Nuño, y Ordoño; also, SB, Ramiro de Guzman; A, as MSB, but ... y salen ... salen Ramiro de Guzmán y el...
   1718. MSBA, Desgracia grande, ten aquessa mano.
   1719. MSBA, assign No se to Fernán; desgracia a sido.❋
   1720. MSBA, vn jarro.
   1721. MSBA, assign to D. Nuño, omit que.❋
   St. dir. before v. 1722. MSBA, omit.
   St. dir. before end of v. 1726. MSBA, Trae Ramiro el agua; J, ... y Ramiro...❋
   1726. MSBA, assign El agua viene to Ramiro.
   1727. MSBA, Dadme.

DAMA 2ª	Es propio de vna fiesta mui solene.	1730
	Vn mal suçeso, vn lastimoso paso.	
RAMIRO	De sí misma pareze que ha caydo.	
FERNÁN	Ella cayó, mas yo perdí el sentido.	
ALFONSO	Hija, ¿no hablas?	
ESTEFANÍA	Ya, señor, me siento	

para hablarte y seruirte.

ALFONSO   No he pensado   1735
jamás que diera amor el sentimiento
                       [fol. 13 v.]
que el tuyo a mis entrañas ha causado.
Sancho, mi hijo, en cuyo naçimiento
alegre le llamaron desseado,
ni Costanza, Fernando y don Garçía,   1740
ygualan a tu amor, Estefanía.
     Quiérote más que a todos.

ESTEFANÍA   Si estubiera
ya muerta, esse fabor me diera vida.

FERNÁN   Esta es mi casa, y oxalá que fuera   ✿
el alcázar de Creso, o del Rey Mida.   1745✿
No está de mármol, como yo quisiera,
ni de oro puro en láminas uestida;
no la adornan los jaspes orientales,
pórfidos, alabastros y cristales.
     Sólo tiene a la puerta esos blasones   1750
y en ese campo azul esos roeles
con aquellos castillos y leones,

1730. MSBA, assign to Ordoño.
1731. MSBA, caso.
1732. MSBA, assign to D. Nuño.✿
1733. B, the designation of the speaker is not clear.
1735. B, hablar.
1736. MSBA, que hiziera amor jamas.
1740. G, u Don Garzia.
1741. MSBA, no ygualan.
1743. MSBA, muerta, tanto fauor me diera vida.
1745. MSBA, y del.✿
1747. J, vestida.
1748. MSB, ni la.
1750. MSBA, omit *a*.✿
1752. MSBA, ganados en contrarios esquadrones.

y despojos de bárbaros crueles.
Yo he ganado los más destos pendones
que sirben a estas puertas de laureles;   1755
mas todo es poco entrando Estefanía,
laurel más noble de la frente mía.

ESTEFANÍA   La casa, para mí, querido esposo,
será mayor alcázar que el de Tebas,   *
honrrado de apellido tan glorioso,   1760
de Hércules nuebo y de vitorias nuebas.

ALFONSO   Basta ser jaula de vn león famoso
que ha hecho entre los moros tantas pruebas.
Entrad los dos donde os gozéis mil años.
                                    [fol.] 14 [r.]

FERNÁN   ¿Qué es esto, çielo?
DAMA 1ª   Agüeros son estraños. 1765

✠ *Dentro ruido, como que la casa se hunde.*

ESTEFANÍA   ¡Bálame Dios, qué estraña desbentura!
NUÑO   Sin duda que la casa se ha caydo.
ALFONSO   Don Nuño, antes de entrar será ventura...
FERNÁN   Gran parte de mi gente abrá cojido.
DAMA 2ª   Vn ombre de entre el polbo se apresura   1770
haçia nosotros.
DAMA 1ª   ¡Venturoso ha sido!
RAMIRO   A, Mudarra pareze, mas la tierra

1754. MSBA, de los pendones.
1755. MSBA, a las puertas.
1756. MSBA, y todo es poco, siendo Estefania.
1757. MSBA, digno.*
1760. MSBA, famoso.
1762. *
1764. *
1765. MSBA, Valgame el cielo; Est. assigned the second part; G, omits.*
St. dir. before v. 1766. MSBA, Hazen que se van a entrar, y suena ruydo
como que se cae la casa.*
1766. MSBAG, Valgame; all but G assign to Castro.
1767. MSBA, assign to Ramiro.*
1768. MSBA, Ramiro.
1770. MSBA, assign to D. Nuño.*
1771. MSBA, assign the second part to Ramiro.*
1772. MSBA, assign to Ordoño.*

pareze que le encubre y uiuo entierra.

✠ *Mudarra, lleno de tierra.*

MUDARRA	Tente, señor, ¿dónde vas?	
FERNÁN	¿Quién es?	
MUDARRA	¿No me has conozido?	1775
FERNÁN	¡O, Mudarra, estás herido!	
MUDARRA	¡Casa vieja nunca más!	*

     Apenas, señor, salía
de aquel quarto de los Castros,
que en mármoles y alabastros   1780
aun es neçio el que se fía,
     quando cruxendo los techos
como quando truena el çielo,
vino su máquina al suelo,
los artesones desechos.   1785

FERNÁN	¿Ha muerto [a] alguno?	
MUDARRA	A Tristán,	

a Fabio, Alberto y Leonido.
Oy de la tierra he salido
como el mismo padre Adán:
     de poluo me hizo Dios,   1790*
de polbo me buelbe a hazer.   *[fol. 14 v.]*

RAMIRO	Si tarda, os viene a coger,	

sin duda alguna, a los dos.
     ¿Por qué ese quarto mandaste
que aderezase Tristán?   1795

ALFONSO	Malas sospechas me dan.	
ORDOÑO	Pienso que esta junta erraste.	

St. dir. before v. 1774. MSBA, Sale Mudarra.
1776. MSBA, Es Mudarra?
1780. B, de alabastros.*
1781. MSBA, quien se fia.*
1782. MSBA, sus techos.
1785. MSBA, sus.
1786. AG, a alguno?; also, G, *Han.*
1787. B, Alberto; A, Leonido,
1789. MSBA, como salio el padre Adan.
1791. B, del.
1792. *

ESTEFANÍA	Ya todo me atemoriza;	
	en triste punto nazí.	
MUDARRA	Oy ha sido, para mí,	1800
	vn miércoles de çeniza.	*
	Yo vi vna tapia caer,	
	que me dixo, y luego çierra:	*
	"acuérdate que eres tierra	
	y en polbo te has de boluer."	1805
	Y viue Dios, si no corro	
	y dexo capa y espada,	
	que fuera tan polbo y nada,	
	que de sepultura ahorro.	
NUÑO	Suplico a tu magestad	1810
	se sirba, aunque es yndezente,	*
	de que yo los aposente	
	en esta neçesidad,	
	que mi casa es la más çerca.	
ALFONSO	Conde, haréysme gran plazer.	1815
FERNÁN	Algo me ha de suçeder. [ap.]	
ESTEFANÍA	Algún daño se me açerca. [ap.]	
NUÑO	Venid, señores, conmigo.	
FERNÁN	Nuño, hazéysme gran merzed.	
NUÑO	Que soy, Fernando, crehed,	1820
	mui de veras v[uest]ro amigo.	

✠ Entrense Estefanía, Fernán Ruiz y don Nuño.   [fol. 15 r.]

MUDARRA	Alguna buena oraçión	
	he reçado esta mañana,	
	mas era cosa mui llana	
	librarme desta ocasión.	1825
	No ay que tener sobresalto;	

1801. MSBA, el Miercoles.
1805. MSBAG, tierra.
1810. B, su.*
1815. MSBA, Nuño.
1818. MSBA, Venios.
St. dir. before v. 1822. MSBA, Vanse Estefania, Castro, y D. Nuño;
G, Vanse Estefania Fernan y Nuño.*

las que a mí me han de coger,
bodegas diz que han de ser,
que no aposentos en alto.
　"Dios te libre," me deçía   1830
mi agüela, y ¡qué buena era!
"de amor de muger ramera,
sereno de noche fría,   ✢
　sol que membrillos madura,
fuelles de amigo soplón,   1835*
de cuchillada a trayzión,
y de casa mal segura."

                    ✠ *Váyase Mudarra.*

RAMIRO   No temas que suçeda lo que dizes,
              que estas son cosas naturales todas.
ALFONSO   Ramiro, ¡plega a Dios!
ORDOÑO   ¡Otro ruido!   1840

        ✠ *Alguaçiles y gente que traen preso vn cochero.*

ALGUAÇIL   Sin cárzel, fuera bien atarle a un palo.
              Tirad con él.
ALFONSO   De lo que fue te informa.
ORDOÑO   ¿Por qué llebáis ese ombre?
ALGUAÇIL   Es vn cochero
              de Fadrique Velázquez de Mendoza.
COCHERO   Señor, a mí, señor Ordoño Vela...   1845
ORDOÑO   ¿Qué ha hecho?
ALGUAÇIL   Sólo por pasar su coche,
              de Rui de Castro ha muerto vn escudero.

1827. MSB, los; A, lo ... ha de.
1828. ✻
1830. ✻
1831. MSA, abuelo, y que bueno era; B, abuelo, y que bueno que era.
St. dir. before v. 1838. MSBA, Vase; G, Mudarra vase.
1840. MSBA, Ramiro plega a Dios, pero en efeto; assign to Alfonso.✻
St. dir. before v. 1841. MSBA, omit; G, Un alguazil y gente que traen
preso un coche[r]o; J, Alguaçil.✻
1841-51. MSBA, omit; 1841. J, vn.
1845. G, ha.

Ordoño	Andad con Dios.
Alguaçil	Pensaua ya librarse;
	camine por ay.
Alfonso	¿Qué es eso, Ordoño?
Ordoño	De Fadrique Velázquez vn cochero 1850

[fol. 15 v.]

	que ha muerto vn escudero a Rui de Castro.
Alfonso	Si contra n[uest]ra fee santa no fuera
	creher agüeros, diera a tantos crédito,
	mas estas cosas son mui naturales.

✠ *Sancho Laynez.*

Sancho	Tened aquesas postas, que ya buelbo. 1855
Ramiro	Sancho Laynez viene.
Alfonso	¿Quál, Ramiro?
Ramiro	El fronterizo de Jaén y Córdoba.
Sancho	Déme tu magestad los pies.
Alfonso	¡O, Sancho,
	bien sehas venido! ¿Qué ay en la frontera?
Sancho	¡Gran mal, señor!
Alfonso	¿Gran mal? ¿De qué 1860
	[manera?
Sancho	Los vandos almorauides
	y los moros almohades
	tuuieron guerra en Marruecos,
	Azamor y Tarudante.
	Murió el Miramamolín 1865
	llamado Alboali-Ben-Zayde;
	pusieron en su lugar

1851. *
1853. MSBA, a todo.
St. dir. before v. 1855. MSBA, Dentro Sancho Laynez.
1855. J, aq̄stas.*
1856. MSBA, buelue.*
1857. *
1859. MSBA, como venis? que ay de.*
1863. MSBA, pusieron cerco a.
1864. M, a Zamora; A, a Azamor.*
1866. MSBA, Almohadi Abenzayde.*

a Abdelmón, hijo de Tarfe,
hombre humilde que era ollero,
como su agüelo y su padre,   1870
de vn astrólogo mouido
para hazañas semejantes.
Como en España tenían
los almoráuides parte,
vn almohadí, que en su seta   1875
era tenido por ángel,
le inçitó con mil enrredos
para que a España pasase
y los consumiese a todos,   [fol. 16 r.]
ganándoles sus çiudades.   1880
Juntó su gente Abdelmón,
y con çiento y quatro nabes,
quarenta mil moros puso
sobre Gibraltar y Cádiz.
Ganólas, ganó a Xerez,   1885
de donde a Seuilla parte,
que, aunque de moros, tenía
muchos cristianos muzárabes.
Huyó su santo arçobispo
Clemente, y el docto frayle   1890*
Arnugo, y otros varones
fueron esperando mártires.
No ay lengua para dezirte
deste ollero las crueldades,
pero basta que te diga   1895

1868. A, *Andelmón* regularly for Abdelmón.*
1870. *
1871. *
1872. MSBA, hazaña semejante.
1874. MSBA, los Almohades tanta parte.
1877. MSBA, insistio.
1879. MSBA, destruyesse.*
1880. MSBA, saqueando.
1881. G, la gente.
1890. MSBA, Armigol y el docto padre.
1891. MSBA, Clemente.*
1893. MSBA, dezir.

que ya es su orgullo tan grande
que han jurado de venir
a Castilla, y no dexarte
hasta que como Pelayo,
en las Asturias te guardes.   1900
Trahen vn pendón...

ALFONSO   Detente,
Sancho, y no temas que passen
de los muros cordobesses
sin que Alfonso los ataje.
No temí reyes de yerro,   1905
de azero, ni de diamante,
¿y temeré vn Rey de barro
y que de la tierra sale?
Ya sabe España que soy
castigo de sus alarbes.   [fol. 16 v.] 1910
Yo juntaré gente luego;
yo nombraré capitanes.

RAMIRO   Aquí tienes a Ramiro
de Guzmán, y ya tú sabes
de qué manera te sirben   1915
los caballeros Guzmanes.   ❋

ALFONSO   Nonbraré a don Nuño Osorio
por general, o al Alcayde
de Toledo.

LAYNEZ   A Rui de Castro,
gran señor, agrauio hazes.   1920

ALFONSO   Es mui reçién desposado;

1896. MSBA, es ya.❋
1897. MSBA, ha.
1898. MSBA, y della echarte.
1899. MSBA, para que.
1901. ❋
1903. MSBA, de los muros de Iaen.
1905. MSBA, no temerè si es de azero; also, B omits *de*.
1906. MSBA, de hierro, ni de diamante.❋
1910. MSBA, açote.
1912. MSBA, y nombrarè.
1913. ❋
1919. ❋

mas mientras de Asturias bajen,
de Galiçia y de León,
nobles, caballos y infantes,
habrán pasado las bodas.   1925

SANCHO   El çielo, señor, te guarde,
para que de España arrojes
los bárbaros almohades.

Fin del 2º Acto

(rúbrica)

1924. A, é infantes.*
1925. MSBA, se auran.
MSBA do not designate *Fin de Acto;* G, Fin del Acto Segundo *(rúbrica).*

3

ACTO

(rúbrica)

MSB, ACTO TERCERO DE LA DESDICHADA ESTEFANIA. AG, omit. J, 3º.

Los que hablan en el 3º Acto

Fortún Ximénez
Olfos
Bermudo
Ximeno
Fernán Ruiz de Castro
Mudarra
Estefanía
Ysabel
Rey Alfonso
Ramiro de Guzmán
Nuño Osorio
Ordoño
Abdelmón, Rey moro

(rúbrica)

MSBA do not repeat the list of characters here; G, Personas que hablan en este acto 3º y ultimo.*

ACTO 3º   *[fol.] Pᵃ [r.]*

Entre Fortún Ximénez y Olfos, lacayo.

FORTUNIO

Años de amor que pasáis
ligeros por n[uest]ras vidas,   1930
a aquella esperanza asidas
que para engañarnos dais,
    ¿cómo me trahéis perdido,
sin onrra entre mis yguales,
porque apenas ven señales   1935
de lo que otro tiempo he sido?
    Dando crédito a una esclaua,
puse los ojos en ti,
ángel de quien yo lo fui
quando libertad gozaua.   1940
    Pedí prendas y fabores
de tu persona y vestido;
no fue más faborezido
ombre que tratase amores.
    Quísete hablar; merezí   1945

MSBA do not repeat this act heading; G, Acto 3º y Vltimo.
    St. dir. before v. 1929. MSA, Salen Fortun, y Olfos; B, omits; G, Fortun
y Olfos lacayo.
    1931. MSBA, nuestra.
    1932. MSBA, dezid donde me lleuays.
    1933-36. MSBA, omit.
    1939. MSBA, Angel quando yo; G, solo fuy.°
    1940. MSBA, de quien libertad.
    1941-68. MSBA, omit.
    1944. °

hablarte por vn balcón,
en que supe tu afizión,
y la supiste de mí.
Mas quando pude gozarte
y amor en tal punto está,   1950
lléganme nuebas que ya
el Rey a la guerra parte.
   Voy con el Rey; gana el Rey *[fol. 1 v.]*
la más notable vitoria
que ha dado laurel y gloria   1955
a capitán de su ley.
   Venze al gallardo Abdelmón,
y luego echarle porfía
de toda el Andaluzía
con su cristiano esquadrón.   1960
   Mas yo, que otra guerra fiera
de mi amor y mi venganza
seguía, con esperanza
de la vitoria primera,
dexo al Rey, el canpo dejo;   1965
y vengo, el de Castro ausente
a ver el sol en su oriente,
pues de su ocaso me alejo.
   Esta vez la gozaré,
que así me lo ha prometido;   1970
cartas suyas he tenido,
y testigos de su fee.
   Olfos.

OLFOS   ¿Señor?
FORTUNIO   ¿Traes la escala?
OLFOS   ¿Hauía de venir sin ella?
FORTUNIO   Quedo. De mi prenda bella   1975

1950. °
1953. °
1965. G, al campo.
1969. MSBA, Gozaua, y la.
1972. MSBA, con que assegura mi fe.
1974. MS, Aura.°

los pasos siento en la sala.
Por aquí me viene a hablar.

✠ *Ysabel, en alto.*

YSABEL   ¿Es Fortún?
FORTUNIO   Tu esclauo soy.
YSABEL   El bienvenido te doy,
                mas no te puedo abrazar.   *[fol.] 2 [r.]*   1980
FORTUNIO   Tus cartas me han engañado.
                Dime, hermosa Estefanía,
                ¿no escriuiste que sería
                de tus brazos regalado,
                y que luego me partiesse?   1985
YSABEL   No niego lo que escriuí,
                mas ay gente por aquí
                y temo que nos oyesse.
                    ¿Traes la escala?
FORTUNIO   Aquí la tiene
                Olfos, fuerte como vn Çid.   1990
YSABEL   Pues por el jardín subid
                mientras el aurora viene,
                    que allí con la escuridad
                de nadie seré sentida.

✠ *Estos hablan, y salen dos criados de
Rui de Castro, Bermudo y Ximeno.*

BERMUDO   Debo, Ximeno, la vida   1995
                a Rui de Castro.
XIMENO   Es verdad.
                Desde niño te crió.
                y te sacó de tu tierra.

1976. MSBA, oygo.
St. dir. before v. 1978. MSA, Ysabel a la ventana; B, omits.
1988. B, oyessen.
1989. *
1990. B, fuerre; MSBA, el Cid.
1992. *
St. dir. before v. 1995. MSBA, Salen Bermudo, y Ximeno.

BERMUDO   A Córdoua fue a la guerra
                y su cassa me encargó;   2000
                    y aunque no ay de qué temer,
                estas noches he sentido
                por este xardín rüido.
XIMENO   Tus çelos deben de ser,
                    que es vn ángel mi señora,   2005
                y está en contina orazión
                por Rui de Castro.
BERMUDO   Ay razón
                para andar çeloso agora.
                    Ximeno, nunca porfíes
                ni desafíes a alguno;   2010
                ni fíes ombre ninguno   [fol. 2 v.]   *
                ni de alguna muger fíes.
                    Porfïar es neçedad,
                desafïar, muerte justa;
                fïar, confianza injusta,   2015
                y en la muger, liuiandad.
                    Mi señora Estefanía
                es ángel, pero es muger,
                que suele a vezes caer
                de su misma gerarquía.   2020
XIMENO   Antes creheré que en el çielo
                ay árboles y en la tierra
                estrellas, vida en la guerra,
                luz en noche, fuego en yelo,
                    que crea que mi señora   2025
                ha hecho tal liuiandad.
                Yo sé bien su santidad,

_____

2001. MSBA, Pero aunque no ay que.
2003. MSBA, en.
2008. MSBA, estar.
2009. *
2011. MSBA, de hombre.*
2015. *
2016. MSBA, libertad.
2018. B, pero muger.
2020. MSBA, propia.
2027. MSBA, honestidad.

	y que a Rui de Castro adora.
BERMUDO	Ximeno, amor es demonio;

sienpre acomete lo bueno.   2030
¡Ay, Dios!

XIMENO   ¿Qué has uisto?
BERMUDO   Ximeno,
¿qué más claro testimonio?
Dos onbres he uisto allí.

XIMENO   Y aun el vno hablando está.
¡Bálame Dios! ¿Qué será?   2035

BERMUDO   Será lo que yo temí:
rebuelta en aquel manteo
que suele traher de día
en la güerta Estefanía,
en la ventana la veo.   2040

XIMENO   ¿Sin luz le ves?   *[fol.] 3 [r.]*
BERMUDO   Luz me dan,
Ximeno, los pasamanos,   ✺
que lo que tocan las manos,
los más çiegos lo verán.
¡Ay del onor quando sale   2045
en manteo la muger!
¿Qué defensa quiere hazer,
pues de ninguna se bale?

XIMENO   Bien dizes, porque si son
armas de la honestidad   2050
los vestidos, liuiandad
arguye.

BERMUDO   ¡O, fiera trayzión!

2030. MSBA, a lo.
2035. MSBAG, valgame.
2037. MSBA, Embuelta.
2041. MSBAJ, la.*
2043. S, que le tocan.
2046. A, de mujer!*
2047. MSBA, puede.*
2048. MSBA, si de.
2050. MSBA, su.
2052. MSBA, arguyen. Ber.—Fuera traycion.

	¿Qué hemos de hazer?	
XIMENO	Escuchar.	
FORTUNIO	Dime, hermosa Estefanía,	
	¿para qué aguardas el día,	2055
	pudiéndome remediar?	
	Baxa, mi bien, al jardín,	
	y ablemos solos y juntos.	
	No traygas a amor en puntos,	
	que en vn punto está su fin.	2060
YSABEL	Aora bien, entra, que yo	
	baxo, de tu amor vençida.	
FORTUNIO	Olfos.	
OLFOS	¿Señor?	
FORTUNIO	Oy mi vida	
	con mi venganza llegó.	
	Entra y tendrásme la escala;	2065
	por el jardín saltaré,	
	que ya Estefanía fue.	
OLFOS	¿Qué dicha a la tuya yguala?	
	Oy gozas de la muger	
	más bella que ay en Castilla.	2070
FORTUNIO	Es muger. No es marauilla, *[fol. 3 v.]*	
	que todo cabe en su ser.	

✠ *Entrense.*

BERMUDO	Al jardín la escala pone.	
XIMENO	Al honor de Castro, di.	
BERMUDO	¡Ha Dios, si estuuiera aquí!	2075

2053. S, escuche; MSBA, assign last word to Bermudo, remainder to
Ximeno.
2055. MSBA, al.
2058. MSBA, omit first *y.**
2059. MSBA, no pongas mi amor.
2062. MSBA, rendida.
2065. MSBA, omit *y.*
2067. MSBA, se fue.
2072. MSB, para en; A, pasa en.
St. dir. before v. 2073. MSBA, Vanse los dos.
2075. MSBA, Ay.

Pero ¡fuera! El Rey perdone,
que le he de matar.

XIMENO   Detente,
que es hija del Rey, en fin.
No alborotes el jardín,
estando su dueño ausente,   2080
  que a mil onrrados maridos
lágrimas de sus mugeres,
y algunos falsos plazeres
suelen çegar los sentidos.
No ay téstigos verdaderos   2085
que no suelen engañar,
y todo suele parar
en daño de los terzeros.
Reniega de voluntades
que en vna cama se acuestan,   2090
que allí las mentiras cuestan
al preçio de las verdades.
  Si algo quieres quando venga,
díselo con discrezión
para que aquesta trayzión   2095
remedio o castigo tenga;
  pero agora es disparate,
y te ha de costar la vida.

2076. MSBA, pero sea.
2078. MSBA, reversed with v. 2079; B, de Rey.
2080. MSBA, y estando.*
2082. MSBA, las mugeres.
2083. MSBA, suelen trocar en plazeres.
2084. MSBA, aquellos gustos perdidos.
2085-88. MSBA, omit.
2089. MSBA, show as v. 2093.
2090. MSBA, show as v. 2094.
2091. MSBA, show as v. 2095.
2092. MSBA, a peso de; show as v. 2096.
2093. MSBA, show as v. 2089.
2094. MSBA, show as v. 2090.
2095. MSBA, para que su execucion; show as v. 2091.
2096. MSBA, show as v. 2092.
2097. MSBA, No hagas tal disparate.
2098. MSBA, que te costarà la vida.

BERMUDO   Ximén, ¡que mexor perdida   *[fol.] 4 [r.]*
             que quando aquéste me mate!   2100
             Pero ven, porque en efeto
             se puede tener por loco
             quien tiene el consejo en poco
             de vn onbre amigo y discreto.

                    ✠ *Fernán Ruiz y Mudarra.*

MUDARRA   Ya con apuntar el día,   2105
             de Burgos las torres veo.
FERNÁN   Tanbién a visto el desseo
             la luz de mi Estefanía.
MUDARRA   La de la Yglesia mayor
             se vee por entre [e]stos çerros.   2110
FERNÁN   Ya quitó el amor los yerros
             de la prisión de mi onor.
             No osaua pedir lizenzia
             al Rey; al fin la pedí,
             viéndome fuera de mí   2115
             a fuerza de tanta ausençia.
             No pienso que me la diera
             si la carta no llegara
             de su parto.
MUDARRA   Es cosa clara,
             y así fue bien que pariera;   2120
             que de su parto naçió

2099. MSBA, Ximen, que mas bien perdida.
2104. *
St. dir. before v. 2105. MSB, Vanse, y sale Fernan Ruyz de Castro, y
Mudarra; A, Vanse. Salen...
2106. MSBA, las torres de Burgos veo.
2110. MSBA, por aquestos.
2111. MSBA, rompio.
2112. MSBA, con esta fuerça de amor.
2115. MSBA, acabar assi.*
2116. MSBA, con el pesar de vna ausencia.
2117. MSBA, No entendi.
2118. MSBA, nueua.
2119. MSBA, omit *Es.*
2120. G, partiera; MSBA, assign *Quien en sus braços la viera* to Castro,
as are vv. 2121-24; MSB also assign 2125-26 to him.*
2121. MSBA, De tu partida nacio.

el tuyo con más dolores,
porque a los partos de amores
¿quál otro parto ygualó?
 Ya desseo ver, señor,   2125
tu hijo, y de Alfonso nieto.

FERNÁN   ¿Que tengo vn hijo, en effeto, *[fol. 4 v.]*
nieto de vn emperador?

MUDARRA   Si eres Castro, ¿qué te espantas?

Famoso en entranbas leyes,   2130
cassáis con hijas de reyes.
Yo he leydo seis ynfantas,
 todas con Castros cassadas;
pues tú, ¿qué debes, señor,
al mexor antezesor   2135
de los Villalbas y Andradas?
 ¿Quién ha venzido más moros,
más desafíos, ni ha hecho
cossas de más fuerte pecho?

FERNÁN   ¡O, Mudarra! No ay tesoros,   2140
 no ay noblezas, no ay cadena
de asçendençia, armas, poder,
que se compare a tener
muger virtuosa y buena;
 pues que si tiene hermosura   2145
con alguna discreçión,
y es noble de condizión,
quinta essençia de ventura,
 bien puedo dezir que tiene
todo aquesto Estefanía.   2150
Que te he de ver, prenda mía.

2122. MSBA, su parto con mil.
2124. MSBA, parto ninguno ygualò.
2125. MSBA, dessea; J, deseo.
2126. MSBA, el nieto.
2130. MSBA, por justas y antiguas.
2131. G, hijos.
2140. MSBA, Ay.
2141. MSBA, nobleza.
2142. MSBA, decendencia.
2145. *

✠ *Entren Bermudo y Ximeno.*

MUDARRA	Ya gente de cassa viene.	
FERNÁN	¿Has [a] alguno conoçido?	
MUDARRA	Dos escuderos, señor.	
FERNÁN	Estraña señal de amor.	2155
BERMUDO	Seas, señor, bienvenido.	
XIMENO	Señor, bienvenido seas. *[fol.] 5 [r.]*	
FERNÁN	¿Cómo assí me reçiuís?	

Mui tibiamente venís.
¿Ay algún mal?

MUDARRA   No lo creas.   2160

FERNÁN   ¿Hase muerto Fernandico?
¿Está mala Estefanía?
Vosotros sin alegría,
yo presente, bueno y rico,
vitorioso y más onrrado   2165
del Rei que xamás me ui,
¿y me reçiuís ansí
quando apenas he llegado?
¿Tú, demudado el color,
Bermudo? ¿Qué tienes? Habla.   2170
Grande desdicha se entabla,
grande profeta es amor.
¿Es muerta mi esposa? ¡O, çielos!
¿Qué enmudeçéis? ¡Viue Dios,
que os dé la muerte a los dos!   2175
¡Hablad! ¿Sois piedras? ¿Sois yelos?

BERMUDO   Ten la espada, aunque lo tomo

St. dir. before v. 2152. MSBAG, place before v. 2156. Salen Bermudo,
y Ximeno.*
2153. MSBA, Es.
2155. MSBA, Notable.
2158. *
2159. MSBA, como tan tristes.
2164. MSBA, yo contento.
2173. MSB, omit *O*; A, ¡Cielo!
2174. MSBA, no respondeys?
2176. A, hielo.
2177. MSBA, Deten la espada, aunque como.*

	por bueno y dichoso agüero.	
Fernán	Tomar la espada primero	
	por dichoso agüero, ¿cómo?	2180
Bermudo	Haz que Mudarra se alexe.	
Fernán	Vete, Mudarra, adelante,	
	porque ni el plazer la espante	
	ni del auiso se quexe,	
	di que llego a Estefanía.	2185
Mudarra	¡O, qué albriçias me ha de dar!	
	¡Que a Ysabel he de abrazar! *[fol. 5 v.]*	
	¡O, sienpre dichoso día,	
	el que llega a la presençia!	
	Todo es gustos, todo abrazos,	2190
	porque se pagan los brazos	*
	de los pesares de ausençia.	
	¿Que he llegado? No lo creo.	
	Bien aya el que ausenzia hizo,	*
	pues que tan bien satisfizo	2195
	con la presençia el desseo.	

✠ *Váyase Mudarra.*

Fernán	¿De qué será la razón	
	de quererme hablar secreto?	
Bermudo	De que eres onbre, en efeto,	
	sujeto a qualquier pasión.	2200

2178. MSBA, lo tomo por mal aguero.*
2179. MSBA, assign to Ximeno.*
2180. MSBA, tomo; assign to Ximeno.
2182. MSBA, Mudarra vete delante.
2183. MSBA, gozo.*
2189. MSBA, Del que.*
2190. MSBA, gusto.
2191. MSBA, gozan.*
2192. MSBA, con el pesar del ausencia.
2193. MSBA, Que en llegando.
2194. MSBA, ausencias.
2195. MSBA, pues con ellas satisfizo; G, tambien.
2196. MSBA, de la.
St. dir. before v. 2197. MSBAG, Vase.
2197. MSBA, Pues que serà la ocasion.
2198. A, querer.

FERNÁN   Honbres, si en mi casa es muerto
                algo que al alma me toca,
                hablad, pues que tenéys boca,
                y sépalo yo de çierto;
                    porque tengo vn corazón   2205
                cubierto de más cabellos
                que la cabeza, y con ellos,
                fuerza, edad y discrezión.
XIMENO   Acaba, Bermudo, y di.
FERNÁN   Dilo ya, Bermudo mudo,   2210
                que no te quiero ver mudo
                después que triste te vi.
BERMUDO   ¿No das en qué puede ser,
                si en casa sobra salud?
FERNÁN   ¿Es cosa que a la virtud   2215
                ofende de mi muger?
                    Ola, abrí mui bien los ojos.   ✿
                No seáis, con çiençia vana,   *[fol.] 6 [r.]*
                los dos viejos de Susana,   ✿
                çiegos de locos antojos.   2220
                    No digáis que entre las yedras
                del jardín no fue fiel, ·
                porque seré Danïel,
                y os haré matar con piedras.
                    Mirad que habláis de vna cosa   2225
                que la he de ver y tocar,
                que yo no he de castigar
                vna muger virtüosa
                    por siniestra ynformaçión;
                que sé que ay enbidia y çelos,   2230
                y correré entranbos velos
                de honor y satisfaçión;

2201. MSA, Hõbre si en mi casa ha muerto; B, *Hõbres si*, rest as MSA.
2207. MSBA, en.
2209-12. MSBA, omit.
2218. MSBA, licencia.
2221. ✿
2222. MSBA, ha sido.
2223. B, serè yo.

y veré quién es culpado
antes que, con poco seso,
ose fulminar proçeso   2235*
contra vn ángel de mí amado.
Porque en razón de creher
de su virtud, no ay dezir
los oydos han de oyr,
que los ojos han de ver.   2240

BERMUDO   ¿Y si vieses con los ojos
alguna noche?

FERNÁN   ¡Ay de mí!

BERMUDO   Dos personas juntas, di,
¿juzgaras que son antojos?

FERNÁN   ¿Con los ojos?

BERMUDO   Sí, señor.   2245

FERNÁN   Hombres, ¿tenéis seso?

BERMUDO   Bueno,
dile la verdad, Ximeno.

XIMENO   Señor, tú estás sin onor.

FERNÁN   ¿Sin honor?   [fol. 6 v.]

XIMENO   Si mi señora
habla a un onbre en el jardín,   2250
¿será p[ar]a onesto fin
o porque tu infamia adora?

FERNÁN   Será por mi desbentura,
por mi muerte, por mi agrabio.

BERMUDO   Señor, tú eres noble y sabio;   2255
remedio a tu onor procura,
que sin duda los verás
con sólo que vengas tarde
vna noche.

FERNÁN   ¡Dios me guarde!

2240. MSBA, y los.
2244. B, ontojos.
2249. *
2252. MSBA, como lo has de ver agora?
2256. MSA, remediar tu; B, remeddio tu.
2257. MSBA, lo.

	No me habléys, no digáis más.	2260
	¡Jesús, qué ynfierno, qué rabia,	
	qué desdicha! Estefanía,	
	hija del Rey, muger mía,	
	cuerda, onesta, santa y sabia,	
	no es posible. ¡Hombres del diablo,	2265
	vosotros mentís!	

XIMENO   ¡Señor!

FERNÁN   ¿Háoslo dicho algún traydor
de los que en Burgos no hablo?
¿Quánto os dan por este enrredo?

XIMENO   ¡Que se lo dixe a Bermudo!   2270

BERMUDO   ¿Esto dudas?

FERNÁN   Esto dudo,
luego, ¿dudarlo no puedo?

BERMUDO   No, señor, si lo has de ver.

FERNÁN   ¿Verlo con los ojos?

BERMUDO   Sí.

FERNÁN   ¿Burláys?

BERMUDO   Sí, señor, de ti,   2275
que dudes lo que es muger.

FERNÁN   "¡Que dudes lo que es muger!" *[fol.] 7 [r.]*
Esto es echo, venid.

XIMENO   Bamos.

FERNÁN   Pues silençio, que llegamos.
En fin, ¿lo tengo de ver?   2280

XIMENO   Con los ojos lo verás.

FERNÁN   ¡O, casa de infamia llena!
Que vna muger que no es buena

2262. MSBA, es posible.
2264. MSBA, omit *y*.
2269. MSBA, el enredo?
2272. MSBA, dudar no lo.
2273. MSBA, Visto.
2275. MSBA, Burlaysos? Ber.—Señor, de ti?*
2277. MSBA, omit.
2278. MSBA, Assign *vamos* to Bermudo.
2280. MSBA, que en fin.
2281. MSBA, assign to Bermudo.
2282. MSBA, A casa de infamias llena.

puede aniquilarla; mas,
    ¿qué sirben esos blasones   2285
en mil dorados pabesses,
esos luzidos arnesses
y esos colgados pendones?
    ¿Qué sirben esos roeles,
de los Castros sienpre honrrados,   2290
ya de la infamia manchados
de aquellas manos crueles.
    Arcos honrrosos, ¡pluguiera
a Dios que aquel mismo día,
sobre mí y Estefanía   2295
v[uest]ra máquina cayera!
    ¿Para qué os aderezé?
¿Para qué con v[uest]ro escudo
puse el de Castilla? Dudo,
temo; no ha sido, no fue.   2300
    Cómo me pudo ofender
muger de tan alto nombre?
Pero díxome aquel ombre:
"que dudes lo que es muger."
    Muger es; si quiso, pudo.   2305
Pudo, pues ausente fui.   *[fol. 7 v.]*
Fui onrrado, ynfame boluí;
pues si es ansí, ¿qué lo dudo?

✠ *Estefanía, Ysabel, aconpañamiento.*

ESTEFANÍA   Si no saliera al camino,
me matara mi desseo.   2310

2285-88. MSBA, omit.*
2289. MSBA, De que siruen los.
2292. MSBA, por vnas.
2299. S, puso.
2300. MSBA, que es verdad, mentira fue.
2301. MSBA, puede.
2303. MSBA, estaua ausente, soy hombre.
2304. MSBA, era muger, fue muger.
2305. MSBA, Pues si fue muger, bien pudo.
St. dir. before v. 2309. MSBA, Sale Estefania; G, y acompanam[to].

	¿Es posible que te veo?	
	¿Si es verdad o lo ymagino?	
	Déxame, mi solo bien,	
	descansar en esos brazos.	
FERNÁN	¡Quién los hiziera pedazos *[ap.]*	2315
	y a quién se los dio tanbién!	
	Dulçíssima Estefanía.	
ESTEFANÍA	Fernando de aquestos ojos.	
FERNÁN	Dulçe paz de mis enojos.	
ESTEFANÍA	Alma desta [a]lma.	
FERNÁN	Luz mía.	2320
	Luz fue, pero ya eclipsada *[ap.]*	
	de infamia, tiniebla es.	
ESTEFANÍA	¿Cómo vienes?	
FERNÁN	¿No lo ves?	
	Llena de sangre la espada,	
	y el alma de amores llena.	2325
ESTEFANÍA	¿Y no me preguntas más?	
FERNÁN	Ya sé, mis ojos, que estás	
	buena. ¡Ay, Dios, si fueras buena! *[ap.]*	
ESTEFANÍA	Mucho me ofende tu oluido.	
	¿No ay más por quién preguntar?	2330
FERNÁN	Después de ti, no ay lugar	
	donde quepa mi sentido.	
	¿Dízeslo por Ysabel,	
	esa esclaba que has criado *[fol.] 8 [r.]*	
	por Ribera, Ortiz y Prado?	2335
ESTEFANÍA	¡Que aya tanto oluido en él!	
	¡Cómo! ¿No saben allá	

2312. MSBA, omit *Si.*
2314. MSBA, entre tus.
2316. MSBA, da.°
2317. MSBA, Bellissima; G, dulcima.
2319. MSBA, bien.
2320. MSBA, Vida del alma.°
2322. MSBA, y tinieblas.
2328. MSA, a Dios, si fuera; B, a Dios si fuere.
2331. MSBA, Fuera.°
2334. MSA, he; B, he comprado.°

que he parido?

FERNÁN   ¡A, sí, por Dios!
Ya lo supimos los dos;
digo, el Rey, que bueno está,   2340
    Dios le guarde, y yo, que fui
a quien más plazer tocó;
mucho del nieto se olgó.

ESTEFANÍA   Tú, poco.
FERNÁN   ¡Yo! ¿Cómo ansí?
ESTEFANÍA   Porque pensé que vinieras   2345
por el camino pensando
en tu retrato, Fernando,
y que en llegando le vieras.
    Vien pareze que no has sido
padre; no sabes lo que es.   2350
FERNÁN   Visto, le querré después,
que es hijo por el oydo.
    Bamos y descansaré.
ESTEFANÍA   De llegar te abrás cansado.
FERNÁN   No descanso, aunque he llegado, [ap.]   2355
que tengo mui bien de qué.
ESTEFANÍA   No sepa nadie de ti.
FERNÁN   Querráme ver la çiudad.
Çielos, ¿si será verdad? [ap.]
Tened lástima de mí.   2360

✠ Entrense.

MUDARRA   ¿Qué tenemos?   [fol. 8 v.]
YSABEL   Ya lo ve.
MUDARRA   ¿Está enojada?

2338. MSB, Ansi.
2342. MSBA, parte.
2344. MSB, a ti.
2352. *
2356. MSBA, mal.
2359. MSBA, aquesto es.
2360. *
St. dir. before v. 2361. MSBA, Vanse, y salen Mudarra, y Ysabel; G,
Vanse.

YSABEL   Vn poquito.
MUDARRA   Çelito será.
YSABEL   ¿Çelito?
             Çielazo dirá.
MUDARRA   ¿Por qué?
YSABEL   Porque se fue sin hablarme.   2365
MUDARRA   Y agora quiero boluerme
             sin hablalla.
YSABEL   Pues si duerme
             despertaréle en mudarme.
MUDARRA   ¡Por vida de la mui...!
YSABEL   ¡Quedo!
MUDARRA   ¿No es perra?
YSABEL   No, sino ydalga.   2370
MUDARRA   Mejor respondiera ygalga.
YSABEL   Y él, ¿quién es?   *
MUDARRA   Deçirlo puedo
             delante del Rey de España.
YSABEL   Ni aun delante del de copas,   *
             si no es porque no son pocas   2375
             las que de vino acompaña.
MUDARRA   Por esso bien, Ysabel,
             que no lo bebió tu agüelo.
YSABEL   Y él ba mui derecho al çielo,
             a echado el plomo y cordel.   2380*
MUDARRA   Yo soy Mudarra de Asturias,   *
             hijodalgo, como el vino
             por aguar, como tozino
             y puedo...

2364. MSBA, celazos dirà. Mud.—De que?*
2365. MSBA, De que se.
2366. MSBA, pienso.
2368. MSBA, despertarle he con.
2371. MSBA, galga.*
2375. MSBA, es ya porque son.
2376. MSBAG, del vino.
2377-80. MSBA, omit.
2382. MSBA, hidalgo como es el.
2383. G, como el.

YSABEL   No más injurias.
                    Abrázame y ve con Dios,   2385
                    no te eche menos Fernando.
MUDARRA   ¿Y el hablarte?   [fol.] 9 [r.]
YSABEL   Ya en llegando,
                    ven a las tres o a las dos.

                              ✠ Sola.

(YSABEL)   Loco, atreuido pensamiento mío,
                    mucho te atrebes, pues que disfraçado   2390
                    con la piel de Esaú, llegaste osado   *
                    adonde hurtar la bendizión confío.
                    Fingí de Estefanía talle y brío;
                    gozé a Fortún, y hauiéndole gozado
                    creçió el amor, aunque es el premio hurtado; 2395
                    que es alma del amor el desbarío.
                    La voz fingida, el háuito me anpara,
                    y el encubrime más que fuera justo.
                    ¡O, quién de amor con libertad gozara!
                    ¡O, quién llegara a verle sin disgusto,   2400
                    que no gozar el gusto cara a cara
                    es ynfamia de amor, trayçión del gusto!

              ✠ Váyasse y entren Fortún Ximénez y Olfos.

OLFOS   Triste vienes.
FORTUNIO   Con razón,
                    Olfos, debo entristezerme.
OLFOS   Quien tiene amor, poco duerme.   2405*

2388. MSBA, luego hablaremos los dos.
St. dir. before v. 2389. MSBA, Vase Mudarra; G, Ysauel sola.
2390. *
2394. MSBA, el talle.
2397. MSBA, la luz.
2398. MSBA, el disfraçarme.
2401. MSBA, del gusto.
2402. *
St. dir. before v. 2403. MSB, Vanse, y salen Fortun, y Olfos; A, Vase.
Salen... ; G, Vase. Fortun Ximenez y Olfos.

FORTUNIO   Vela sienpre el corazón.

OLFOS   ¿Qué te aflixe?

FORTUNIO   El ver presente
a Rui de Castro.

OLFOS   ¿Qué ymporta?

FORTUNIO   ¿No ymporta si el ylo corta
del fabor que tuue ausente?   2410

OLFOS   ¿Por esso le has de perder?

FORTUNIO   Y quando no le perdiesse,
¿no es justo que el ver me pese
al lado desta muger   [fol. 9 v.]
todas las noches vn ombre?   2415

OLFOS   No es hombre el aborrezido.

FORTUNIO   ¡Ay triste, que es su marido!
No lo dudes; basta el nombre,
y tras ausençia, no ay cosa
que alegre vna casa más.   2420

OLFOS   Ymaginatiuo estás.

FORTUNIO   Amando, es cosa forzossa
a tales curiosidades,
ymaginando, lleg[u]é,
que de çelos me abrasé.   2425

OLFOS   Pues, ¿a qué te persüades?

FORTUNIO   A que la goza, que basta,
y de enuidia desatino;
que después que Vlises vino,   *
no fue Penélope casta.   2430
No tiene amor en su çiençia
más profundo pensamiento
que el que tratamos, ni aun siento,

2406. *
2410. MSBA, al saber que estuue.*
2413. MS, que verme; BA, que ver me.*
2415. MSBA, a vn.
2416. *
2421. MSBA, Con dichas celoco estàs?
2425. *
2427. MSBA, goze.
2429. *
2431-42. MSBA, omit.*

para tratarle, paçiençia.
    Sábenlo solos aquellos   2435
que al tomar la posesión
de vn bien, a quien la ocasión
dio contados los cabellos,
    vieron venir vn ausente
que a su lado se acostó,   2440
y descuidado gozó
lo que se le dyo presente.
    No sé qué tengo de hazer.   *[fol.] 10 [r.]*

OLFOS   Di, señor, ¿no me dezías
que solamente querías   2445
la ynfamia desta muger,
    y luego pasarte a Françia
a publicar la desonrra
de Rui de Castro?

FORTUNIO   En su onrra
hize vn lanze de ymport[anci]a   2450
    y con él ymaginé
que me vengaua, mas mira
como, amando con mentira,
verdad la mentira fue;
    porque hauiendo ya gozado   2455
a la bella Estefanía,
la noche del mismo día
que esto tuue ymaginado,
    me picó tanto el desseo
la brebedad del fabor,   2460
y una cometa de amor
en el çielo de vn manteo,

2438. J, cortados.*
2442. G, se le hizo.*
2449. MB, honor.
2450. MSBA, omit *vn.**
2454. *
2455. *
2458. B, ymaginada.
2460. MSBA, de vn.
2461. MSBA, omit *y*; J, vna.

aquellas brebes cariçias
que enloquezen de manera
que a quien de mí me dixera,   2465
le diera el alma en albrizias.
Ella es quien es, en efeto.

OLFOS   Sí, mas mira a toda ley.
Que es, tras ser hija de vn Rey,
prenda de vn ombre discreto.   2470
Guarda no cayga en el casso, *[fol. 10 v.]*
que tras ser discreto, es hombre
que hará que este exenplo asombre
a España y al mundo.

FORTUNIO   Paso,
que no estoy para consejos.   2475
Dame aderezo de noche,
pues ya de su negro coche
va el sol diuino tan lejos.

OLFOS   Luego, ¿allá piensas entrar?

FORTUNIO   No más de por el jardín.   2480

OLFOS   Los que no piensan el fin . . .

FORTUNIO   ¿Qué suelen hazer?

OLFOS   Errar.

FORTUNIO   Ya es tarde, echóse la suerte ;   *
Estefanía querida,
ni quiero sin ti la uida,   2485
ni temo por ti la muerte.

✠ *Váyanse y entren, rebozados, Fernán Ruiz, Bermudo y Ximeno.*

2463. MSBA, Que aquellas.*
2464. MSBA, me enloquecen.
2467. J, si ella es. . .*
2468. *
2469. MSBA, que tras ser hija de Rey.
2470. MSBA, es prenda de hombre.
2471. *
2472. MSBA, el hombre.
2473. MSBA, hara que esta hazaña.
2475. *
2479. *
2481. MSBA, miran.
2486. *

St. dir. before v. 2487. MSBA, Vanse, y salen Castro, Bermudo, y Ximeno de noche; G, Vanse. Salen rebozados . . .

FERNÁN	¿Sintiéronnos entrando?
BERMUDO	No pudieron,

que está el jardín tan lejos de tu quarto,
y hazen tanto ruido fuentes y árboles,
los vnos murmurando de los otros,   2490
que el hauernos sentido es inposible.

FERNÁN   Murmurarán, Bermudo, de mi afrenta
y de que se detiene la venganza.

BERMUDO   Antes, señor, mirando que la intentas,
deben de estar en tu alabanza ablando.   2495

FERNÁN   ¿Por dónde entra ese ombre?

XIMENO   A estas paredes
pone vna escala y salta en estas murtas.
                              [fol.] 11 [r.]

FERNÁN   ¿Que no sabéis quién es?

XIMENO   De ningún modo.

FERNÁN   ¿Pudístesle matar?

BERMUDO   Yo lo intentaua,
pero temiendo lastimar tu onrra,   2500
aguardé que viniesses.

FERNÁN   Bien has hecho.
Pero deçidme, ¿cómo estáis tan çiertos
de que estando yo en Burgos, osaría
baxar a este jardín Estefanía?

BERMUDO   Como saliste fuera y le dixiste   2505
que acaso no vendrías hasta el alba,

2487. MSB, en entrando?
2488. *
2489. S, tonto.
2490. MSBA, omit.
2492. B, mormururán.
2493. MSBA, en ver que.
2495. AJ, omit *de.*
2496. MSBA, este.
2497. MSBA, entre estas.
2498. MSBA, assign *De ningún modo* to Bermudo.
2499. MSBA, Pudistele matar. Ber—Ya; G, Pudistele.*
2505. MSBA, la.

	respeto de vn negoçio de ynportançia	
	que el Consejo de Estado al Rei escriue,	
	sospecho yo que baxará, sin duda,	
	a gozar la ocasión; que las mugeres	2510
	que dan en liuiandades semejantes,	
	ninguna pierden que ganarla puedan.	
FERNÁN	¿Quién será este onbre en Burgos? ¿Será noble?	
XIMENO	Ya que perdió el onor y la vergüenza,	
	el balor de la sangre y el respeto	2515
	debido al tuyo, abrá escojido vn ombre	
	tan bueno que en su muerte la disculpe.	
FERNÁN	No caygo en onbre de inport[anci]a.	
XIMENO	¿Cómo?	
FERNÁN	Todos sirben al Rey.	
BERMUDO	Aquí han quedado	
	algunos mozos destos que no sirben	2520
	sino de infamia en las mugeres nobles,	
	ymitando sus trages y cabellos.	
FERNÁN	¿Será Sancho Laynez?	
XIMENO	Es gallardo.	
FERNÁN	¿Será Bernardo Alfonso?	
XIMENO	Libre mozo.	

[fol. 11 v.]

FERNÁN	¿Yllán Anzures?	
BERMUDO	La locura misma.	2525
FERNÁN	¿Gonzalo Osorio?	
BERMUDO	El mismo atreuimiento.	
FERNÁN	¿Rui Ponze Díaz?	
XIMENO	Quedo, que he sentido	
	arrojar el cordel.	

2507. MSBA, que hasta el Alua, señor, no boluerias.
2508. MSBA, que al Consejo de Estado el.*
2511. B, libertades.
2512. MSBA, gozar la.
2517. MSBA, que su muerte le.
2518. MSBA, assign ¿Cómo? to Bermudo.
2523. MSBA, assign Ximeno's speech to Bermudo.
2525. *
2528. MSBA, vn cordel.

FERNÁN   ¡Bálgame el çielo!
            Cubríos destos árboles.

        ✠ *Entren Olfos y Fortún Ximénez.*

OLFOS   Repara
            en que dixo el papel que si salía   2530
            Fernán Ruiz de cassa...
FORTUNIO   Maxadero,
            si no supiera yo que estaua fuera,
            ¿viniérame a poner en tal peligro?
            Déxame hazer la seña.
OLFOS   No la hagas,
            que quien espera no ha menester seña.   2535

        ✠ *Ysabel con vn reboziño rico y manteo con oro cubierto.*

YSABEL   ¿Eres mi bien?
FORTUNIO   ¡O, bella Estefanía!
BERMUDO   ¿Oyes aquello?
FERNÁN   Calla.
YSABEL   ¿Cómo vienes?
FORTUNIO   Para seruirte vengo. ¿Tienes puestas
            espías en la puerta?
YSABEL   Ysabel queda
            mirando quando viene Rui de Castro.   2540
FORTUNIO   Pues éntrate detrás de aquestos árboles.
            Ablaremos vn rato, que me has muerto
            de çelos esta noche.
YSABEL   ¿Çelos tienes?

    St. dir. between v. 2529. MSBA, Salen Fortunio, y Olfos; G, Fortun y
Olfos.
    2531. MSBAG, de Castro.
    St. dir. before v. 2535. MSBA, Sale Ysabel a la ventana.
    2537. MSBA, omit *Ysa.—¿Cómo vienes?*, replaced by *For.—Tienes pues-
tas*, from v. 2538.
    2538. MSBA, omit *para seruirte vengo.**
    2539. MSBA, a la.*
    2540. MSBA, venga.
    2541. MSBA, aquellos.

FORTUNIO   Ay mucho que. reñir.
YSABEL   Gallardo vienes.

                  ✠ *Entrense.*

FERNÁN   Sobrándome corazón   2545
                  para solo acometer
                  mil moros, le vengo a ver
                  cobarde en esta ocasión.
                     Debe de ser que la cara
                  de la afrenta me espantó,   2550
                  que aun no ymaginaua yo   *[fol.] 12 [r.]*
                  que tan fea la mirara.
                     Mientras los voy a matar,
                  ese onbre los dos asid.
BERMUDO   ¿Matarémosle?
FERNÁN   Aduertid   2555
                  que le quiero luego ablar.

                  ✠ *Entrese Fernán Ruiz, lleguen a Olfos los dos.*

XIMENO   ¡Suelta las armas, cuitado!
OLFOS   ¡Muerto soy!   ✻
BERMUDO   ¡Suéltalas presto!
XIMENO   ¡Tenle firme!
(Dentro)   ¿Qué es aquesto?
FERNÁN   Castigo de vn afrentado.   2560
YSABEL   Mísera de mí, ¿qué haré?
                  Rui de Castro lo ha sentido.

                  ✠ *Salga huyendo Ysabel por vna puerta y entre por otra.*

2544. B, omits *Ysa.—Gallardo vienes.*
St. dir. before v. 2545. MSBA, Vanse Ysabel, y Fortunio.
2549. ✻
2551. MSBA, omit *aun.*
2553. MSBA, la voy.
2554. MSBA, el paje.
St. dir. before v. 2557. MSBA, Vase; G, Vase Fernan Ruiz. . .
2558. MSBA, Ber.—Sueltalas. Xim.—Sueltalas presto.
2559. MSBA, Olf.—Valgame el cielo. Fort.—q̄ es esto?
St. dir. before v. 2560. MSBA, Dentro.

(Dentro)	¡Muerto soy!
FERNÁN	¡Onbre atreuido!
YSABEL	¡Triste de mí! ¿Dónde yré?

                     Mas debaxo de la cama   2565
                     me entraré de mi señora.

✠ *Entrese y salga Fernán Ruiz con la espada desnuda.*

FERNÁN	¿Adónde está la traydora
	que mi noble sangre infama?
BERMUDO	Al aposento se fue

                     donde duermes, si entendí   2570
                     bien lo que dixo.

OLFOS	¡Ay de mí!
XIMENO	De aqueste infame, ¿qué haré?
FERNÁN	Llébale y çierra mui bien,
	y tú a Mudarra lebanta,
	y tray vn acha.
OLFOS	¡Que tanta 2575

                     fue mi desdicha!

FERNÁN	Di, ¿quién
	es el hombre que venía
	contigo?
OLFOS	Fortún, señor.
FERNÁN	¡Fortún! ¡O, ynfame traydor! *[fol. 12 v.]*

                     ¿Con Fortún Estefanía?   2580
                     Matalde por el auiso
                     mientras a matarla voy.

St. dir. before v. 2563. MSBA, omit.
2563. MSBA, assign *¡Muerto soy!* to Fortunio; J, assigns to ysa.
St. dir. before v. 2567. MSBA, Sale huyendo Ysabel, y Castro siguiendola.*
2570. MSBA, duerme.*
2572. MSBA, assign to Bermudo.
2573. MSBA, Atale, y asle muy bien.
2574. MSBA, omit *a.*
2575. B, vna.
2577. MSBA, Fue de aquesta aleuosia.
2578. MSBA, el dueño.
2579. MSBA, A infame, ay mi noble honor.
2582. MSBA, yo a.

✠ *Entrese.*

OLFOS	Señores, criado soy,	
	mi mala suerte lo quiso.	
	¿No hizieran vuesas merzedes	2585
	lo que Castro les mandara?	
BERMUDO	Lágrimas y lengua para,	
	villano saltaparedes.	✿
	¡En casa de vn noble, o perro!	
OLFOS	¿Confesarme no podré?	2590
XIMENO	¿Dónde?	
OLFOS	Luego bolueré.	
BERMUDO	¿Darémosle?	
XIMENO	Désta çierro.	✿
OLFOS	¡Sin confisión! Esta pido;	✿
	cristianos soys; luego vengo,	
	que aquí en la parroquia tengo	2595
	vn clérigo conozido.	
	Todos somos honbres flacos.	
XIMENO	Mátale ya.	
OLFOS	¡Confisión!	
	¡Muerto soy!	
BERMUDO	Tal galardón	
	tiene quien sirbe a bellacos.	2600

✠ *Entrense y salga Fernán Ruiz con la espada desnuda.*

FERNÁN	¿No ay quien me dé vna luz? Pero ¿qué espero?
	En la cama he sentido algún ruido;

St. dir. before v. 2583. G, Vase; MSBA, omit; J, Entrense.
2585. A, vuestras.
2588. M, salta parede.
2589. MSBA, omit o.
2592. MSBA, assign Bermudo's speech to Ximeno and vice versa.
2593. MSBA, esto.
2594. MSBA, Christiano soy.
2598. MSBA, assign Ximeno's speech to Bermudo.
2600. MSBA, lleua.
St. dir. before v. 2601. MSBA, Vanse. Sale Castro con la espada desnuda;
G, Vanse. Sale Fernan con la espada desnuda.✿

no disimules el delito fiero,
que del çielo el castigo te ha venido.
Correr corrido la cortina quiero,   2605
pues ya la de mi afrenta se ha corrido.

[fol.] 13 [r.]

✠ *Corra vna cortina y véase vna tarima y cama y en ella*
  Estefanía, vestida, sobre la colcha de seda, y
  almohadas, con vn niño en brazos.

Aquí su cuerpo atiento; finjes sueño,
siendo despierta, de mi infamia dueño.
¡Muere, muere, cruel!

ESTEFANÍA   ¡Dios mío! ¡Dios mío!
¿Qué es esto? ¿Quién me ha muerto?

FERNÁN   Yo, traydora.   2610

ESTEFANÍA   ¿Tú, mi señor, tan grande desbarío?

FERNÁN   ¿Quién llora aquí tanbién?

ESTEFANÍA   Tu hijo llora.
Abrig[u]éle en mis brazos por el frío;
no me acosté por esperarte. ¿Agora
me matas y oy me has echo tantas fiestas?   2615

FERNÁN   ¿Qué vozes son tan diferentes éstas?
      Muger, ¿no estauas con aquel que he muerto
agora en el jardín?

ESTEFANÍA   ¿Quién te ha engañado?

FERNÁN   ¿Yo no te ui con él?

ESTEFANÍA   ¡Qué bien, por çierto,
mi amor y obligaçiones has pagado!   2620

FERNÁN   ¡Bálgame todo el çielo! ¿Estoi despierto?

ESTEFANÍA   Si en Córdoba mi padre te ha enojado,
¿qué culpa tube yo, dulçe bien mío,

2603-2604. MSBA, show as vv. 2605-2606.
      St. dir. before v. 2607. MSBA, Entra dentro, parece Estefania en la
cama herida; A, Aparece; J, y salga Fernán Ruiz con la espada desnuda.
y...*
      2607. MSBA, aqui siento su cuerpo, finge sueño.
      2608. MSA, afrenta el dueño; B, despierto de mi afrenta el dueño.
      2609. MSBA, Muere cruel. Est.—Dios mio, Iesus mio.
      2623. B, te ha nojado.

	quando tu hijo entre mis brazos crío?
FERNÁN	¿Cómo respondes eso?
ESTEFANÍA	¡A, Castro, Castro! 2625
	En mí te vengas de pasiones vanas.
FERNÁN	¿Qué sangriento rigor, qué influxo de astro
	me ha puesto aquí, qué furias inumanas?
	¿Yo no entré en el jardín siguiendo el rastro
	de tus pisadas locas y liuianas? *[fol. 13 v.]* 2630
	¿Yo no le vi en tus brazos, tú en los suyos?
ESTEFANÍA	¿Yo [e] estado en otros brazos que los tuyos?

Mudarra con vn acha, Ximeno y Bermudo.

MUDARRA	¿Fernán Ruiz a mi s[eño]ra ha muerto?
BERMUDO	Calla, Mudarra, que su onor le quita.
FERNÁN	Ola, llega esa luz.
MUDARRA	El daño es çierto. 2635
	¡Señora de mi alma, alma bendita!
	¿Cómo has echo, señor, tal desconçierto?
FERNÁN	Este villano a que le mate inçita.
	¿Quién duda que abrá sido el alcagüete?
BERMUDO	¿De qué lloras, Mudarra? Calla o vete. 2640
ESTEFANÍA	Mudarra, mi señor me ha m[uer]to.
MUDARRA	¿Cómo?
	¡Triste de mí!
ESTEFANÍA	No sé, por desdichada.
MUDARRA	Luego, señor, desde la punta al pomo

2625. MSBA, A Castro, a Castro; G, Ha Castro.
2627. MSBA, dolor.*
2628. MSBA, fieras.
2630. MSBA, torpes.
2631. G, estando.
St. dir. before v. 2633. MSBA, Sale Ximeno, y Bermudo, y Mudarra con vna hacha. Also A, Salen ... un hacha.*
2635. MSBA, Allega acà.*
2637. G, mo has.*
2639. MSBA, que le aurà sido alcahuete.*
2640. MSBA, assign to Ximeno.
2642. MSBA, Por solo desgraciada.
2643. MSBA, Llega señor, y de la.

me atrauiesa el azero de esa espada.

FERNÁN   Tristes sospechas del suçeso tomo.   2645

XIMENO   La cama tienbla.

FERNÁN   De mi onor culpada.

BERMUDO   Mira lo que ay aquí.

FERNÁN   ¡Jesús! ¿Qué es esto?

    Es Ysabel

✠ *Sáquenla.*

FERNÁN   Pues, ¿cómo aquí te has puesto?

MUDARRA   El reboziño y el manteo tiene
    de mi señora.

FERNÁN   ¡Triste yo! ¿Qué hize?   2650

YSABEL   Tarde o tenprano, al fin la culpa viene
    a pagarse.

MUDARRA   ¿No escuchas lo que dize?

YSABEL   Amor, que no ay cordura que le enfrene,
    aunque al mundo mi engaño escandalize,
    me hizo de Fortunio enamorada,   2655
    gozarle desta suerte disfrazada.
    Fingí ser mi señora Estefanía,
            [fol.] 14 [r.]
    y huyendo tu furor, aquí me he puesto.

FERNÁN   Angel del çielo, dulçe esposa mía,
    este demonio fue la causa desto.   2660

2644. J, atrauiese.*
2645. MSBA, Triste sucesso en tal sospecha tomo!*
2646. MSBA, assign Ximeno's speech to Bermudo.
2647. MSBA, Mud.—Mira lo que ay aqui. Castr—Pues que es aquesto?
St. dir. between v. 2648. MSBA, Sacan a Isabel detras de la cama; place between v. 2647; G, omits.*
2648. MSBA, Ysa.—Echò fortuna a mi desdicha el resto.
2649-50. MSBA, omit.
2651. MSBA, al mal castigo.
2652. MSBA, Cas.—Es Ysabel?
2654. MSBA, Interpolated between vv. 2654-55 is: aunque disculpa de si, y [BA, de] otros tiene, / no la quiera tener del mal que hize.
2655. MSBA, yo soy quien de.
2656. MSBA, le goze desta.
2658. MSBA, omit y.
2659. MSBA, amada esposa.

	¡Maldiga Dios de mi venida el día!	
ESTEFANÍA	¿Cómo que dieses crédito tan presto	
	a quien te puso en tan notable engaño?	
FERNÁN	¡Ay, infames testigos de mi daño!	
	¡Quitaos de aquí que por el çielo...!	
ESTEFANÍA	Esposo,	2665

esto es echo; yo muero, aunque ynoçente;
que fue a tus manos tengo por dichoso
suçesso. Oyeme vn poco atentamente:
cría este niño, y en mi entierro onrroso
pondrás para memoria de la gente: 2670
"Aquí, muerta sin culpa..."

FERNÁN   ¡Ay, prenda mía!

ESTEFANÍA   "...yaze la desdichada Estefanía."
       Abrázame, y adiós. Hijo querido,
no os puedo yo criar. Mi sangre os queda,
que de vna desdichada habéis naçido.   2675

MUDARRA   ¿Murió?

YSABEL   Murió.

FERNÁN   ¿Que aquesto sufrir pueda?
       Yo me sabré matar.

MUDARRA   ¿Tienes sentido?

FERNÁN   Al seso es bien que el sentimiento exçeda.
       Çierra aquella cortina. ¡Ay, dulçe suerte,
si mis ojos çerrara assí la muerte!   2680
       Angel, mártir, hermosa, virtüosa
Estefanía, al fin la desdichada,   *
effeto natural del ser hermosa.
¿Que te perdí? ¿Que te mató mi espada?

2664. G, Ha; B, notables.
2666. MSBA, yo muero como ves.
2668. MSBA, y se tendrà perpetuamente; J, sucesso.
2671. B, murio sin.
2672. J, yace.
2673. MSB, a Dios.
2679. MSBA, cierra aquessas cortinas, triste suerte; G, aquesa; J, cierra
aq̄sta.
2681. MSBA, Angel del cielo, y mi querida esposa.
2683: MSBA, de ser.*
2684. MSBA, piadosa.

Viue el çielo en que estás, alma dichosa,   2685
            [fol. 14 v.]
de tantos ynoçentes coronada,
de hazer por ti el más graue sentimiento
que aya cabido en triste pensamiento.
   Al Rey yré, para que luego al punto
me corte la cabeza. Tú, esa esclaba   2690
me pon en viuo fuego.

         ✠ *Váyase Fernán Ruiz.*

MUDARRA   No pregunto
si estaua con Fortunio o si no estaua,
ni me ha de responder en contrapunto,
ni sacar lagrimitas del alxaua,
sino que solamente...

YSABEL   ¿Qué me quieres?   2695
Me diga lo que son...

YSABEL   ¿Quién?
MUDARRA   Las mugeres.
YSABEL   Las buenas son, Mudarra, soles, çielos,
vnico bien, seguras confïanzas;
las malas son tinieblas, yras, çelos,
ynfiernos, desbenturas y mudanzas.   2700
MUDARRA ¿Qué merezen las buenas?
YSABEL   Que con velos
se cubran sus diuinas semejanzas,

2686. MSBA, rodeada.
2687. MSBA, tan graue.
2688. MSBA, que te sirua de tumulo sangriento.
2689. MSBA, me yrè.
2690. MSBA, triste esclaua.
2691. MSBA, ponla en vn.
St. dir. between v. 2691. MSBA, Vase; G, omits.
2694. MSBA, ni dezir que le amaua, o no le amaua.
2697. A, son a padres.*
2698. MSBA, segura confiança; J, vnico.
2700. MSBA, mudança.
2701. *
2702. MSBA, se cubra su diuina semejança.

	y las adore el ombre.	
MUDARRA	Bien, y luego	
	las malas, ¿qué merezen?	
YSABEL	Muerte y fuego.	
MUDARRA	Tu causa has sentençiado. ¡Ven, perrona,	2705
	que te quiero tostar!	
YSABEL	Mudarra mío,	
	ya tiene aquella mártir su corona.	
MUDARRA	Quitarte quiero de ese miedo el frío.	
	No es tienpo ya de burlas, no. Perdona.	
YSABEL	Confieso a Dios mi grabe desbarío.	2710
MUDARRA	Pues a fee que no mueres inoçente.	
	[fol.] 15 [r.]	
YSABEL	Merezco este castigo justamente.	

✠ *Rey Alfonso, caxas y vanderas y alarde; Ordoño, el conde*
Nuño Osorio, Ramiro de Guzmán, Abdelmón, presso, y
moros cautibos.

ABDELMÓN	Digo que soi, Alfonso, tu cautibo,	
	y que confiesso tu balor notable;	
	justamente en España te han llamado	2715
	Enperador por tus famosos echos.	
ALFONSO	Rey Abdelmón, aduierte que te he dado	
	libertad contra el boto de mi gente.	
	Cúnpleme la palabra de que luego	
	te enbarcarás al Africa, llebando	2720

_____

2703. *

2708. MSBA, Quitarla quiero el miedo de esse frio; J, dese.

2709. MSBA, de llanto, ven perdona.

2710. MSBA, grande.

2712. MSBA, Mereci.

St. dir. before v. 2713. MSBA, Vanse, y salen el Rey Alfonso, y Ordoño Ramiro, y Sancho Laynez marchando, y trae a Audelmon cautiuo; also, A, omits first and second *y*; and *traen.*

2713. G, Confieso.

2714. A, omits *y.*

2715. MSBA, te llamaron.

2717. G, Aduiertan Abdelmon como te he dado.*

2720. MSBA, te bolueras.

	los moros almohades que truxiste.	
ABDELMÓN	Todas las nabes tengo aperçiuidas,	
	y yo sé que tan pocos me han quedado	
	que en menos se podrán pasar al Africa.	
	Bien te puedes boluer a tu Castilla	2725
	sin temor de que quiebre la palabra.	
VN SOLDADO	Fernán Ruiz de Castro por la posta	
	acaba de llegar.	
ALFONSO	Sea bienvenido	
	porque goze tanbién desta vitoria,	
	que su venida aumentará mi gloria.	2730

✠ *Entren 4 escuderos de luto delante, y detrás, Fernán*
Ruiz con vn vestido de sayal y una soga al cuello.

FERNÁN	Rey Alfonso de Castilla,	[fol. 15 v.]
	alto Emperador de España,	
	a tus pies vengo a pedirte	
	de Fernán Rüiz venganza.	
ALFONSO	¡Çielos! ¿Qué miro? ¿Quién eres	2735
	que desa suerte me hablas?	
FERNÁN	Fernán Ruiz de Castro soy,	
	el Castellano me llaman.	
ALFONSO	Hijo, pues ¿de esa manera?	
	¿Quién en mi reyno te agrauia?	2740
	Aquí están mis ricos ombres,	

2721. MSBA, traxiste; G, has traydo.*
2722. *
2723. MSBA, y pienso que; A, omits *me*.*
2726. MSBA, temer que te quiebre.
2727. MSBA, assign to Ordoño.
2728. MSBA, llegado.
St. dir. before v. 2731. MSBA, Sale Fernan Ruyz cubierto de luto, y
vna soga al cuello.
2732. *
2733. *
2735. S, quien er.
2736. MSBA, desta.
2738. MSBA, que el.
2739. MSBA, Pues hijo.
2740. MSBA, mis Reynos.

	aquí mis soldados; habla.	
FERNÁN	Yo propio me agrauio a mí.	
	Oye.	
ALFONSO	¡Nouedad estraña!	
FERNÁN	Partí de Córdoba, Rey,	2745

con tu liçençia, a mi cassa,
pero antes de entrar en Burgos,
çerca de sus torres altas,
dos escuderos hidalgos
que crié p[ar]a mi ynfamia   2750
me dizen que Estefanía
vn ombre en mi ausençia trata.
No doy crédito, porfían,
llego, disimulo, aguardan,
y en vn jardín vna noche   2755
me ponen las doze dadas.
Veo baxar a dos honbres,
a las dos, con dos escalas,   *[fol.] 16 [r.]*
y una muger con las ropas
de mi esposa disfraçada.   2760
Mato el hombre, que era, Rey,
Fortún Ximénez, que andaua
por vengarse a lo cobarde,
si la trayçión es venganza.
Las espaldas me ofendía   2765
por no atreberse a la cara,
que en efeto la muger
es del ombre las espaldas.
Sígola y fuese a esconder
debaxo mi propia cama.   2770

2743. MSBA, me agrauio Rey.
2747. MSBA, y antes de llegar a.
2751. MSBA, a Estefania.
2752. MSBA, mi casa.
2758. MSB, por vna escala; A, a los dos por una escala; J, a los dos.*
2760. *
2761. MSBA, matè al vno.
2766. MSBA, ofenderme la.
2767. *
2769. MSBA, omit *y.*

Llego a escuras y a mi esposa
la doy çinco puñaladas.
Despierta a morir del sueño,
que con tu nieto abrazada
esperaua a que viniese,   2775
ynoçente, linpia y casta.
Traen achas, oygo ruido,
y allo, señor, vna esclaua
que era dueño del enrredo,
de Fortunio enamorada.   2780
Mi culpa confieso, Rey;
no quise pasarme a Françia,
sino morir, como es justo,
quien los inoçentes mata.

ALFONSO   ¡Que al fin de tantas vitorias   *[fol. 16 v.]*   2785
este fin se me esperaua!
¡Ay, cómo saben los çielos
poner en el bien templanza!
Fernando, no siento aquí
que me ayas dado en el alma   2790
las çinco heridas que diste
al cuerpo de aquella santa,
sino que falte del mundo
la muger de mexor fama,
la que pude yo cassar   2795
con lo mejor de Alemania.
Pleyto te quiero poner.

NUÑO   Llorando va su desgr[aci]a.

2772. MSBA, le.*
2775. MSBA, aguardaua.
2777. MSBA, Traygo vna hacha, hago ruido.
2782. MSBA, pagar.
2786. MSB, guardaua; A, aguardaba.
2787. MSBA, a.
2791. *
2793. MSB, como que; A, del modo.
2794. *
2798. MSBA, assign to Ordoño; J, assigns to Mu.*

ALFONSO   Juezes tengo en Castilla,
            ellos sentenzien la causa.   2800

                    ✠ *Váyase el Rey.*

ORDOÑO   ¡Gran dolor!
RAMIRO   ¡Gran desbentura!
ORDOÑO   Aquí la tragedia acaba,
            aunque Belardo os conuida   ✦
            a lo que la historia falta
            para segunda comedia,   2805
            que esta primera se llama
            la Desdichada Ynoçente
            que lloran Castros y Andradas.

                            1 d v.j.os.

En Toledo a
12 de nouienbre   M Lope de Vega Carpio *(rúbrica)*
de 1604

                                    [folio, unnumbered, recto]

[1] Examine [e]sta comedia, cantares y entremeses della el
S[ecretari]o Thomás Gracián Dantisco y dé sus censuras en Madrid a 9 de hen[er]o, 1607 años.

                        (rúbrica)

[2] Esta comedia intitulada Estefanía la desdichada se podrá
representar reseruando a la vista lo que fuera de la lectura se

---

2799. MSBA, ay.
2800. MSBA, que sentencien esta.
St. dir. before v. 2801. MSBA, omit; G, Vase el Rey.
2801. MSBA, assign Ramiro's speeches to Ordoño and vice-versa.✦
2802. MSBA, assign to Sancho.
2804. MSBA, a la.
MSA add *Fin de la Tragicomedia de la desdichada Estefania;* B, *Fin
de la tragedia de la desdichada Estefania;* G, *Finis Coronat Opus;* En
Toledo ... *(rúbrica) (rúbrica).*✦

offreçiere, y lo mismo en los cantares y entremés. En Madrid a
9 de enero, 1607.

Thomás Gracián Dantisco
(rúbrica)

[3] Podráse representar esta comedia, cantares y entremeses della,
guardando las censuras en ella dadas en M[adri]d a 12 de
hen[er]o, 1607.

[4] Por mandado de los señores Inquisidores y Juezes Apostólicos
de Vall[adoli]d, vi esta comedia y no ay en ella cosa contra la fe
católica ni buenas costumbres, sino que [e]s la historia a la letra
de los Conde[s] de Lemos y del S[eño]r Rey don Alo[nso], y
así se le puede dar la licen[ci]a de representarla en S[an]
Fran[cis]co de Vall[adoli]d, 29 de abril 1607.

Frai Gregorio Ruiz
[folio, unnumbered, verso]

[5] Los s[eñor]es Inquis[ido]res Apostólicos de Vall[adol]id,
auiendo visto el parecer de atrás de Fray Gregorio Ruiz, lector
de theulugía de S[an] Fran[cis]co desta ciudad, dieron lisençia
para que se pueda representar esta comedia yntitulada Estefanía
la desdichada en la çiudad de Vall[adol]id, 29 de abril de 1607.
(rúbrica).

Juan Martínez de la Vega
(rúbrica)

[6] Por comisión de los señores probisores deste arçobispado, bi
esta comedia llamada Estefanía la desdichada y con las çensuras
que tiene se representará en esta çiudad de Burgos en 7 de
set[iem]b[re] de 1607 años.

El licen[cia]do Inigo López [?]
[folio, unnumbered, recto]

[7] Por mandamiento del Arzob[isp]o, mi señor, he bisto esta
comedia de Estefanía la desdichada y digo que se puede repre-

sentar, reseruando p[ar]a la bista lo que es fuera de la lectura, así lo firmo en Çaragoça a 25 de octubre, año 1608.

El d[oct]or Villalua
(rúbrica)

[8] Conforme al mandam[ien]to de su s[eñorí]a el Illustriss[im]o de Plas[enci]a, vi esta comedia y no ay en ella cosa que se pueda reformar contra lo dispuesto en los sacros cánones y concilios y así la pueden representar ff° en Trugillo, treze de julio de 1609 a[ños].

El D[octo]r Al[ons]o Núñez
de Camargo *(rúbrica)*

[9] Não tem cousa por onde se não possa representar. Em L[isbo]a a 12 outubro de 609.

Fr. Manoel Coelho

[folio, unnumbered, verso]

[10] Por mandado del s[eño]r l[icencia]do Gonzalo Guerrero, Canónigo de la doctoral y Provisor General deste obispado, uide esta comedia llamada Estefanía la desdichada y no ai en ella cosa contra nuestra s[ant]a fe católica, y assí podrá, a mi parecer, representarse, dada [en ?] Jaém a 18 de julio de 610.

D[oct]or Antonio de Godoi Chica

[11] En la çiudad de Jaén, a dies y ocho días del mes de julio de mill y seisçi[en]to[s] y diez años, su m[erce]d el s[eño]r licen[cia]do G[onzal]o Guerrero, Prouisor General deste obispado, aviendo uisto el testimonio de uisitar la [?] comedia yntitulada Estefanía la desdichada, fecho por mandado de su m[erce]d por el dotor Ant[oni]o de Godoy, Prior de San P[abl]o, dijo que daua y dio lic[enci]a y facultad a A[ntoni]o Granados, autor, p[ar]a que la rrepres[enta]se en la çiudad y obispado, y lo firmó de su nonbre.

El L[icencia]do Gonçalo Guerrero
[An]te mí
Joam de Matam[oros] *(rúbrica)*

[folio, unnumbered, recto]

[12] Vi esta comedia y se puede representar en Gr[ana]da 6 de henero de 1611.

El D[oct]or Fran[cis]co
Martínez de Rueda

[13] Por mandamiento del Arçob[isp]o, mi señor don Pedro Manrrique, he visto esta comedia de Estefanía y digo que se puede representar en Çaragoça a 26 dell año 1611.

El D[oct]or Villalua
(rúbrica)

[folio, unnumbered, verso]

[14] Podesse reprezentar esta comedia intitulada Estefanía la desdichada em Lisboa 8 de outubro 617.

Dantisco

[15] O mesmo me parece.

J. F. Salazar *(rúbrica)*

MANUSCRIPT NOTES

Cross. A simple cross, without the over-writing of JM or JMJ, is found on the title page and the folios giving the *reparto* for each act. See the Introduction, p. 16.

Title. The title page shows one of two instances in the play of Estephanía as an alternate spelling for Estefanía (the other occurs in the *reparto* for Act I). Now referred to as *La desdichada Estefanía,* the play was listed in Medèl del Castillo's *Indice* as simply *Desdichada Estefanía.* Fajardo and La Barrera have changed Lope's *Andradas* (see vv. 2136 and 2808) to *Andrades* in their secondary title (see the Introduction, p. 20, n. 9).

Rúbrica. Lope's rubric is here written in conjunction with an M, which stands for Micaela de Luján. It was a common practice of the period to thus refer obliquely to one's *amante.* See Hoge, *El príncipe,* p. 2 and n. 5, for a listing of other autograph manuscripts in which Lope used the M. The *rúbricas* of the *repartos* and the folios numbering acts do not have the M, though it appears with Lope's signature at the end of the play.

Actors. An unnumbered folio, *recto,* which precedes the title page shows the following assignment of actors to roles:

Actor	Rui de Castro
Castro	Mudarra
Antonio Mejía	Fortún Jiménez
Salbador	Olfos, Cerbin, Alcaide
Çamora	Jimén
Belasco	Rey Luis, Abdelmón
Santos	Bermudo
Santiago	Alfonso, Rey de España
Hernando	Almoadí, Nuño
Ribadeneira	Sancho y el májico, Miramamolín
Dama	
[?] Marta	Estefanía
Mari López	Ysabel

To the left of Ribadeneira is written *y alcaide.* J reads *Autor* for *Actor; Zamora* for *Çamora,* which was started originally with an S, then changed to *Ç;* omits *Dama; Albu* for *Olfos.* J was unable to read *májico,* and did not notice that Ribadeneira was assigned to the roles of both Sancho and

Miramamolín, which is made clear from the long dash between the name of actors and the role or roles to be played. There is no dash between *Dama* and what, at first glance, is the next role listed. *Dama* was evidently added at a later time between the names of *Ribadeneira* and the next member of the troupe.

See page 15 of the Introduction for a description of notations on another unnumbered folio which precedes the title page. J omits reference to the notation in the upper left margin, and states inaccurately that the reference to Antonio Granados is repeated three times, for it appears only twice.

TII. These letters appear to the right of the title page, parallel with the margin. There are various ink blots, doodlings, and what appear to be water stains on the title page; J omits mention of these additions. A photograph of the title page is available in *BAE*, XXII (1935), *lámina* XV, facing p. 636.

The verso of the folio containing the *reparto* for Act I has the following listing:

Rey de Françia	Belasco
Rey Alonso	Santiago
Fernán Ruiz	Granados

J makes no reference to this listing.

Act I, reparto. A variety of symbols precede the names listed: dashes, circles, triangles, X's, often superimposed on each other. Behind the names are X's, dashes, small circles joined by a dash which extends to the left (sometimes crossed by a short vertical line with another line, extending obliquely upwards from the left end of the dash, forming a "4"). A simple cross has been written between each character's name and the following, except between Ysabel and Mudarra.

Folio P, verso. Ya que ha llegado mi dia Mas Pues m Granados *(rúbrica)*; not mentioned by J.

Stage directions. Lope did not use the cross potent in stage directions at the beginning of an act. He failed to use it only once, in the directions before v. 2633.

1. Lope abbreviates characters' names when they are indicated as speakers. In addition, a name is often given in its abbreviated form for the sake of versification (e.g., Fernán-Fernando, Fortún-Fortunio). In the latter case, Lope's reading is maintained, but in the former situation, speakers' names are given in their full form.

5. *y en fin* deleted, replaced by *señor*; J proposes *yo estoy* for the deleted words. A comparison of final *-y* in vv. 1, 3, 5, initial *f-* in vv. 37, 42, 48, internal *-s-* in vv. 1, 3, 6, and *estoy* in v. 3, indicates the inaccuracy of J's reading.

9. *a esta* are written as one word, with partial blotting of the *esta* portion, not with Lope's usual circular deletion. J omits comment here.

21. M adds *os*, which alters the sense of Luis's speech. It is he who is receiving hospitality, not Alfonso. Such changes are frequently made without regard to their effect.

26-40. A horizontal line above this verse meets a vertical line in the left margin, which extends downward through v. 40. Each verse is underlined. To the left *no* has been written, probably an *autor's* indication that in a particular performance the section was to be omitted. In other performances, the section in question may or may not have been retained. In some cases, a section marked in this fashion is also omitted in the variant editions, or is changed (e.g., vv. 2713-2716, 1841-1854). These passages are often characterized by having a confusing array of *sí's* and *no's* in the margin, plus heavy underlining of the verses, making for difficulties in transcription. J has also noted this tendency in his *Observaciones preliminares*, p. 9.

27. B's *vos* is probably a printer's error.

28. MSBA's *nombre* is an unwarranted change, since Luis has just referred to Castilla. The subsequent reference to Alfonso completes a sequence which goes from the general to the particular.

41. It should be noted that in this, as in many future cases, the variants omit or change words which do not alter the meaning of a verse nor the meter (see also vv. 77, 91, 109, 114, etc.). The omission was probably an effort to avoid elision in the original verses.

46-50. A vertical line in the left margin intersects the underlining of vv. 46-50. *No* is written to the left of the passage.

51. A non-Lopean cross has been placed to the left of this verse, probably to indicate that the text was to be followed again; J indicates alignment of the cross with v. 50.

56-75. Each verse is underlined, with a vertical line along the left margin. *No* appears in the left margin at v. 60 and again at v. 74 on the following folio. The underlined section of folio 2r has been damaged by water or ink smears, presenting difficulties in transcription.

78. When two or more speakers are involved in one verse, Lope did not start a new line for each. For the sake of regularity, each time there is a change of speaker a new line is begun.

81. *español* deleted, replaced by *es Español*.

82. *pa* (?) deleted before *se*.

83. *y* (?) *del* deleted, replaced by *Su; Franzés* deleted after *pecho*, with *en crisol* added after *es oro*.

84. *desta que* written and deleted after *y sólo*, twice; J proposes *deste q̄* for the first deletion and *dese q̄* for the second.

86-90. Completely boxed from the text, with very light underlining visible, from contact with the previous page, which was heavily underlined in the corresponding section; J fails to note this underlining.

100. *hablad delante los dos* changed to *delante hablad de los dos; de* is formed by use of the unaltered portion of *delante* in the original.

102-105. A rough simple cross and *sí* appear in the left margin, a large *sí* in the right. A horizontal line above the verse joins the usual vertical line which extends to v. 105, where it is intersected by a short dash. J mentions only one *ṡi*.

104. *con el silenzio,* written in the margin, is followed by the deletion *mi pecho* (?); J proposes no solution for the deletion.

106. A cross potent in the left margin indicates resumption of the text after the above boxed-off section; J omits mention of the cross.

111-115. Boxed off at the left, top and bottom; *diçe* in the left margin is heavily smudged, with *diçese* written directly below it. J reads *No* for *diçe* (a printer's error continues the word *tachado* in italics, as if it were part of J's report of the marginal note). Close scrutiny shows that the initial letter of the smudged word and the *di-* of *diçese* below are identical, leading to the proposal of *diçe* for the notation. J does not indicate that there are three groupings of verses separated from the text in the section 111-130.

116-121. The line making the separation of the previous section meets a vertical line in the left margin, distinct from that of the above passage. A simple cross appears in the left margin even with v. 116. J omits reference to the cross.

122-130. A vertical line in the left margin, extending from the top of the page to v. 130 (which is underlined) separates this passage from the text. A large cross is opposite v. 126 in the left margin, above a large *sí*. A word in the margin before *por* of v. 128 is heavily smudged, making it illegible. J does not mention this marginal deletion.

126. *fingi* deleted at the beginning of the verse, then written at the end of the line, to rhyme with *ti* (v. 128) and *mí* (v. 130). Since the line follows the marginal limits of previous and following verses, this change was most likely made at the moment of composition, as Lope was deciding what information to present in the following lines, and how to express it. MSBA omit this passage, depriving the audience of the specific connection between Alfonso's inquiry into the reasons for Luis's apparent unhappiness, the latter's initial answer, and then his true reason for making his pilgrimage. Clarity is important at this point to establish motives for the audience.

131. A cross in the left margin indicates the resumption of the text after the separation of the above passage.

134. *mi* deleted at the end of the verse, but is used to begin the following; J omits reference to this deletion.

138. *v[uest]ra* deleted, replaced by *tu*.

162. Deleted, replaced by *en paz a perpetua guerra.*

176-200. The entire page is boxed off, with a smaller section at the top divided from the rest of the page. *No* is in the left margin eight times, crossed out six times, once written heavily over *sí*; J notes only three *no*'s.

One other *sí* is in the left margin, and an enormous one in the right margin. A cross is in the upper left at v. 181.

187. (?) *qual le ves* deleted, replaced by *de ygual poder.* The change is important for Fortunio's following argument that he did not flee from Spain because of cowardice, but that his service to Luis was of a legitimate nature. J proposes *tal qual le ves* for the deleted portion.

192. *del Cid y* deleted, replaced by *El Rey de. El* (?) deleted, replaced by *deziende.* J proposes *el primero* for the second deletion.

194. *que ofende* (?) *es el decoro* deleted, replaced by *y esto no inporta al decoro.* J proposes *más el decoro* for the deleted section, indicating that the first portion was undecipherable.

196. Word deleted after *que.*

199. *de ser bueno y capitan* deleted, *ser capitan* beneath it deleted, replaced by *de ser bueno y ser guzman.* The original line would involve exact rhyme with v. 197.

201. A cross, underlined, appears in the left margin.

203. *q̃* is written in the far left margin.

210. Word deleted before *mengua,* could be *Mengua* (?).

211-12. B's alteration results in nonsense verse.

227. Lope apparently wrote *al,* then changed it to read *lui.*

235. MSBA make Fortunio appear worse than he is accused of being.

249. *Soto* crossed out in the left margin; J interprets the deletion as *solo.*

251. *su ma* deleted at the beginning of the line, probably intended to be *su magestad,* which is placed at the end, to begin a new set of *quintillas.* This line begins a boxed-off section, with lines at the top, right and left margins, and the bottom, running through v. 260. Underlining appears for vv. 251-55. *No* is to the left of the passage three times, crossed out twice; *sí* twice, both lined through. J notes only one *sí* in the left margin. To the right a large *sí* is lined through twice, a *no* written directly above it.

254. A cross is to the left of this line.

260. *Maria* is in the left margin, in a hand other than Lope's; *y* deleted before *corra;* J does not mention these notations.

262. A cross, directly under *alon,* in the far left margin; not noted by J.

271. This line starts a boxed-off section, with lines at the top, bottom and sides, through v. 275. A large *sí* is in both margins, a *no* is crossed out between vv. 272-73, a cross is in the left margin between vv. 273-74. A printer's error continues J's *substituido* in italics, as if it were part of his notation of marginal writing. J does not note the large *sí* in the right margin.

275. *deçi* (?) deleted at the beginning of the line; J proposes *Decid.*

290-302. These verses are underlined. A wavy marginal line at the left runs from v. 291 to v. 295. A straight line continues through to v. 302. Two short vertical lines appear at the end of v. 293. To the left of v. 294 there is a V, with a short underline from its point, extending to the right; J notes: "... hay algo que parece una Y." A large *no* is written to the left of v. 298.

292. Menéndez y Pelayo (*Ac.*, VIII, p. 334b, n. 1), indicates that B has *Anzures*, while it actually shows *Ançures*, as do MS. The autograph reads *Ansures*. While J has noted *Ruiz* for *Rui*, vv. 171, 216, and *Constanza* for *Costanza*, vv. 279, 304, he does not note A's rendering of *Ansurez* for *Ansures*.

294. *fue hija del* replaced by *fue hija doña*. Lope evidently decided to provide Sancha's name for Luis before continuing with her lineage; J notes *Fue hija de* for this deletion.

300. *pues* deleted at the beginning of the line.

312. Deletion after *es;* possibly Lope left out a letter of *religiosa* and re-wrote?

Stage directions. The stage directions before v. 321 are set off from the text by a line at the top and at the bottom; sometimes Lope used a continuous line for this type of separation, but often an interrupted one. No further note will be made of this practice.

321. MSBA's change from "to sum up" to "at last, finally," is uncalled for, and indicates a mis-interpretation of this device to indicate that conversation has been in progress.

324. MSBA obscure the clarity of the original here by elimination of what *onrra* conquered.

328. Word deleted at the beginning of the line; J's proposed solution is *pues*. MSBA's alteration makes an illogical allusion to royalty.

329. Deletion at the beginning of the line; J proposes *no.*

331. MSBA evidently consider that Fernán's outburst was a manifestation of insanity, or that he lost consciousness.

348. MSBA anticipate a conjugal situation.

369. *aq[ue]sta manera* deleted after *de;* changes to a *rima aguda.* J suggests *aunq̄ est* ... as a resolution of the deleted section.

381. *guerra y en paz* replaced by *toda Castilla.* The new reading provides a contrast with Africa (geographically), and implies the war versus peace image stated specifically in the original reading.

402. Deletion after *en* and after *tu;* J proposes *en la tuya.*

412. Menéndez y Pelayo (*Ac.*, VIII, p. 335b, n. 1), says "Rayo, dice la primera edición pero en este caso me parece preferible el texto de

Barcelona (brazo)." Actually, the autograph and MSA have *brazo,* while B has *rayo.*

415. *a detener* replaced by *a conuertir.*

419. *por* deleted at the beginning of the line, for the sake of versification. J proposes a deleted *Pues,* but a close comparison of this deletion and Lope's *porq̃* of v. 413 shows the same type of connecting line between *por* and *q̃* in both instances. In addition, the deleted word does not occupy sufficient space for a four-letter word such as *pues.*

423. MSBA's change destroys the meaning of the simile.

430. Deletion before *entre.*

434. Several words deleted after *le.* J shows *mo[do],* which, though smeared, is clearly *modo* in the autograph.

449. *pues por Dios* replaced by *pues a fe,* avoids repetition of v. 445.

460. Lope's image is destroyed by MSBA'S change.

473. A's oversight in directing Fernán's remark to Alfonso is startling in its implications.

478. MSBA's reading is not consistent with the previous action.

497. J does not note A's variant reading *Prendedle,* nor does he provide exit directions for Fernán's departure, which Lope omitted.

507. *Rei* precedes *Alfo,* which is altered by the addition of an *o* after *l,* in a hand other than Lope's; J does not record this marginal notation.

510. Deletion after *te;* J proposes *me* as a solution. As in cases mentioned above, a printer's error was not corrected; J's *Falta* is included in italics as if it were part of the textual variant.

515-16. Boxed off from the text and separated from the following six verses (which have also been marked for omission).

517-22. A large *sí* is in the left margin at v. 517. Although the initial letter of *huelgo* has been tampered with, not necessarily by Lope, G's transcription *huelgo* supports the reading suggested here rather than J's *güelgo.* These lines are separated from the text by vertical lines in the right and left margins, and a horizontal line between vv. 516 and 517.

521-22. There is marginal writing at the lower right of the page; smudges make transcription difficult, but *2ª,* closed off on the top, left and bottom, followed by *no puede ser* are visible. *No* appears in the left margin at v. 521; J does not refer to these marginal additions.

523-24. Marked for omission by a vertical line in the left margin and light underlining under v. 524.

525. *Rey* (?) deleted at the beginning of the line; J proposes no solution for this deletion.

530. A cross appears in the far left margin.

531. *vn fabor me* replaced by *vna mrd me. habría* changed to *has;* J proposes *habéis.*

553. *Quiso* deleted before *Arias; dar* after *Gonzalo;* J suggests *Quien* and *armó* (?) for the deletions.

556. *por salir a pelear* replaced by *y a la canpaña salio.* The deletion separates *canpa-ña; a pelear* is not deleted in Lope's usual manner. J's version of the deletion is *para salir a pelear.* In this case the configuration of the deleted letters suggests *por* rather than *para.* J's note offers *campa,* although he correctly transcribes *canpaña* in the text.

568. J does not record A's omission of *os* in this verse.

581. In the stage directions before this verse, J renders *[T]odos se van [y Y]sabel . . . ,* although the elements in brackets are clear in the manuscript; the connecting *y* before *Ysabel* is unnecessary.

589. A large *sí* is written in the left margin; J does not record this marginal notation.

595. MSBA would have Ysabel and Fortunio be middle-aged by their indication that Ysabel has known and loved him secretly for ten years.

597-604. This passage is boxed off for omission; two large *sí's* are in the left margin, between which is a large *no,* lined through twice.

606. The *s* of J's *quizio[s]* is clear in the autograph.

607. The *ntos* of J's *vie[ntos]* is clear in the autograph.

608. The *cios* of J's *frontispi[cios]* is clear in the autograph.

609. The *s* of J's *atento[s]* is clear in the autograph.

610. The *ios* of J's *ofiç[ios]* is clear in the autograph.

612. Deletion before *entrañas.*

622. Deletion at the beginning of the line; J suggests *quiebren.*

Folio 12 v. Random lines appear in the upper-left corner of the page; J omits mention of them.

639. B makes a place name of Durandarte by replacing *tu* with *a.*

653. *tanto* deleted before *la; quiere* deleted before *amorosa.* J was unable to decipher the second deletion.

Stage directions. The stage directions before v. 685 are separated from the text by interrupted underlining, ending in the Z figure described by Fichter (*El sembrar en buena tierra,* p. 2 and Notes, pp. 177-78), indicating that the stage is empty at this point; J does not note the Z. J brackets the first letter of four words, but in all cases the autograph is clear.

692. A printer's error in B?

700. A cross in the left margin; the last three vv. of the page are underlined, intersecting with a vertical line in the left margin. The underlining is continued through v. 709. MSBA omit 700-704 of this passage.

706. *astros* (?) deleted, replaced by *otros.* J suggests no solution for this deletion.

710. There is a cross in the left margin indicating resumption of the text after the above passage; J places the cross at v. 709.

712. *que me quieres* replaced by *de mi que infieres.*

715-722. Boxed off and underlined for omission. There is a profusion of *sí*'s and *no*'s to the left of the section, one *no* to the right. MSBA omit 715-19 of this section.

725-734. Underlined and boxed off from the text. A heavy *sí* is written over a *no* in the left margin; J inaccurately indicates that this section begins at v. 726.

733. *pues mas o menos* replaced by *pues vna materia,* which is more in keeping with the point that he is making in comparing Abdelmón's creation with that of Alá, making it more definite.

735-44. Underlined and boxed off from the text. *No* appears in both margins.

742. *e:ta de ti* (?) deleted at the beginning of the line; J suggests *Estás* for the first word, and proposes no solution for the remainder of the deletion.

745. *alb,* indicating the speaker, is repeated unnecessarily here. The hand resembles Lope's *alb* of vv. 690 and 687, but could be that of the person who marked the previous section for omission. *Sí* appears to the left of the section; J omits reference to the marginal *sí*.

748. *que a los cristianos con el* deleted after *del.*

750. Deletion after *solo;* J suggests the original version *A Dios.*

758. J does not record A's reading *la da.*

760. J does not record A's reading *será acierto.*

762. B's alteration results in nonsense.

765-69. This passage is separated from the text by short vertical and horizontal lines in the upper and lower left margin. *Sí* is written to the left of the section; J inaccurately refers to a *sí* in the right margin.

779. A heavy line runs from left to right under this verse. A large *no* is written after *Lisardo* in the stage directions immediately following, separated from the name by a vertical slash; J does not mention this *no*.

780. The line begins a long section in which each verse is underlined, with a vertical line at the left margin, through v. 825. A simple cross is to the left of *alm* at v. 780; J does not refer to the cross.

783. *No* is crossed out to the left of *lis.* A's rendition indicates the probably unconscious modernization of the text.

787. *No* is lined through in the left margin; J does not record this *no*.

788. *ordenan* (?) deleted before *intentan.*

789. The *o* of J's *conçiert[o]* is clear in the autograph.

791. *zerb* is lined through, *alm* written to the left, not in Lope's hand. Gálvez shows Zerbino as the speaker; J does not mention these marginal notes.

795. S's reading is nonsense.

806. *do* is written directly above *m.* Menéndez y Pelayo (*Ac.*, VIII, p. 340a, n. 1) records *surco* for B, but MSBA all show *curso.*

812. MSBA destroy Lope's forceful image, replacing it with nonsense.

815. M's reading may be a printer's error; if not, the image of a *yugo temeroso* stretches poetic imagination.

816. A small, curved vertical line, intersected by a short line to the right, is written to the left of *almo,* with an *x* directly below the speaker's name. J does not record these notations, nor note A's assignment of Zayde as speaker.

822. J does not record Zerbino as speaker in A.

824. B's referent is questionable. Another printer's error?

829. *es por es* deleted at the beginning of the line, possibly the beginning of *eso* (?); J suggests *el pa . . . es.*

830. The *e* of *tres* has been altered to resemble an *a,* but other samples of *tres* tend to corroborate this reading (v. 992, etc.). Other instances of this type of alteration occur (e. g., *tendréla,* v. 1710). G reads *tres;* J does not refer to this alteration.

834. In the left margin there is a cross with deleted writing immediately below, too smudged to decipher. To the far left is a *rúbrica* of complicated form, appearing to be a *D* over interlacing lines. None of these are Lope's; J does not mention the *rúbrica.*

862. *es* replaced by *llaman,* which is then used to rhyme with v. 865, *ynfaman;* J suggests no solution for the deletion.

885. *y es* (?) *onbre de gran sujeto* is replaced by *desde agora le prometo.* Mudarra thus continues his *mona* topic, rather than reacting to what Fernán is saying concerning the Miramamolín; J suggests *y es entre . . . sujeto.*

891. *nu* deleted before *jamas,* probably intended to be *nunca.*

894. This line begins a long underlined passage, with a vertical line in the left margin, extending to v. 941. J indicates inaccurately that the marked passage begins at v. 892 and continues through v. 942.

895. What appears to be *lea* has been blotted out, and *alb* substituted, not in Lope's hand. This occurs again in vv. 963, 964, 968, 971 and 984. It is difficult to determine whether the substitutions are all Lope's or not. Since Learín appears in the stage directions, it would seem to follow that it is his name that should be used, not Albumasar's. This is substantiated by G's reading of Learín in all the above-mentioned cases. J, however, reads *Alc.*, and uses this designation in the indicated verses. He refers to an *alcalde,* instead of an *alcayde* in his note on p. 45. He also omits this verse number on p. 43.

899. Lope abbreviated *cristiano* as *Xpiano,* so it is resolved in the text without brackets; J transcribes *Xtiano.*

912. *en* altered to read *a.*

962. Every line from this point to the end of the act (v. 1019) is underlined, including the stage directions. A vertical line at the left margin is interrupted only at those points where it would cross through a line of stage directions.

976. J did not correct a printer's error which renders *Falta* in italics in his note.

Stage directions. The *s* of J's *uno[s]* in the stage directions before v. 990 is clear in the autograph.

992. The last word is not shown completely, due to a tear in the manuscript. However, context calls for the reading *quatro,* which G also has; J does not refer to this difficulty.

994. FERNAN RUIZ is printed in heavy capital letters; illegible writing under *RU.*

995. J does not record A's variants here.

998. J does not record A's variants here.

1000. J does not show that A designates Zayde as speaker here.

1001. *lis* is blotted, another hand has written *Lis* to the left, below an *x.* Deletion after *Fez.*

1003. J omits A's addition of instructions here.

1005. The second speaker's name has been heavily blotted out, *alb* substituted above it (by Lope?). G records *Albumasar.*

1006. *lis* has been blotted out, which would make his speech a continuation of the previous speaker's, the substituted *alb.* This is G's reading.

1007. Deletion before *no;* J does not note this deletion.

1015. *almo* has been written above *lis,* in what seems to be a hand other than Lope's; *lis* has not been crossed out. GJ record *almo* as the speaker here. The repetition of *Lis* as speaker in the next line becomes unnecessary.

1016. J does not record the assignment of *¿Quién vive?* to Andelmón in A.

1017. A heavily inked cross, not Lope's, is in the left margin. The arms are elongated, unlike any other appearance of the symbol. Below the right arm, *fer* is unnecessarily duplicated, possibly by Lope.

1018. The *d* of *defendamos* is written over Lope's abbreviation *q̃*. This is not noted by J.

Folio 18r. Act I's last folio is filled with dialogue, leaving no space for Lope's usual *Fin de Acto* indication.

Act. II, reparto. Like the symbols described earlier for the *reparto* to Act I, this one shows the simple cross between characters' names, but only for the first four, and again between Ordoño and Fernán. Circles with "tails" appear after seven names, heavy slash marks are after ten names. A cross is written before Ramiro de Guzmán and Sancho Laynez, with dashes preceding the other names, except for the Alguazil and the Cochero, which are both lined out, corresponding to the lined out passage in which they were to appear at the end of Act II. *Dentro* (the voice of the *tornera*), Dama 1ª and Dama 2ª do not appear in the *reparto* (see v. 1238 and v. 1719). J also notes the intention of deleting roles and scenes; see his *Observaciones preliminares,* p. 9.

1035-46. Boxed off from the text, *no* written in the left margin at v. 1040; v. 1039 underlined.

1047-1069. Boxed off from the text, two large *no*'s appear in the left margin at vv. 1055 and 1062; v. 1069 underlined.

1057. MSBA's change presents the strange image of a *carro español,* which has no meaning in the context.

1058. Though it appears to be *al,* tampering with the manuscript is obvious, much in the same manner as *tres* of v. 830. G reflects uncertainty with writing which could be interpreted as an *a* or an *e;* J makes no note of this tampering.

1063. Deletion before *tus;* J suggests *Vros.* as the reading.

1075. A horizontal line at the top of the page joins a vertical wavy line in the left margin, which extends to v. 1084, and is underlined. A large *no* appears in the left margin at vv. 1079-80.

1080. *ymposible* replaced by *grande exçeso.*

1082. *con* (?) *mi poder inbenzible* (?) *a lo que profeso / ni el que al sol le quita el carro,* deleted, replaced with the more ordered *ni llebar, aunque vil peso / al que al sol le quita el carro.* J proposes . . . *ni q̃ al sol* . . . and . . . *con el balor q̃ profeso.*

1087. J adds *h* to *hoy,* without providing brackets.

1090. *no* deleted in the left margin, not noted by J.

1094. J does not italicize A's variant reading here.

1100. A line above this verse intersects a vertical wavy line which extends to v. 1102. J omits A's variant reading *José.*

1103-04. Separated from the text by lines above and below. J records *amándole* in v. 1103, but the autograph clearly reads *amandola,* which is corroborated by G.

1110-14. Boxed off from the text, *no* blotted out in the left margin.

1112. MSB misinterpret Lope's *ara* as a future of *hacer,* which then results in nonsense verse.

1115. A cross is written in the left margin. To the left of it is a smudged *sí.*

1118. *Ordoño* has been altered by a hand other than Lope's, but is still legible. J accepts the alteration as Lope's, proposing *el día* as the deleted words, or *El signo* as the deletion, and as a consequence is required to add *[en]* to lend coherence to the speech, which is still awkward. MSBAG support a reading of *Ordoño* here.

1123. *la* (?) deleted after *no.*

1128. MSBA have Alfonso give an order that Ordoño be called in order to bless the couple. See the Notes to the Text.

1143. MSBA's alteration makes no sense.

1147. Deletion after *se.*

1150-59. Boxed off from the text. A second vertical line in the left margin joins the underlining of v. 1158. Three *sí*'s appear in the right, three in the left margin. Three *no*'s in the left, one in the right margin; J mentions only one *sí* and only three *no*'s. A omits v. 1151.

1170-75. Boxed off from the text, *no* written in the left margin.

1180. The stage directions preceding this verse show the underlining which ends in the symbol described in n. 685, used when the stage is left empty. J does not refer to this symbol.

1209. *con* replaced by *yo;* it is then placed after *yo.*

1212. J does not record A's variant reading *en quien.*

1221. Menéndez y Pelayo (*Ac.,* VIII, p. 345a, n. 1) shows *ha hecho* for B. In reality, B reads *hizo;* the autograph and MSA have *ha hecho.*

1238. There is no indication in the *reparto* for the voice of the *tornera,* represented as *Dentro.*

1243. *la criada o la señora* replaced by *o el laberinto de Troya.*

1244. The form *vusted* which MBA give was first observed in 1619 in the *Diálogo* by Juan de Luna (see Pla Cárceles, "La evolución del tratamiento 'vuestra merced,'" *RFE,* X [1923], p. 265n).

1261. Deletion before *amen.*

1276. S asks a strange question of the *tornera* here. Her answer, if given, would be "Jesús".

1283. *le dio* replaced by *llebó.*

1330. *dezir* deleted after *sirbe.*

Folio 6 r. Random marks appear in the lower right margin.

1332-41. A wavy line to the left, a curved line to the right, and underlining of v. 1341 separate this section from the text. A large *NO* is written in the left margin at vv. 1336-37.

1333. J does not record A's transposition of *ya* in this verse.

1342-43. A cross is written to the left of each of these lines.

1348-59. Ditto marks appear to the left of each line. A large number symbol is written to the left of vv. 1351-52. MSBA omit vv. 1352-55.

1355. The autograph clearly reads *varios;* compare with *ello* of v. 1241, where the *o* of *ello* connects with *es* following; J reads *varias.*

1356. *amor* (?) replaced by *temor,* which reveals better the tenor of Fernán's feelings, in keeping with *sospecha, çelos,* etc. J does not suggest a solution here.

1361. *pinta* (?) deleted at the beginning of the line. MSBA omit this verse.

1366. J omits reference to A's variant reading of *amor.*

1375. *vealo* (?) *en sus letras* replaced by *si ves en ellas.* J suggests *Viendo las letras.*

1378-85. MSBA's omission of this passage was possibly in answer to a lack of understanding of what it meant within the larger context of Fernán's speech.

1381. *llegar* replaced by *pasar,* since Fortún did arrive, but did not enter the city.

1388. The variants make an illogical alteration here, as if Fernán was to remain dressed in his Moorish costume. The tone suggests that Mudarra is about to be punished. The underlining of the verse is not noted by J.

1389. Underlined; not noted by J.

1403. A short vertical line at the left margin intersects with a short horizontal line under the first word of this verse. The same notation is made at v. 1411, giving the appearance of a section marked for possible omission; not noted by J.

1411. J does not note A's variant reading of this verse.

1416. Underlined; J notes only that A omits the first *que,* not referring to the underlining or the omission of the second *que.*

1417. Shows an underlining consisting of a long dash, a wavy line, then another long dash, etc.

1429. J omits A's variant.

1442. Originally *quedizes,* an *s* inserted between the *e* and *d, lo q̃* written above the line, reading *que [e]s lo que dizes.* The variant readings, especially G, have different solutions; J adds the *e* without providing brackets.

1444. *le* (?) deleted at the beginning of the line; J does not suggest a solution.

1447. The second *r* of *honrreme* is written above the line.

1457. The context and the autograph call for a feminine demonstrative here, the referent being *esposa;* G supports the reading *aquellas* versus J's *aquellos.*

1471. Deletion after *sobre;* J suggests *borde* as the original.

1479. Deletion at the beginning of the line.

1489. *no prosigo* (?) deleted after *fort,* replaced by *perdon pido.*

1504. A slash is written after the first *soy;* J does not note this.

1512. MSBA miss the point that the original makes, that Fortunio had not courted Estefanía as Fernán had.

1517. The word order in MSBA's rendition of this verse is strange.

1523. J does not refer to A's reading *¡Ah . . .!,* which effects a basic change of meaning if accepted.

1536. Mudarra uses a third person, not speaking directly to Ysabel. A possible *s* on *ve* is heavily blotted, not noted by J.

1537. The *o* of *con* seems to have been the circle of Lope's *q̃,* not noted by J. The *c* has been written as a capital letter, the lower circle merging with the tail of the *q̃.*

1558. J inaccurately indicates that the long section of changes in the text which begins here, as reflected in A, begins at v. 1557.

1566-87. Boxed off from the text; four *no*'s appear in the left margin, *esto se dice* at v. 1570 in the left margin, a cross below it at v. 1574. MSBA omit vv. 1568-75 and 1579-84.

1567. *para* (?) *que* deleted at the beginning of the line; J suggests *Porq̄,* though the *a* is clear, and space considerations indicate something more than *Por-.*

1578. *a la* deleted at the beginning of the line; not noted by J. His note to v. 1584 reads "A *la,* ídem.,", probably referring to this note, which was not included; there is no deletion in v. 1584.

1583. *cay perdi las* replaced by *dexe; y* (?) replaced by *perdi estribos,* which elaborates more in detail Fortunio's fall; J inaccurately notes these deletions as appearing in v. 1593.

1585. *pero si* deleted at the beginning of the line.

1586. *he* is clearly absent before *podido* in the autograph. GJ have probably corrected Lope's line unconsciously.

1593. A short horizontal line above this verse joins a vertical line in the left margin, which extends to v. 1607. A simple cross below an 8 (?)

is to the left of v. 1594, *sí* written under the right arm of the cross. A large asterisk is found in the right margin between vv. 1606-07. J does not mention the cross.

1608. *For* is repeated in the left margin, not in Lope's hand; this verse begins after the section marked off from the text, described above in n. 1593.

1609. *hable* deleted at the beginning of the line.

1613. *za* deleted after *noble;* J suggests no solution for the deletion.

1648. *For* is repeated in the margin here, in a hand other than Lope's. A simple cross appears to the left. J accepts the writing as Lope's and omits mention of the cross.

1653. *pidele por cortesia* appears at the right of this line. An *autor* has boxed off the section between this line and v. 1693, writing the cue line for the next speech to be used. vv. 1653-67 are completely boxed off, with four *sí*'s in the right margin, two in the left, and a *no* between the latter two. MSBA's omission has the effect of making Fortún accept too quickly the offer which Ysabel is making him, destroying the dramatic suspense of the original.

1661. *pero es justo que me quiera* replaced by *oja a los uientos ligera,* in keeping with the image of woman's *mudanza* which Lope has been developing.

1668-77. A large asterisk in the left margin at v. 1668 interrupts the vertical line which continues from the previous passage; v. 1676 is underlined; J does not note the asterisk nor the underlining.

1670. *estimada* deleted after *que;* J proposes *está rendida.*

1678-82. Boxed off from the text, v. 1681 is underlined; not noted by J.

1683. A large asterisk in the left margin is joined by a line which descends from it, curves upward, then down again; J does not note the marginal writings, and states inaccurately that this verse is underlined.

1687. J does not record A's variant reading.

1693. *de parte mia* is replaced by *por cortesia;* there is a large asterisk in the left margin even with this verse, not mentioned by J. MSBA's shifting of verses from one place in the text to another responds to no apparent logic, nor does it enhance the reading.

1694. *vn cordon* is deleted at the beginning of the line. J's indication that A omits *un* is inaccurate; see below, n. 1695.

1695. J does not indicate that A omits *un;* an error in line identification.

1696. *escuche mi pasion* (?) replaced by *goze la ocasion;* J suggests *pensión.*

1697. There is a simple cross in the left margin, not noted by J.

1698-1702. Boxed off from the text, a large *no* written over a smaller *no* at v. 1699, in the left margin; J notes only one *no.*

1706. Deletion after *estas.*

1709. *el cabello* pluralized to *los cabellos;* J does not note.

1710. *tendrela* altered to *tendrala;* see n. 830 and n. 1058 for similar changes that were probably not made by Lope. J does not note.

1716. *ya me Vene* (?) replaced by *oy me Vengo;* J suggests *Ya me ven . . .*

1719. *Or* altered to read *1ª d[am]a.*

1721. *Dama 2ª* altered to read *Nuño,* not in Lope's hand.

1726. In the stage directions before this verse J adds an *y* before *Ramiro* without adding brackets. *Dama 1ª* altered to read *Ram* as speaker here, not noted by J.

1732. *fort* appears to the left of *Ra,* not in Lope's hand, not mentioned by J.

1745. Deletion at the beginning of the line; J proposes *la de.*

1750. J fails to correct a printer's error which records *Falta* in italics as if it were part of A's variant reading.

1757. Deletion at the beginning of the line; J proposes *gala.*

1762. A word has been added to the line *(con[?]),* but it is omitted to maintain the rhyme pattern and the syllable count; J fails to note the addition.

1764. Underlined, with a vertical line in the left margin which runs from the top to the bottom of the page. A large *sí* is written in the lower left margin.

1765. *que es esto çielo* is underlined, separating it from the following stage directions, but the rest of the line is not. The second half of the line is assigned to a *dama,* the original speaker's name is written over; J notes only that section 1765-90 is separated from the text.

Stage directions. Only *dentro ruido* of the stage directions before v. 1766 have underscoring. A short vertical line in the left margin intersects the underlining of v. 1765 and that of the stage directions; J does not note.

1767. *Nuño* is written over another speaker's name.

1770. *Dama 2ª* is written over *Nuño;* J suggests no solution.

1771. *y se le* (?) replaced by *haçia nosotros. Dama 1ª* is written over *Ord;* J suggests *y se lebanta.*

1772. There is a slash after *pareze.* J fails to note that A assigns this line to Ordoño.

1780. Deletion after *en;* the verse is underlined. J proposes *Mar* for the deletion.

1781. The verse is underlined.

1792. The speaker's name has been altered by a hand other than Lope's. It was originally *Ra*, with an *f* placed between the two letters; it is resolved as *Ramiro*, which Gálvez also has. J omits the speaker designation, thus continuing Mudarra's speech, and suggests no resolution for the speaker designation. His statement that the sense of the speech indicates that it should belong to Mudarra is not necessarily true. Since Mudarra was at the scene, it may be presumed he was aware of Fernán's orders, but Ramiro was not present, and might be expected to make this observation, and then ask this question.

1810. Illegible writing to the left of *nu*, which has been lined through; not mentioned by J.

Folio 14 v. At the bottom of this folio there appears *fin de 2ª*, written in a hand other than Lope's. The act could have conceivably been ended at this point, but it would then eliminate the background information concerning the *moros almohades* and Alfonso's preparation for battle, which explains Fernán's absence in Act III. The additional *malos agüeros* would also not appear, nor Alfonso's reaction to them.

Stage directions. In the directions before v. 1822 there is a deletion after *entrense*. J proposes *Y salga*. J brackets *[e]ntrense* and *[F]ernán;* both letters are visible in the autograph.

1828. A short horizontal line intersects a short vertical line in the left margin; J does not note.

1830-37. Boxed off from the text.

1840. A line above *or. — otro ruido* joins a line under the first part of the speech; a vertical line extends from the cross in the left margin to the bottom of the page. The stage directions and vv. through 1854 are lined through. *No* appears in the left margin between vv. 1842-43. J reads *Alguaçil* in the directions, though the manuscript clearly has *alguaçiles.* MSBA omit this scene entirely.

1851. J's *stro* of *Ca[stro]* is clear in the manuscript.

1855. There is a large cross in the left margin, indicating resumption of the text after the preceding passage, which was to be omitted. J places the cross at v. 1854.

1856. J's *o* of *Ramir[o]* is clear in the manuscript. *Laynez* is written over *Ram;* J suggests the original was *Ramírez*, but the *-nez* of *Laynez* is plainly not overwriting.

1857. There is a deletion in the middle of the word *cordoba.*

1859. J omits A's variant reading *¿Qué hay de la frontera?*

1864. Menéndez y Pelayo (*Ac.*, VIII, p. 352a, n. 1) records *Zamora* for B, while it really has *Azamor,* as do SAGJ and the autograph; M has *Zamora.*

1866. Deletion between *Be* and *n* of *Ben Zayde.* J lists A's variant reading as appearing in v. 1886.

1868. Deletion before *hijo;* not noted by J.

1870. A short line above *como* intersects a short vertical line in the left margin.

1871. A short line above *de* joins a vertical line in the left margin, which extends to the bottom of the page. *No* is in the left margin at v. 1872; not noted by J.

1879. A vertical line runs from the top of the page through v. 1896, which has the start of underscoring. A short horizontal line crosses the vertical line at v. 1881; *no* is written in the left margin at v. 1891, but J locates it inaccurately at vv. 1893-96.

1891. Deletion at the beginning of the line.

1896. J omits A's variant reading *es ya.*

1901. *d* deleted before the speaker indication *alf;* not noted by J.

1906. Deletion after *azero;* J suggests *mármol.*

1913. *x* is written to the left of *ra;* not noted by J.

1919. *Sí* is written in the left margin. Lope changed *or* to read *Laynez.*

1924. *caballos* appears between slash marks; *y* before *infantes* written twice.

Act III, reparto. The symbols used in Acts I and II are present in this *reparto* also. There is a dash before each name (in some cases several). There is a circle with a line extending from it after each name except Fernán Ruiz de Castro, Mudarra, and Rey Alfonso. After Olfos and Ordoño a vertical line crosses that from the circle. The circles after Bermudo and Ximeno are joined by a line extending to the right, meeting a vertical line at mid-point. The *soldado* of the last scene is not indicated in the *reparto.* J does not note the foregoing.

Folio Pªr. The dialogue on this page is boxed off at the top and sides; v. 1940 is further set apart with horizontal lines which meet the vertical lines of the margins. In the left margin there is a *no* at v. 1934, *sí*'s at vv. 1940 and 1943. A *sí* appears in the right margin at v. 1945. MSBA omit 1933-36 and 1941-52. J notes only one *sí.*

1939. MSBA's alteration makes no sense.

1944. *se* of *tratase* is written above the line, replacing what appears to be the deletion of *de.*

1950. There is a word deleted at the beginning of the line.

1953. Marginal lines set off the dialogue of this page to v. 1972; no line at the top, indicating a continuous deletion from the previous page. There is a non-Lopean cross to the left of v. 1965 with a vertical line descending to v. 1968, and then under it. MSBA omit 1953-68. J does not note the additional section set off from the text.

1974. Menéndez y Pelayo (*Ac.*, VIII, p. 353a, n. 1) reads *habré* for B; the autograph and BAG have *auia* (or spelling variants thereof), MS read *aura*.

1989. The middle of *escala* has been deleted. In the left margin a piece of paper has been attached to the manuscript; J does not use italics for *escala* in his note.

1992. There is a small deletion at the beginning of the line; J inaccurately identifies this deletion as appearing in v. 1991.

2009-10. These lines are separated from the text by lines at the left, top and bottom. *No* is written in the left margin.

2011. A heavy vertical line runs from the top of the page to v. 2020, intersecting with the underlining of each verse. The lines under 2012 and 2016 are joined at the right by a loop; a heavy *no* almost obliterates the *sí* under it (to the left of v. 2015). Another *no* in the left margin between vv. 2016-17 has been crossed out. Immediately below it there is a simple cross with an extended right arm which crosses the vertical line from the top of the page, almost reaching the first word of v. 2017. A large *sí* is directly below the cross. For the marginal notations, J notes merely: "En el margen: *No, Sí.*"

2015. *fue* deleted after *fiar*, maintaining the elliptical construction of the previous verse; J suggests no solution.

2041. J changes Lope's verse to *le*, stating: "Lope escribió *le* en vez de *la* por equivocación." This type of change in the text is not consistent with the goals of a paleographic edition.

2046. In the right margin there is a sign with the appearance of an asterisk with a tail extending from it to the right.

2047. J does not note A's variant reading *puede*.

2058. J's note of A's variant does not specify that it is the first *y* that is omitted.

2080. A vertical line in the left margin extends to v. 2096, with horizontal lines above v. 2080 and under v. 2096, which join the vertical line. vv. 2089-92 are also underlined, with an asterisk to the right of v. 2091. A *no* is written to the left of v. 2085, a simple cross below it.

2104. Broken underlining separates v. 2104 from the following stage directions.

2115. Deletion at the beginning of the verse.

2120. J does not report the assignment of A's altered line to Fernán.

2145. This and the following three verses are underlined.

2152. The stage directions in this folio are enclosed in a frame which is utilized in no other part of the play. It consists of a "wing" line for the top, straight lines on the sides, with 45° angles enclosing the last two letters of Ximeno. There are several small curlicues at the top and the bottom. J does not record the altered stage directions of A, nor their changed position.

2158. *fer*, appearing twice, has been blotted heavily, but is still recognizable; J does not note.

2177. *aun* is written in the right margin, not in Lope's hand, evidently to clarify the heavy over-writing of the word *aunque* in the verse.

2178. MSBA destroy the impact of the original reading.

2179. J neglects to report A's assignment of Fernán's speech to Jimeno.

2183. J repeats Lope's words instead of A's variant reading *gozo*.

2189. A deletion after *el que* es replaced by *llega a la presençia;* J suggets as the original verse *el q̄ da fin a la ausencia.*

2191. *todo amor* (?) *es todo lazos* deleted, replaced by *porque se pagan los brazos,* which is underlined, as vv. 2192, 2194, 2195 and 2196, also are.

2221. *piedras* (?) deleted before *yedras.*

2249. *si mi* (?) deleted after *honor.* Lope probably started the next speech, then realized that he had not indicated a new speaker. J suggests that Lope first wrote *Ber(mudo),* then changed the speaker. However, the first letter is obviously an S; compare with the *s* of *si* following.

2275. *ber* has been written heavily over what seems to be *xim;* not noted by J.

2288. Deletion after *y esos* replaced by *colgados pendones;* J suggests *morriones.*

2316. *y a quien le engendra tan* deleted, replaced by *y a quien se los dio tanbien;* J suggests *y a quien le ... dio tan.*

2320. J provides an additional *a* for Lope with *desta alma,* which he does not place in brackets.

2331. J does not note A's variant reading.

2334. J does not note A's variant reading.

2352. Underlined.

2360. Partially underlined; not noted by J.

2364. *mud* is written heavily over what was originally *ys.*

2371. J renders *y galga,* avoiding the word play on *ydalga.*

2390. A series of ditto marks under *Ysa* continues through v. 2402, which is underlined by a line in four sections. J records inaccurately that the ditto marks begin at v. 2389. He does not note that Lope wrote *Ysa* again at 2389, unnecessarily.

2402. *es trayçion al amor* deleted, replaced by *es ynfamia de Amor.*

2406. Underlined, even with a cross in the left margin, directly above a vertical line which runs to the end of the page. A series of three *sí*'s (the first to the left of the cross) is also in the left margin; J notes only one *sí*.

2410. MSBA show nonsense verse here.

2413. J's *e* of *pez[e]* is clear in the manuscript.

2416. Underlined, completing the passage to be omitted from the previous page. *No,* also underlined, is to the left of the section.

2425. A large *sí* has been written over a *no* in the left margin.

2429. Underlined.

2431. This line begins another boxed-off passage, separated from the text by an encircling line. Five *no*'s have been smudged out in the left margin, and possibly two in the right; J notes only one *no* and one *sí*. The text is resumed after v. 2442. MSBA omit 2431-42.

2438. Several words deleted at the beginning of the line; J proposes *Mostró.*

2442. *lo que se deben presente* replaced by *lo que se le dyo presente.* The deletion is also smudged out before v. 2443; J proposes *lo que le...*

Folio 10 r. At the top left appear several superimposed crosses, and many renderings of *olf,* blotted by circular deletion marks.

2450. A heavy line crosses the entire page here, meeting a lighter line running from the top of the page to v. 2468. A small *no* is to the left of the vertical line, even with v. 2450.

2454. *verdad* deleted after *mentira.*

2455. *no* in the left margin has been covered by a heavy circular smudge. This situation appears again next to vv. 2461 and 2465.

2463. Deletion after *aquellas.*

2467. J has picked up a *sí* from the marginal notations and included it in Lope's text, not noticing the very clear difference in handwriting. He naturally assumes then that A has omitted a *si.*

2468. A cross is in the left margin next to *olf,* at the end of the passage marked for omission.

2471. A vertical line runs from the top of the page to v. 2474 and intersects with a short line under it. *no* in the left margin has been crossed out, *sí* written above it.

2475. Lope's *q̃* has been written directly over *ya.*

2479. A *no* has been blotted out to the left of *olf;* not noted by J.

2486. A broken line from left to right, ending in a *rúbrica* in the right margin. It may be an altered Z used to indicate an empty stage. J does not note the *rúbrica.*

2488. J's *o* of *quart[o]* is clear in the autograph.

2499. J does not note A's variant reading.

2508. *real* (?) deleted after *consejo;* J proposes *escri...*

2525. Another hand has written *xim* over *ber;* J accepts the alteration as Lope's.

2538. A speaker's name (*for?*) after *vengo* has been deleted. J's *s* of *puesta[s]* is clear in the manuscript.

2539. J does not note A's variant reading *a la puerta.*

2549-50. Underlined.

2567. *Fortun con* (?) *la* deleted next to *salga* in the directions preceding this verse.

2570. *entendi* is heavily smudged.

2574. BA's omission of *a* renders the passage illogical.

2601. J's *o* of *esper[o]* is clear in the manuscript.

2607. J repeats the previous stage directions here, from v. 2601, though they are not repeated in the autograph.

2627. J fails to note A's reading *dolor* for *rigor.*

2633. Lope omits the cross potent here. J notes a lighter cross just below the stage directions; however, it is not of the same style as Lope's.

2635. J's *o* of *çiert[o]* is clear in the manuscript.

2637. The only case where G copied only part of a word. J's *o* of *desconçiert[o]* is clear in the manuscript.

2639. J's *e* of *alcagüet[e]* is clear in the manuscript.

2644. J's inaccurate reading of *atrauiese* is unfortunate, as the autograph clearly shows *atrauiesa.*

2645. MSBA's change leads to tortured syntax.

2648. J does not record A's stage directions here.

2683. Deletion before *hermosa.*

2697. A makes an arbitrary and unjustified change here.

2701. *mil consuelos* replaced by *que con velos.*

2703. Slash mark after *bien.*

2713-16. These lines have been lined through in a manner different from Lope's usual markings.

2717. *Rey* is lined through, and what appears to be *aduiertan* is written above the line. *aduierte* is also lined through, with *como la e dado* substituted above it, neither change by Lope.

2721. *truxiste* replaced by *a traydo,* not by Lope.

2722. Deletion before *todas;* J suggests *Abd.*

2723. J inaccurately identifies A's variant reading here as appearing in v. 2722, and fails to note A's omission of *me.*

2732. Deletion after *alto;* J inaccurately places this deletion at v. 2731.

2733. Word deleted at the beginning of the line; J inaccurately places this deletion at v. 2732.

2758. AJ's reading would have Lope repeat information given in the previous verse instead of giving the hour. The autograph clearly reads *las,* which is supported by G.

2760. *Estefania* deleted after *de.*

2767. An asterisk appears in the right margin.

2769. J fails to note A's omission of *y.*

2772. J fails to note A's *le* for *la.*

2791. Word deleted before *diste.*

2794. Word deleted after *muger;* J inaccurately reports that the deletion appears before *muger.* He proposes *más* for the deletion.

2798. The autograph clearly reads *Nu,* and there is no indication in the stage directions that Mudarra is to be present here.

2801. Illegible writing over *Ra;* not noted by J.

Folio 16 v. *ldvjos.* "laus Deo, Virgini, Jesu [et] omnibus Sanctis." For Lope's use of abbreviated pious ascriptions at the end of acts and particularly at the end of his plays, see Fichter's note in *El sembrar en buena tierra,* pp. 233-34, where he specifically mentions our play, and refers to a Maggs Brothers' catalogue plate showing the ascription in *La desdichada Estefanía* (Plate XCVI, Cat. No. 555 — *Books Manuscripts,* etc., London, 1931).

Signature. See the beginning of the Manuscript Notes for a reference to Lope's custom of using the initial M before his signature.

The *censuras* (a censor's approval of the text of the play) and the *licencias* (the permission for presentation of the play) are numbered for identification, and will be commented upon where necessary, in the order of appearance. Amezúa, *Colección,* p. 43, accepts without comment the faulty listing of *censuras* and *licencias* of the *Catálogo,* p. 9, number 17 (which are discussed below), noting only that G omits some of them. J's readings are presented in the Appendix.

1. G reads *su censura.* For information concerning Thomás Gracián Dantisco and his cordial relationship with Lope, see Fichter's *El sembrar en buena tierra,* p. 236.

2. The *Catálogo* does not indicate that "9 de enero, 1607" appears in two distinct entries: first, for the order to examine the play; second, in the report of Dantisco. G reads *entremeses de ella,* omits *en* before *Madrid,* writes *de* before 1607.

3. G reads *Podrá representarse, eella* before *guardando,* omits *en* before Madrid, has two *de*'s before *henero,* another before 1607.

4. G omits the longer *licencias* and those which are extremely difficult to read, an unvoiced comment on the probable poor state of the manuscript even in 1762.

5. G omits. The *Catálogo* fails to indicate two separate entries for "29 de abril de 1607."

6. G omits.

7. G reads "lo que fuera de la lectura fuere malo." The *Catálogo* also lists 1608 as the year for this entry. A comparison of Lope's and Villalua's writing of the number eight tends to support this reading, though a case could be made for transcription of a six. Villalua ends his signature with a flourish resembling as S (indicated as a *rúbrica*), a fact not reported by other editors. Hoge, *El príncipe,* p. 3, maintains Américo Castro's transcription "Villalva" which is clearly "Villalua" in the manuscript (see "El autográfo de *La corona merecida* de Lope de Vega," RFE, VI [1919], pp. 307-308, note. Three folios at the beginning of *La corona merecida* have *licencias* for *El príncipe despeñado*). Amezúa transcribes Gálvez's "Villalba" in *Benavides (El Primero)* in *Colección,* p. 31, and for *El príncipe despeñado,* p. 53. In the former play, the reading should be "Villalua" (A. G. Reichenberger examined the *licencias* for the play, and furnished this information in a letter to the editor, dated March 4, 1964, University of Pennsylvania, Philadelphia, Pennsylvania). The latter play shows "Villalua" in the autograph. G writes "Villalva" for *La desdichada Estefanía.*

9. G omits. Amezúa, *Colección,* p. 29, quotes a Coelho *licencia* as it appears in the Gálvez manuscript of *La batalla del honor* as, "en Sevilla, a 22 de julio." Our autograph clearly shows Coelho's abbreviation for Lisboa, recognized also as Lisboa by the *Catálogo.*

10. G omits.

11. G omits. Hoge, *El príncipe,* p. 139, reads: "Joan de Mata;" Reichenberger, *Carlos V en Francia,* p. 190, has: "Joan de Mata n[otorio]"; but Montesinos, *El cuerdo loco,* p. 130, has "Joan de Matams," which reflects more closely the signature as it appears in *La desdichada Estefanía* (also shown very clearly in the autograph of *La prueba de los amigos*). Only Reichenberger mentions the *rúbrica* after his name.

12. G reads "marzo de 1611."

13. G omits. The *Catálogo* shows "20 septiembre," but there is nothing in the entry to indicate the month.

14. G reads *de* before 617. The *Catálogo* reads "8 de diciembre de 1611," for what is clearly "outubro 617." The signature following this entry has been reported illegible by various editors (Schevill, *La dama boba,* [Berkeley, 1918], p. 250; Harlan, *El desdén vengado* [New York, 1930],

p. 123). The writer is probably citing Dantisco as a recognized authority for the presentation of the play, in the same way as judicial cases are cited to lend weight to court decisions. The theory that someone is citing Dantisco is further supported by the handwriting in *El desdén vengado*, obviously not the same as that of *La desdichada Estefanía* and *Carlos V en Francia*, but very similar to the hand in *La dama boba*. At least two persons are using the same formula and copied signature. A comparison of the one found in *El cordobés valeroso Pedro Carbonero* (1603) and *La discordia en los casados* (1611), in the same hand, shows the *P* of *Podesse* and the *D* of *Dantisco* to be quite different, which is not so obvious in entries of other plays. It is clear that Gálvez tries to imitate the handwriting of the signatures he is copying. His rendition of *Dantisco* in *La desdichada Estefanía* shows a degree of uncertainty for the second half of the name, but he, also, has clearly read *Dan-* for the first half, strongly supporting the interpretation of Dantisco as the correct signature. The section to which Schevill refers as, "No date, rest illegible," is "9 de henero de 616. Dantisco."

NOTES TO THE TEXT

13-15. Understand "it's no wonder that Castile extends its hospitality to a King of France."

30. *fuistes*. This preterite form could end in *-tes, -tis,* or *-teis* during the period. See Rufino José Cuervo, *Obras inéditas, editadas por el P. Félix Restrepo* (Bogotá, 1944), pp. 343-47. Hoge, *El príncipe*, p. 150, n. 480, calls attention to the form in that work: "¡Ay, esperanzas! Quán lebes/ fuistes en t[iem]po tan poco!" (vv. 479-80).

37. *fee*. One syllable, by crasis. Hoge, *El príncipe*, pp. 142-43, n. 55, calls attention to the various meanings of the word as they are used by Lope, citing also Van Dam's *El castigo sin venganza* (Amsterdam, 1928), p. 376, n. 2172.

43. *balor*. Here, "méritos". See Hoge, *El príncipe*, p. 157, n. 813, for *balor* as "nobleza".

63. A detailed historical account of Luis's pilgrimage to Santiago and his real reasons for making the trip can be found in the *Primera crónica general de España*, ed. M. Pidal (Madrid, 1955), II, pp. 656-58. See also the Introduction, pp. 29-33.

86. *pribanza*. Refers to the relationship between a king and his closest nobles. As Lope explains in the next verse, *confianza* is a major element in the relationship. Fichter notes the meaning *criado* in *El castigo del discreto* (New York, 1925), pp. 252-53, n. 2081. See also Reichenberger's edition of *Carlos V en Francia*, p. 214, n. 1098, for the related *pribado* (cf. v. 90 of *La desdichada Estefanía*).

109. *y ygual*. 17th-century form permitted this construction, and "the use of *e* in such circumstances was due to a conscious effort for elegance," J. M. Hill and M. M. Harlan, *Cuatro comedias* (New York, 1941), p. 146, n. 1367.

120. *arguya*. "Del verbo latino *arguo, is,* vale contradezir, tentar, calumniar, acusar, reprehender," (Covarrubias, *Tesoro*). Here Luis uses the word to mean *contradezir,* for Costanza displays the breeding of nobility and legitimacy, not that of a bastard, and these qualities deny the reported illegitimacy.

132. *cautela.* "El engaño que uno haze a otro ingeniosamente, usando de términos ambiguos y de palabras dudosas y equívocas," (Covarrubias, *Tesoro*). Here, "without deception."

138. "Vos: era mirado como un tratamiento demasiado familiar. 'El primero título y más bajo es tú, que se da a los niños o a las personas que queremos mostrar grande familiaridad o amor. *Vos* se dice a los criados o va-allos.' ... De *vos* tratamos a los criados y mozos ... y entre amigos adonde no hay gravedad ni cumplimiento se tratan de vos," (Américo Castro, ed., *Vida del buscón* [Madrid, 1911], pp. 217-18, n. 17; see also Lapesa, *Historia*, pp. 251 and 356).

164. *rayo.* Serge Denis, *Lexique du théatre de J. R. de Alarcón* (Paris, 1943), gives "la menace suprême," one meaning for this frequently used word (see vv. 166, 410, 622, 1093, etc.).

165. *Conde Julián.* The arch-traitor who, to avenge the dishonor done to his daughter Florinda (called *la Cava* by the Moors) by King Rodrigo, opened the way for the Moor's invasion of Spain by delivering Ceuta to them. See *BAAEE*, X, p. 404 for treatment of the subject in *romances*.

170. *Pelayo.* Successful leader of the resistance forces who won the battle of Covadonga in 718, the first success against the invading Moors, and considered the point of departure for the Reconquest. As a result of his success, Pelayo was named King. See *BAAEE*, X, p. 411 for ballads concerning him. Fernán's reference here to the *ventura de Pelayo* carries out the idea of right versus wrong in the challenge which he delivers to Fortunio.

178. *la cruz roxa.* Fortunio alludes to the Order of Santiago, the religious-military order founded in 1161 to protect pilgrims on their way to Santiago de Compostela, and to guard the borders against the Moors. One of their standards showed a red cross.

192. *el Rey de Alfonso deziende.* "In 1010 Alfonso V was imprudent enough to confer the hand of his sister on Mohammed, King of Toledo, a prince who was subsequently raised to the throne of Córdova," (S. A. Dunham, The History of Spain and Portugal [London, 1832], III, p. 147). Fortunio makes use of this matrimony and the implication of service of a Christian King to a Moor to illustrate his (Fortunio's) service to Luis as acceptable. Speaking of this type of defense, Montesinos says: "... acuden a nuestra memoria numerosas reminiscencias: ecos de la vieja querella entre feministas y antifeministas, recuerdos de aquella moral humanística obstinada en medir las acciones humanas todas, refiriéndolas a los paradigmas heroicos de la antigüedad. Lope sintió muy hondamente este último, y la profesión que repetidamente hace de una ética 'historizada', o mejor 'heroificada', explica numerosos pasajes de sus comedias. ... Lo humano y lo monstruoso, las pasiones, las virtudes, los vicios se justifican o no según pueden referirse a 'la historia'," (from his edition of *Barlaán y Josafat* [Madrid, 1935], p. 241). See also n. 196 and n. 553 for further use of history to lend weight to an argument.

196. *Guzmán el Bueno.* Guzmán served Abeyuzef, the monarch of Algeciras, on condition that he not have to fight Christian troops. Don Sancho wrote him that: "Merecedes ser llamado *el Bueno,* y ansi vos lo llamo, y vos ansi vos llamaredes de aqui adelante." Upon his return to Spain, Guzmán's trip was made a triumphal march, honored by all. Fortunio continues citing examples from history to establish precedent for his actions.

239. *pondré carteles en Fez.* Menéndez y Pelayo (*Ac.,* VIII, p. lxxii, n. 2) refers to an historical *desafío* of D. Alonso de Aguilar and the Conde de Cabra, found in *Relaciones de algunos sucesos de los últimos tiempos del reino de Granada, que publica la Sociedad de Bibliófilos españoles* (Madrid, 1868), pp. 69-145. The work referred to consists of a series of letters by D. Diego, Conde de Cabra, to D. Alonso de Aguilar, repeatedly demanding satisfaction, by duel, for offenses received. There also appear in Arabic, with translation, *cartas de seguro* from the ruler of Granada. The precedent for dueling by Christian nobles in Moorish territory was well established for Lope's use of such a device.

258-59. *Hiziérala aquí / si en esto no hubiera ley.* The attached object pronoun anticipates *ley* of the next line, "I would make it [a law] here if there weren't a law concerning it."

278-79. *Sancho, Fernando, don Garçía, / y Costanza Ysabel.* See the Introduction, p. 33, for the *Primera crónica's* listing of Alfonso's children.

294. *Doña Sancha.* See the Introduction, p. 34, for a comparison of Lope's lineage and that of Sandoval for doña Sancha.

319. *Eslo.* "[Es estremo] en discrezión."

325-26. *Pasiones son naturales / yra y amor.* See Morby, *La Dorotea,* p. 442: "La ira y el amor son nuestras dos passiones principales." He also notes the appearance of this *sentencia* in *Si no vieran las mugeres* (*Ac.,* I, 577a): "Pero ¿cuál es la mayor / pasión de las que tenemos / los hombres naturalmente? / . . . Dejando afectos diversos, / son la ira y el amor."

387. *como el ángel de Abrahán.* Abraham, about to sacrifice his beloved son Isaac, has his hand stayed by an angel. See *Genesis,* 22: 11-12.

403. *lo que el Çid con el judío.* In an anonymous ballad, a Jew approaches the body of the Cid to pull his beard; but as his hand is reaching out to do so, he sees that the Cid has started to remove Tizona from its sheath:

> Muy grand pavor ha cobrado:
> Tendido cayó de espaldas
> Amortecido de espanto.
> Halláronlo allí caido
> Los que en la iglesia han entrado.

As a result of the "milagro," the Jew becomes a Christian. See *BAAEE,* X, p. 572.

425-26. *como Hércules fiero / a Licas.* For a representation of Hercules about to dash in Lycus's head, see the *Enciclopedia Universal* (Madrid, 1925), XXVII, p. 1139. Hercules, upon his return from Hell, discovers Lycus's plan to kill the former's wife and children, the plot of Euripides's and Seneca's tragedies *Hércules furioso.*

432. *ynterpretas.* Covarrubias, *Tesoro,* gives "declarar; interpretación, o declaración, ... o declaración de cosa escura, como enigma."

443. *monesterio.* In *El castigo del discreto,* Fichter cites Menéndez Pidal's *°monesterium,* "de donde el culto monesterio" (p. 266, n. 2427). But A. Zamora Vicente, in his edition of *El villano en su rincón* (Madrid, 1961), notes that "monesterio es forma casi general hasta el Siglo de Oro; deriva de una variante vulgar, *monisterium,* frente a la forma culta," (p. 124).

464. *Atienza.* In Central Spain, on the outskirts are remains of fortifications and a castle. *Almonaçid.* There are several such places in Spain, one in Zaragoza Province (de la Sierra), another is Almonaçid del Marquesado, etc.

473. *Bellido.* According to legend, Bellido Dolfos offered to show Sancho II the most vulnerable points of the walls of Zamora, which the King had under siege. As they walked in the darkness, a short distance from the King's accompanying troops, Dolfos killed the King and fled. See J. H. Silverman, "Peribáñez y Vellido Dolfos," *BHi,* LV (1953), pp. 378-80, for use of the traitor's name in curses. *BAAEE,* X, pp. 504-507 has ballads involving the legend.

479-82. Estefanía is the angel who made Fernán refrain from attacking Fortunio (cf. vv. 385-88), the second time such a reference has been made to *ángel* (Denis, *Lexique,* gives "désignant la femme aimée."). Fernán's *condiçión* is his bravery and his duty as a noble to maintain his honor, which he feels has again been besmirched by Fortunio.

487. *Çeuta.* Twenty-eight miles northeast of Tangier, opposite Gibraltar.

491. *cabeza de caza.* Related to *cabeza de lobo,* "tomado de la costumbre de los cazadores o pastores que habiendo muerto alguno de estos animales nocivos, traen la cabeza y con ella piden contribución como premio" (J. Cejador y Frauca, *Fraseología o estilística castellana* [Madrid, 1921], I, p. 215. See also his edition of *Lazarillo de Tormes* [Madrid, 1926], p. 195, n. 2). From the foregoing, the meaning of our expression becomes clearer. Fortún's *lengua,* the alleged source of the conflict which has brought Luis to Spain, will be the proof for Fernán that Fortún has been chastised in battle. As a trophy it will proclaim his victory over the evil that Fortún represents.

553. *Arias Gonzalo.* Accused of being a traitor, Arias Gonzalo refused to remain at home while his sons avenged him. Even though he was aged:

> El quiere ser primero
> porque en la muerte no ha estado
> de Don Sancho ... (See *BAAEE,* X, p. 513)

In this and subsequent references (cf. vv. 558-59), Estefanía utilizes historical precedent to convince Luis that before she can marry Fortunio he must have cleared his name, and the only way to do so is for Fortunio himself to meet Castro in battle.

558. *murieron en estacado.* A search of the ballads referring to the Condes de Carrión reveals no mention of their death. The sequence of the *Poema de mio Cid (Cantar de Corpes)* where Pedro Vermúdez and Martínez Antolínez challenge the Condes, and ballads describing the battle, end without their death. As referred to here, their death suggests a popular, mythical extension of what was to be expected in a *desafío*, according to cultural heritage — a popular addition to the written ballads as they are found today. For a discussion of myth in the *Poema*, see P. N. Dunn's "Theme and Myth in the *Poema de Mio Cid,*" *Romania*, LXXXIII (1962), pp. 348-69.

559. *Rui Velázquez.* Mudarra González, half-brother of the ill-fated Infantes de Lara, avenged his brothers' death by challenging and killing Rui Velázquez, who had engineered their murder. See *BAAEE*, X, p. 457 for ballads concerning the subject. It is of interest to note that Lope gave the name Mudarra to the *gracioso* of this play, the only instance where the name is applied to a non-Moor.

612. *y se queda Ysabel con mis entrañas.* Repeated as a refrain in vv. 620 and 628.

621. *sober.* Should be *sorber,* which MSBAG all show. In the autograph manuscript of *La mayor virtud de un rey* (v. 98), Lope wrote *domiré* for *dormiré.*

622. *baxen rayos de amor.* J. F. Montesinos, in *Barlaán y Josafat,* pp. 285-86, identifies this concept as one from Alciato's *Emblemas* (Aligerum fulmen fregit deus aliger igne / Dum demonstrat uti est fortior ignis amor), noting its appearance in other plays by Lope. Here, Mudarra's speech represents a comic intensification of the image, for the bolts are to descend to splinter objects (i.e., reduce legs to their component parts, etc.).

627. *pues me voy donde no ay vino y castañas.* Cf. *La doncella Teodor, Ac.,* XIV, p. 149b:

> ¿Que voy donde no hay vino ni tocino?
> ¡Trágueme el mar!

631-35. The *gracioso* now parodies sentiments commonly found in the poetry of Petrarch and his followers.

639. *Durandarte.* The knight who served Belerma without receiving favor from her until his death; expressed a last wish to have his heart taken to her as a reminder of him. See *BAAEE*, X, p. 260 and pp. 283-84 for a burlesque of the ballad. Lope used the name Durandarte for characters in *Los celos de Rodamonte (Ac.,* XIII), and *El Marqués de Mantua (Ac.,* XIII).

645-47. Mudarra's reference to the fickleness of women, rendered comical in this context, assumes graver importance in the main plot (cf. vv. 1643-45, 1660-62 and 2275-77) as Ysabel, Fortunio and the servants define *muger* in terms of *mudanza.* See Morby, *La Dorotea,* p. 259, n. 148, for further occurrences of this concept. Hoge, *El príncipe,* p. 154, n. 691, also notes the frequent use of the comparison in that work.

670. *Las postas dexo en cassa.* Mudarra indicates that he and Fernán are prepared to leave for Fez immediately. *Las postas,* rented horseback transportation (see Hoge, *El príncipe,* p. 166, n. 1685), came to be identified with speed (see Schevill, *La dama boba*, p. 254, n. 25 for other examples). See v. 1855, where Sancho Laynez says, "Tened aquesas postas." The urgency of his message for Alfonso is underlined by the use of *postas*.

671. *Fernán González de alabastro*. Mudarra is probably referring to Fernán.

676. *perrigalga*. The form is noted by Santiago Montoto in his "Contribución al vocabulario de Lope de Vega," *BAE*, XXVIII (1948), p. 472, citing its use in *La difunta pleiteada* (Ac., IV, p. 559) and *El mayor dudoso* (Ac., VII, p. 489). He gives *perrenga* for *La desdichada Estefanía*, the reading of MSBA. Denis, *Lexique*, notes the use of *galga* to refer to a *mora*, a term of scorn, and the use of *perro* to designate a non-Christian, but cf. Martín Alonso, *Enciclopedia del idioma* (Madrid, 1958), "dícese de la persona inquieta, que anda de acá para allá."

681. *angeo*. "Es una tela de estopa o lino basto que se trae de Francia o de Flandes" (Morby, *La Dorotea*, p. 129, n. 16). See also Fontecha, p. 22.

685. *almilla* in the stage directions. "Especie de jubón, con mangas o sin ellas, ajustado al cuerpo" *(RAED)*. G's transcription clarified this previously doubtful reading.

719. *trino*. "Que contiene en sí tres cosas distintas, o participa de ellas" *(RAED)*. In astrology the conjunction of planets determines prognostication, and the term *aspecto trino* refers to a favorable position of the planets. See also Morby, *La Dorotea*, p. 437, n. 159.

770. *vía. Veía, reía*, become *vía, ría* by elision. See Federico Hanssen, *Gramática histórica de la lengua castellana* (Halle, 1913), p. 107, and M. Romera Navarro, *Registro de lexicografía hispánica* (Madrid, 1951), p. 984.

784. *Miramamolín*. Morley-Tyler, *Nombres*, I, p. 150, list this name as a "nombre fingido," but in Diego Catalán's article, "La *Crónica de Ca tilla* y la *Historia de Africa* del sabio Gilberto, en la *Estoria de los Reyes del Señorío de Africa* del Maestro Gilberto o Sujulberto: Una obra del siglo XIII perdida," *Romance Philology*, XVII (1963), p. 350, we see: "...su padre era miramamolín, que quiere tanto dezir commo enperador." The title "Commander of the Faithful" is listed in: Hans Wehr, *A Dictionary of Modern Written Arabic* (Ithaca, 1961), p. 27; R. Dozy and W. H. Engelmann, *Glossaire des mots espagnols et portugais dérivés de l'arabe* (Leyde, 1869), p. 314; A. Socins, *Arabische Grammatik* (Berlin, 1909), p. 91. See also Covarrubias, *Tesoro*, s.v.

807. *moros almohades*. The name of the fourth dynasty of Berber princes who overthrew the *almorávides* and reigned in northern Africa and part of Spain from 1146 to 1269. The founder, Al-Mahdi, preached religious reform and suppression of the religious tolerance practiced by the *almorávides*. See Angel González Palencia, *Historia de la España musulmana* (Madrid, 1945), pp. 83-111, for the influence of these two groups in Spain.

826. *de camino* in the stage directions. "For travel, the seventeenth-century Spaniard ordinarily wore a colored costume, with plumed hat, boots, and spurs" (J. Hill and M. Harlan, *Cuatro comedias* [New York, 1941], p. 446, n. 1075).

835. *Tetuán.* Approximately thirty miles southeast of Tangier, the city dates from the beginning of the 14th century.

864. *aquí por las monas van.* In this and in subsequent speeches, Mudarra's use of *mona* involves its secondary meaning of *borrachez* and *borracho.* See J. E. Gillet's *Study of the Propalladia and Other Works of Bartolomé de Torres Naharro* (Menasha, 1943), III, p. 532, n. 247. Cf. vv. 1404-07 in Act II, where the word play is continued.

866. *no era mejor yr a Coca ... a cazar monazos uiejos.* "Castilla la Vieja, tierra sedienta, producía al borde de los hilos de agua que la surcan, viñedos pródigos en famosos vinos. A orillas del Eresma, cosechaba Coca uno de los más nombrados en el siglo XVII" (M. Herrero García, *La vida española del siglo XVII* [Madrid, 1933], p. 47). Coca, famous as it was for wine, and *mona* (with its meaning *borrachera*), form another word play, continuing to emphasize Mudarra's interest in wine.

867. *Alaejos.* "La región vallisoletana servía también ricos mostos a la mesa española. El rey de estos vinos castellano-leoneses era el de Alaejos. Su nombradía iba vinculada al dicho proverbial: 'Vino de Alaejos, que sustenta niños y viejos'" (Herrero García, *La vida española*, p. 48). See also Morby, *La Dorotea*, p. 154, n. 75: "...y aunque es verdad que soy más aficionado a vna bota de Alaejos que a las trecientas de Iuan de Mena, ..." *San Martín.* In the Province of Madrid, also famous for its wine. See Herrero García, *La vida española,* pp. 6-7.

876-81. Mudarra's accumulation of illnesses and symptoms to create a grotesque effect is found in other plays of Lope. Montesinos has gathered examples in *Barlaán y Josafat,* pp. 282-83. One sample is:

> Viva el príncipe cien años,
> que lo demás son congojas,
> corrimientos, reuma y tos,
> hipocondría y la gota.

921. *que tenga el alma en los dientes.* Cejador y Frauca, *Fraseología,* p. 71, lists this expression as meaning "en peligro de muerte."

1019. *¡Mas que me voy a España sin la mona!* Mas que here means "I bet that," noted by Hill and Harlan, *Cuatro comedias,* p. 126, n. 168. See also E. H. Templin, "An Additional Note on *mas que*," *H*, XII (1929), pp. 163-170; S. A. Wofsy, "A Note on *mas que,*" *Romanic Review*, XIX (1928), pp. 41-48; John Brooks, "*Más que, mas que* and *Mas ¡Qué,*" *H*, XVI (1933), pp. 23-34.

1032. *vn rebelión.* Could be either gender, but usually masculine in Lope. See Hoge, *El príncipe,* p. 171, n. 2357.

1056. *bizarro.* Listed by Lapesa in his *Historia*, pp. 195-96 (the 3d edition, Madrid, 1955), as a word of Italian origin, with a semantic shift to the meaning *extravagante, extraño.* Noted in *Carlos V en Francia* by Reichenberger, pp. 219-20, n. 1344, with the meaning *gallardo.* J. Corominas, *Diccionario crítico etimológico de la lengua castellana* (Madrid, 1954-57), indicates that it derives from the Italian *bizzarro (iracundo, furioso)*, documented from the XIIIth and XIVth centuries in Dante, Boccaccio, etc.

The word is not listed in J. H. Terlingen's *Los italianismos en español* (Amsterdam, 1943), and reference to it does not appear in Lapesa's fourth edition of his *Historia* (Madrid, 1959).

1066. *nación almohadí.* The use of *almohadí* as an adjective is noted by Montoto, "Contribución...," *BAE*, XXVI (1947), p. 289; the example is from *La desdichada Estefanía.*

1069. *Rodrigo por la Caua.* La Cava is the name given to Conde Julián's daughter by the Arabs. Because she was violated by Rodrigo, "último Rey Godo," her father's revenge caused the peninsula to be overrun by the Moors. Fortunio envisions a like situation for Spain unless Alfonso hastens to the defense of the frontier. See *BAAEE*, X, pp. 401-03, for ballads concerning the subject.

1100-1102. Jacob agreed to serve Laban for seven years, after which time he was to marry Rachel; but Laban gave him Lia and Jacob had to spend another seven years of service before he could marry Rachel. Jacob is noted for his great affection for Rachel and their son Joseph.

1120. *vn ora.* Hoge, *El príncipe*, p. 151, n. 566, indicates that *un* before *ora* is rare, "even in early Spanish," citing H. M. Martin, "Termination of Qualifying Words before Feminine Nouns and Adjectives in the Plays of Lope de Vega," *MLN*, XXXVII (1922), pp. 398-407. The phenomenon occurs also in *Peribáñez*, vv. 656 and 2666 (see Hill and Harlan, *Cuatro comedias*, p. 134, n. 656), so its occurrence in Lope's plays was not a rarity.

1125. *Mormojón.* In the Province of Palencia, the exterior of the castle still stands (see Carlos Sarthou Carreres, *Castillos de España* [Madrid, 1931], pp. 147-48).

1126. *Palençuela.* Also in Palencia Province, north-central Spain (León). *Castromocho.* Located in the "Tierra de Campos," characterized by L. Martín Echeverría as a monotonous and sad area, "del que son verdadero complemento los pueblos grises y polvorientos ... y los restos de antiguos castillos y fortificaciones (... Castromocho ...)" (*Geografía de España* [Barcelona, 1932], II, pp. 53-54).

1128-29. Ordoño Vela is ordered to have "them" call someone to bless the couple. For another instance of the full name of this character, see v. 1845.

1179. *Yo diré "sí", el alma "no".* Estefanía's determination to remain true to Fernán Ruiz "en el alma" parallels the story of Costanza in Dante's *Paradiso;* she was forced to leave a nunnery and was married against her will, but "non fu dal vel del cor già mai disciolta" (see C. H. Grandgent's edition of *La divina commedia* [Boston, 1933], Paradiso, Canto III, p. 682).

1191. *voy temiendo la nuez.* Covarrubias, *Tesoro*, gives "nuez de ballesta, donde prende la cuerda y se encaxa el virote, por la semejança de la nuez," so Mudarra is afraid they will be attacked because of the Moorish costumes they are wearing.

1194-95. *el echar la bendiçión / al pueblo con los talones.* Apretar los talones has the figurative meaning of "to hurry"; Mudarra, continuing the image from the previous lines, fears they will be chased out of town.

1196. *Ya que Dios nos escapó.* "Since God liberated us," "freed us"; see also Morby, *La Dorotea*, p. 73, n. 48. Cf. "Fendyonda, la mi Fedyonda, / 'eskápame de 'estas 'olas" (S. G. Armistead and J. H. Silverman, *Diez romances hispánicos en un manuscrito sefardí de la Isla de Rodas* [Pisa, 1962], p. 30).

1226-27. The *torno* and *muger* are equated; both change from moment to moment, a further word play on *muger-mudanza* noted in vv. 645-47.

1240-43. Mudarra may be breaking the dramatic reality of the play as he discourses on the *tramoya* ("máquina para figurar en el teatro transformaciones o casos prodigiosos," with an additional meaning of "enredo dispuesto con ingenio, disimulo, y maña" [*RAED*]) of the *torno* in the convent, a device to receive articles and messages from outside without the person inside being seen. He likens it to a *çerbatana* ("cañuto en que se introducen bodoques u otras cosas para despedirlas o hacerlas salir" [*RAED*]). The identity of the *tornera* is not known, so Catalina and Juana, common names, are suggested for the lay person in charge of the *torno* (see Montesinos's edition of *El Marqués de las Navas*, pp. 191-92, for the use of similar names to indicate vagueness). The last indication of an *enredo* is presented in the reference to the *laberinto de Troya*. As far as is known, Troy had no labyrinth like that of Crete, where the legendary Minotaur was hoursed, or the Egyptian Labyrinth of Arsinoe.

1258. *quartillo.* In liquid measure, a quarter part of an "açumbre" (see Covarrubias, *Tesoro*).

1259. *laúd.* "Instrumento de cuerdas ... difiere de la vihuela por quanto no tiene el vientre o cuerpo quadrado sino redondo y giboso, hecho de muchas costillas delgadas, sutilmente pegadas, unas con otras" (Covarrubias, *Tesoro*). The comparison is doubly humorous if one considers the shape of the *laúd* and Mudarra's possible rotund figure, and the secondary meaning of *perezoso* for *floxo*.

1264-65. *cada uno pide / aquello que ha menester.* Cf. "cada cual lo que le toca," a traditional expression of the time and the title of a play by Rojas Zorrilla (see Hill and Harlan, *Cuatro comedias,* p. 280, n. 68).

1270. *es yda.* Ser was commonly used with intransitive past participles (*es venido, es muerto,* etc.). See Hanssen, *Gramática,* p. 232. Hill and Harlan, *Cuatro comedias,* p. 144, n. 1296, refer to its continued use today. Cf. v. 1288, "Muerto soy."

1278-79. For the equivalency *amor-llama,* see Montesinos's edition of *El cuerdo loco* (Madrid, 1922), p. 220, n. 1738, where he identifies it as a theme from Ovid.

1290. *Bálame.* This form is used instead of *válgame* when referring to Dios (see v. 1766, etc.). Fichter, in *El castigo del discreto,* p. 236, n. 1294, and Gillet, in his *Study of the Propalladia,* III, pp. 503-504, also note the form.

1298. *el Andaluzía.* By analogy with the old form of the feminine singular definite article *ela*, now reduced to *el*, and used only before nouns which begin with a stressed *a*, other feminine nouns which begin with unaccented *a* were also seen with *el*. See A. Bello and R. Cuervo, *Gramática de la lengua castellana* (Paris, 1925), pp. 70-71.

1308-1309. *Que ver la amada prenda / gozar al enemigo es grande afrenta.* This refrain appears (with slight variations) in vv. 1365-65 and 1394-95.

1311-22. Mudarra's speech here, and his next (vv. 1328-47) show the typical juxtaposition of attitudes of the *galán* and the *gracioso*, giving the latter's philosophy of life as counterpoint to Fernán's *quejas*. See J. F. Montesinos, *Estudios sobre Lope* (Mexico, 1951), pp. 35-55, and J. H. Silverman, "El gracioso de Juan Ruiz de Alarcón y el concepto de la figura del donaire tradicional," *H*, XXXV (1952), pp. 64-69.

1342. *notomías.* "En la acepción 'esqueleto' aparece anatomía ya en Cervantes, y esta acepción toma comunmente la forma notomía..." (Covarrubias, *Tesoro*). *Hacer la anatomía*, to dissect, hence to examine closely.

1360. *Angélica y Medoro.* Fernán compares himself to the suitors of the beautiful Angélica who met in battle to determine which would win her hand. Medoro, the young Moor, slipped away with her while the knights were in battle, depriving the victor of his prize. Fortunio is represented by Medoro, while Estefanía is cast in the role of Angélica. The allusion is faithful to the circumstances of *Peribáñez,* whose sonnet (vv. 603-616) is noted as an inexact reference to the incidents of Ariosto's *Orlando furioso* (Canto XIX) (see Hill and Harlan, *Cuatro comedias,* p. 133). See also *BAAEE*, X, pp. 269-71, and Dámaso Alonso's study of Góngora's *Romance de Angélica y Medoro* (Madrid, 1962). The latter work has detailed information on the theme in Spanish literature.

1376. *más amores que razones.* Cf. "... amor no se gouierna / por discurso de razón," (Fichter's edition of *El castigo del discreto,* vv. 69-70, p. 78). For further examples, see his note to the verses, p. 207.

1390-1393. "I want to dishonor (do injury to, insult) Fortunio, if it is possible that I still can, as he is honored by Estefanía and I am without her and without my honor."

1397. *carta vieja.* "Es carta vieja el anciano que sabe los rincones del lugar y linajes" (Gili y Gaya, *Tesoro lexicográfico* [Madrid, 1947]).

1399. *¡Más mal hay en el aldea!* Cf. n. 1298 for *el* before *aldea* (also Zamora Vicente, *El villano,* p. 130, n. 1600: "y al aldea vengo a pie"). For the meaning "corte," see Karl Vossler's note for *aldea* in *La poesía de la soledad en España* (Buenos Aires, 1946), p. 70, n. 1: "Aparece reiteradamente esta palabra en las églogas de Sá de Miranda con el sentido traspuesto de 'corte, sociedad mundanal, temporal, sensual, afán estrepitoso, hasta pecaminoso;' ..." It is not used as the opposite of *corte* (as in *Menosprecio de corte y alabanza de aldea,* by Antonio de Guevara), nor does it refer to the temporal world as posed in contrast to the spiritual world (see Morby, *La Dorotea,* p. 82, n. 74). Cejador y Frauca records: "En el aldea que no es buena, más mal hay que suena" (*Refranero Castellano* [Madrid, 1928], I, p. 30) but Mudarra's words reflect just the quality of a *refrán*, he is not quoting one directly.

1403. *martas flamencas*. A *marta* (martin) is sought for its valuable pelt, and is noted for "el daño que hace a la caza" (Martín Alonso, *Enciclopedia del idioma* [Madrid, 1958]). The adjective "Flemish" is not clear here; as a masculine noun it has the meaning "especie de navaja."

1406. *la más alegre mona*. See n. 864.

1409. *ojeras*. "Copita de cristal que sirve para bañar el ojo con alguna medicina" (*RAED*). From its relationship with *copa*, Mudarra continues his word play on drinking.

1410. *aranbeles de Mahoma*. Gili y Gaya, *Tesoro lexicográfico*, cites Palet (1604), "façon de tapisserie," and Vittori (1609), "alquerifa, tapis de Turquie à long poil; tapeto de Turchia a lungo pelo." Reichenberger notes the existence of a pejorative meaning, "andrajo" (see *Carlos V en Francia*, p. 234, n. 2313).

1411. *tiritañas*. "Tela antigua de lana o seda" (*RAED*).

1413. *Babieca*. Mudarra here refers to the Cid's famous horse. The *gracioso's* use of such a name in this context contributes to his high-flown, pseudo-intellectual speech, which is the comic parallel to Fernán's anguished discourse upon hearing of Estefanía's bethrothal to Fortunio.

1414. *envés*. Fichter notes the colloquial use of this word for "rump" in *El castigo del discreto*, p. 268, n. 2488-90.

1472. *Tarudante*. In the Empire of Marruecos, in the valley of the river Sus, surrounded by walls of some extension. The name also appears in H. Ziomek's edition of *La nueva victoria de D. Gonzalo de Cordoua* (New York, 1962), p. 162, v. 1550.

1482-83. Morby, *La Dorotea*, p. 449, n. 202, notes the pride of Spaniards in their reputation for telling the truth, an accusation of lying being one of the greatest insults possible.

1488. *quanto más que a t[iem]po estamos*. For *quanto más*, "moreover," see Keniston's *Syntax of Castilian Prose* (Chicago, 1937), p. 354.

1495. *muchos*. Refers back to *servir* or to *seruiçios* in a type of brachilogy.

1525-27. *que he hecho lo que he podido / ... / fortuna lo que ha querido*. This is the first of four appearances of the "viejo blasón castellano" (see J. F. Montesinos, *Ensayos y estudios de literatura española* [ed. J. H. Silverman; Mexico, 1959], p. 9) within the next lines. Arjona mentions in "Defective Rhymes and Rhyming Techniques in Lope de Vega's Autograph *Comedias*," *HR*, XXIII (1955), p. 113, that this is a quotation from a famous *letrilla satírica* of Quevedo (see *BAAEE*, LXIX, p. 301, no. 663 for the poem to which he refers), but Montesinos, clarifying his reference above to a "viejo blasón", says: "a) Esa comedia, que es de 1604 [*La desdichada*

Estefanía], no creo que pueda ser posterior a la letrilla de Quevedo donde
b) los versos del mote no creo que puedan tenerse por invención del poeta,
quien, como otras veces, está glosando algo tradicional" (from a letter to
Professor J. H. Silverman, dated December 30, 1963, University of California,
Berkeley). Professor J. O. Crosby agrees that it appears to be "a gloss of
something traditional" (from a letter to Professor J. H. Silverman, dated
January 21, 1964, University of Illinois, Urbana). See the Introduction, p. 46,
for the sequence "caído-podido-querido" in *romance* in vv. 1585-87.

1529. *Perdióse el remedio mío. Remedio,* meaning "marriage," has been
noted by various editors (see Fichter, *El castigo del discreto,* p. 206, n. 50
and examples, and Hill and Harlan, *Cuatro comedias,* p. 158, n. 1974).
Ysabel's *remedio* would have been the marriage of Estefanía and Fortunio.

1538-39. *Pues a fee que más de vn çiego / olgara de haberme visto.*
This refrain-like expression is similar to that found in Torres Naharro's
Comedia Calamita: "Tengo por fe que / los ciegos holgarían de me ver"
(see Gillet's *Study of the Propalladia,* III, p. 643, n. 27).

1541. *¿Bienes bueno?* This use of an adjective in an adverbial function
occurs also in *Peribáñez:*

> PERIBÁÑEZ ¿Estás buena?
> CASILDA Estoy sin ti.
> ¿Vienes bueno? (vv. 1190-91)

(see Hill and Harlan, *Cuatro comedias,* p. 82).

1567. *Faetón.* According to the myth, Faetón asked his father to allow
him to drive the coach of the sun for just one day in order to prove his
ability. He lost control of the horses, left the customary path, and burned
the heavens and the earth. Zeus killed him by a bolt, and he fell into the
river Po. The remains of his destruction are seen as the Milky Way.

1634. *que no te quiera, cobarde.* The idea that love is not for the
fearful has been expressed by Lope in other plays (see Montesinos, *El cuerdo
loco,* p. 219, n. 1678 for examples. "O no hay amor en los dos, / o no es
posible haber miedo; / miedo y amor no andan juntos ..." [vv. 1678-80]).

1677. *pensión.* For the meaning *carga, gravamen,* cf. Morby, *La Dorotea:* "A nadie sin pensión la [hermosura] ha dado el cielo" (p. 131, and
n. 24, where Morby cites Fichter's *El sembrar en buena tierra,* pp. 218-19).

1718. For a discussion of the fall, see the Introduction, p. 73.

1726. *agua en salua* in the stage directions. Zamora Vicente, *El villano,*
p. 85, n. 182, writes: "*Bandeja.* Se trata de la pieza de plata o de oro
en la que va puesta la copa ..."

1744. Fernán's speech indicates that the group has moved from the
church to his house. See H. Rennert, *The Spanish Stage in the Time of
Lope de Vega* (New York, 1909), pp. 86-91, regarding the demands of the
plays of the period on the imagination of the audience in visualizing a
change of scene.

1745. *alcázar de Creso.* The richness and opulence of the King of
Lydia's palace was renowned, serving as a symbol of wealth and grandeur.

See Pero Mexía's *Silva de varia lección* (Madrid, 1934), II, p. 301: "...vino [Solón] a la corte del famoso y riquísimo rey Creso de Lidia. El cual, después de haber hecho a Solón grande demostración de riquezas y aderezos, puesto en su trono y aparato, le preguntó si había visto otro espectáculo más ordenado y más hermoso." Solón's reply, in effect, said that riches do not guarantee happiness. See Zamora Vicente, *El villano*, pp. 111-12, for a more elaborate use of this theme.

1759. *Tebas.* Located north of Athens, Thebes was a leading city of the Boeotian League, consequently much of the wealth of the League was concentrated there and it became symbolic of riches.

1777. *¡Casa vieja nunca más!* Mudarra's exclamation has the quality of a refrain, but only the approximation which follows has been located: "Casa vieja, pronto arde," and "Casa vieja, todas son" — o "todo se vuelve goteras" (F. Rodríguez Marín, *Refranes castellanos* [Madrid, 1926]). The meaning is clear that Mudarra will never again have anything to do with an old house.

1790-91. *de poluo me hizo Dios / de polbo me buelbe a hazer.* See *Genesis* 3:19: "...for dust thou art, and unto dust shalt thou return."

1801. *vn miércoles de çeniza.* An allusion to the custom of placing a mark of ash on one's forehead on Ash Wednesday, the first day of Lent.

1803. *çierra.* The meaning "to attack" for this verb is noted by E. Kohler in his edition of *El perro del hortelano* (Paris, 1951), p. 9, n. 61.

1811. *yndezente.* "Inconveniente" (see Martín Alonso, *Enciclopedia del idioma*).

1833. *sereno de noche fría.* "Comúnmente llamamos sereno el ayre alterado de la prima noche con algún vapor que se ha levantado de la tierra" (Covarrubias, *Tesoro*).

1835. *fuelles de amigo soplón.* For *fuelles,* "persona soplona," and *soplón,* "chismoso," see Martín Alonso, *Enciplopedia*. The idea is to avoid a gossipy wind-bag.

1861. *almorauides.* For the stress on the penult of a *palabra esdrújula,* see S. G. Morley, "La modificación del acento de la palabra en el verso castellano," *RFE,* XIV (1927), pp. 270-71.

1864. *Azamor.* City in the Kingdom of Morocco, on the north coast of Africa.

1866. *Alboali Ben-Zayde.* Sandoval's *Chrónica* calls the Miramaolín Alboali (p. 151); the *Crónica general* names him Alboahli (p. 659a).

1890-91. See the Introduction, p. 39, for historical references to these men from Sandoval's *Chrónica.*

1916. *los caballeros Guzmanes.* The military reputation of the Guzmanes, "muy peynados, / presumiendo de esforçados / y siruiendo por antojos," is noted by Gillet in his *Study of the Propalladia,* III, p. 411, n. 199ff, along with other samples illustrating the high esteem they enjoyed as soldiers.

2011-12. *ni fíes ombre ninguno / ni de alguna muger fíes.* Cf. Gillet, *Study of the Propalladia,* III, p. 558, n. 181ff: "¿Y no has leydo aquel testo, / que maldito deue ser / honbre que en honbre se fía? (from the *Comedia Ymenea).*

2042. *pasamanos.* An adornment of various materials (silk, cotton, wool, gold, etc.). Cf. "son pasamanos de plata," noted by Van Dam in *El castigo sin venganza,* p. 292, n. 15. Bermudo recognized Estefanía's *manteo* which evidently had a distinguishing ornament.

2059-60. *No traygas a amor en puntos / que en vn punto está su fin.* Fortunio beseeches the woman he believes to be Estefanía to stop being coy with him, for he is aware of the importance of time in their relationship, or in any affair of the heart. Love, so fragile, can cease "en un punto," and any obstacle merely wastes precious time. For *punto* as a space of time, see R. Marín's edition of *Don Quixote* (Madrid, 1947), VI, p. 180, n. 9.

2129. *¿qué te espantas? ¿Qué?* is used for *¿Por qué?* Cf. Fontecha, p. 300, and Morby, *La Dorotea,* p. 71.

2148. *quinta essençia de ventura.* Gillet cites Torres Naharro's use, in his *Prohemio,* of the expression from *Proverbs* 12:4: "Es corona del varón / la mujer qu'es virtuosa" (*Study of the Propalladia,* III, p. 619, n. 151f), indicating that the verse appears in the works of Fray Luis de León, Cervantes, Santillana, etc. The irony of the situation is that after heaping praise on Estefanía, Fernán is informed that she has been unfaithful.

2191. *porque se pagan los brazos.* "Se contentan los brazos"; cf. Fontecha, p. 263.

2194. *Bien aya el que ausenzia hizo.* A direct contrast to the attitude of Fernán in vv. 1285-88 and 2307-2308.

2217. *ola.* For *Hola* as an impolite form of address, even for servants, see Fichter's *El castigo del discreto,* p. 220, n. 631; also noted by Schevill in *La dama boba,* p. 291, n. 984, and J. Castañeda in *Las paces de los reyes y judía de Toledo* (Chapel Hill, 1962), p. 241, n. 1354. Fernán speaks to a servant in this fashion again in v. 2635, which is an indication of his state of turmoil and agitation.

2219. *los dos viejos de Susana.* Susana was accused of adultery by two old men, whose advances she had repulsed. She was about to be stoned by a crowd when Daniel, gifted with a superior vision, made the people recognize her innocence and informed them of the iniquity of the old men.

2235. *fulminar proçeso.* In the legal sense, "to draw up in proper legal form, to formulate," noted by Hill and Harlan in *El burlador de Sevilla* (*Cuatro comedias,* pp. 447-48, n. 1135).

2276. *que dudes lo que es muger.* Understand "me burlo de ti porque es posible que dudes lo que es mujer," an obvious matter in light of the many references to the combination *muger-mudanza,* and an idea expressed by Fernán himself on previous occasions (vv. 1284-87, 1370).

2372. *y él, ¿quién es?* For a third person singular used as direct address, Zamora Vicente says that: "Se ve que Lope ... quiere imitar el habla rural" (*El villano en su rincón*, p. 87, n. 256). Fichter notes that this form of address expresses familiarity or displeasure, and it was used on the stage mainly by servants (*El castigo del discreto*, p. 225, n. 807).

2374. *Ni aun delante del de copas.* Refers to playing cards and is involved in a pun on *copas de vino.*

2380. *a echado el plomo y cordel.* This verse suggests that Ysabel's grandfather suffered torture (*cordel*, indicating the ropes used on a rack; *plomo*, weight[s]) because of his faith, but by being faithful to it, went directly to heaven (the torture consisting of his desire for wine and *tocino*, forbidden to the believers of Mohammed?).

2381-83. *Yo soy Mudarra de Asturias, / hijodalgo como el vino / por aguar, como tozino.* A common method of establishing one's standing as a *cristiano viejo* was to claim origin as a *montañés* and to display a relish for wine and *tocino.* See J. H. Silverman, "Judíos y conversos en el *Libro de chistes* de Luis de Pinedo," *Papeles de Son Armadans,* XXIII (1961), pp. 295-97, for other *graciosos* who ". . . afirman ser, ya en forma plenamente burlesca, 'más hidalgo que un tocino.'" Note also Schevill, *La dama boba,* p. 255, n. 44, where he misinterprets a similar allusion.

2391. *la piel de Esaú.* Isaac, planning to give Esau his blessing (which was the equivalent of making him his sole heir), was tricked by Rebecca into blessing Jacob, Isaac's brother.

2405. *Quien tiene amor, poco duerme.* E. S. O'Kane lists the following similar expressions in *Refranes y frases proverbiales españolas de la Edad Media* (Madrid, 1959):

> Quien amores tyene non los puede çelar.

> Ciego ya de amores,
> los días biviendo en pena,
> las noches con mill dolores.   (p. 50b)

> Amanesi no ez di díe, quen duloris tiene
> mal adurmesi.   (p. 105a)

2429-30. *que después que Vlises vino / no fue Penélope casta.* Fortunio expresses a jealousy which is husbandly in nature, but is intensified by his imagined position as Estefanía's lover. He assumes the proprietary feelings of a wronged spouse. Since Ulysses, upon his return, "a su lado [de Penélope], acostó," it is to be expected that Fernán will exercise the same privilege — it is this bitter thought that he now voices.

2483. *Ya es tarde, echóse la suerte.* A Spanish version of the famed words of Caesar after he crossed the Rubicon, marching on Rome.

2558. *¡Muerto soy!* See n. 1270 for the use of *ser* with an intransitive past participle.

2588. *villano saltaparedes.* Defined as "galán que escala tapias" by Fontecha (p. 328), used by Melibea in Fernando de Rojas's *La Celestina* (ed. Clásicos Castellanos; Madrid, 1955), I, p. 179, as she refers to Calisto. The term has been used here in a general sense to include a servant, while Fortunio (Calixto's counterpart) is later merely called a *bellaco* (v. 2600).

In v. 2066 Fortunio says: "por el jardín saltaré." Sandoval, *Chrónica*, p. 81, translates "saltando las paredes" from the Portuguese version of the incident.

2592. *Désta çierro.* "Cerrarse de campiña es determinarse a no conceder lo que le piden o demandan, sino negarlo" (Covarrubias, *Tesoro*).

2593. *confisión.* "La *i* causa mutación en la vocal inacentuada que precede. Sus efectos son ... *e* se convierte en *i*. ... También algunos vocablos doctos tienen mutación: ... confisión ..." (Hanssen, *Gramática*, p. 33. See also, Romera Navarro, *Registro*, p. 294).

2682-83. Morby, *La Dorotea*, p. 420, n. 108, discusses beauty and its relationship to misfortune. See also Herrero García, "Ideas estéticas del teatro clásico español," *Revista de ideas estéticas*, II (1944), pp. 103-104.

2803. *Belardo.* This is the poetic name which Lope used in closing many of his plays. See S. G. Morley, *The Pseudonyms and Literary Disguises of Lope de Vega* (Berkeley and Los Angeles, 1951), pp. 429-34.

BIBLIOGRAPHY

Adam, Francis Osborne, Jr. "Some Aspects of Lope de Vega's Dramatic Technique as Observed in his Autograph Plays." Unpublished Ph.D. dissertation, University of Illinois, 1936.

Alonso, Dámaso, ed. *Romance de Angélica y Medoro* (Luis de Góngora). Madrid: Ed. Acies, 1962.

Alonso, Martín. *Enciclopedia del idioma*. Madrid: Ed. Aguilar, 1958.

Anibal, C. E. "Lope de Vega's *Dozena Parte*," *MLN*, LXVII (1932), pp. 1-7.

———. "Observations on *La estrella de Sevilla*," *HR*, II (1932), pp. 1-38.

Aragone, Elisa, ed. *El Cardenal de Belén* (Lope de Vega). Zaragoza: Ed. Ebro, 1957.

Arjona, J. Homero. "Defective Rhymes and Rhyming Techniques in Lope de Vega's Autograph *Comedias*," *HR*, XXIII (1955), pp. 108-128.

———. "Improper Use of Consonantal Rhyme in Lope de Vega and its Significance Concerning the Authorship of Doubtful Plays," *Separata de Hispanófila*, No. 16 (1962).

———, ed. *La desdichada Estefanía: edición paleográfica* (Lope de Vega). Madrid: Ed. Castalia, 1967.

———. "The Use of Autorhymes in the XVIIth-Century *Comedia*," *HR*, XXI (1953), pp. 273-301.

Armistead, Samuel G., and Joseph H. Silverman. *Diez romances hispánicos en un manuscrito sefardí de la Isla de Rodas*. Pisa: University of Pisa, 1962.

Avalle Arce, Juan Bautista. "Poesía, historia, imperialismo: *La Numancia*," *Anuario de Letras*, II (1962), pp. 76-98.

Bacaicoa Arnáiz, Dora. *Notas hispano-marroquíes en dos comedias del siglo de oro*. Tetuán: Imp. del Majzen, 1955.

Bello, Andrés, and Rufino J. Cuervo. *Gramática de la lengua castellana*. Paris: Imp. Andrés Blot, 1925.

Biblioteca Nacional. *Catálogo de la exposición bibliográfica de Lope de Vega*. Madrid: Gráfica Universal, 1935.

Boorman, S. C., ed. *Othello* (William Shakespeare). London: University of London Press, 1962.

Brooks, John. "Más que, mas que and Mas ¡qué!," *H*, XVI (1933), pp. 23-34.

Brown, Robert B. *Bibliografía de las comedias históricas, tradicionales y legendarias de Lope de Vega*. Mexico: Ed. Academia, 1958.

Buchanan, M. A. Note in "Reviews, Bibliographical Notes," *HR*, III (1935), pp. 74-75.

Campoamor, Ramón de. *Obras poéticas completas*. 3 vols. Barcelona: Sopena, 1903.

Castañeda, James A. *A Critical Edition of Lope de Vega's "Las paces de los reyes y judía de Toledo."* Chapel Hill: University of North Carolina Press, 1962.

Castro, Américo. "Algunas observaciones acerca del concepto del honor en los siglos xvi y xvii," *RFE*, III (1916), pp. 1-50, 357-386.

————. "Alusiones a Micaela de Luján en las obras de Lope de Vega," *RFE*, V (1918), pp. 256-292.

————, ed. *Vida del buscón* (Francisco Quevedo). Madrid: Espasa-Calpe, 1911.

Catalán, Diego. "La *Crónica de Castilla* y la *Historia de Africa* del sabio Maestro Gilberto en la *Estoria de los Reyes del Señorío de Africa* del Maestro Gilberto o Sujulberto: Una obra del siglo xiii perdida," *Romance Philology*, XVII (1963), pp. 346-363.

Cejador y Frauca, Julio, ed. *La Celestina* (Fernando de Rojas). 2 vols. Madrid: Espasa-Calpe, 1955.

————. *Fraseología o estilística castellana*. 4 vols. Madrid: Tip. Revista de Archivos, Bibliotecas y Museos, 1921-25.

————, ed. *Lazarillo de Tormes* (anon.). Madrid: Espasa-Calpe, 1926.

————. *Refranero castellano*. 3 vols. in 2. Madrid: Ed. Hernando, 1928.

Chaytor, H. J., ed. *Dramatic Theory in Spain*. Cambridge: Cambridge University Press, 1925. Lope de Vega's "Arte nuevo de hazer comedias en este tiempo," pp. 15-29.

Cioranescu, Alejandro. *El barroco o el descubrimiento del drama*. La Laguna de Tenerife: University de La Laguna, 1957.

Cirot, G. "Une chronique latine inédite des rois de Castille (1236)," *BHi*, XIV (1912), pp. 30-46, 109-118, 244-274, 353-374.

Corominas, Juan. *Diccionario crítico etimológico de la lengua castellana*. 4 vols. Madrid: Ed. Gredos, 1954-57.

Correas, Gustavo. "El doble aspecto de la honra en *Peribáñez y el Comendador de Ocaña*," *HR*, XXVI (1958), pp. 188-199.

————. "El doble aspecto de la honra en el teatro del siglo xvii," *HR*, XXVI (1958), pp. 99-107.

Covarrubias, Sebastián de. *Tesoro de la lengua castellana o española*. Barcelona: Ed. de Martín de Riquer, 1943.

Cuervo, Rufino J. *Apuntaciones críticas sobre el lenguaje bogotano*. Bogotá: Ed. El Gráfico, 1939.

————. *Obras inéditas, editadas por el P. Félix Restrepo, S. J.* Bogotá: Ed. Voluntad, 1944.

Delano, Lucile K. "An Analysis of the Sonnets in Lope de Vega's *Comedias*," *H*, XII (1929), pp. 119-140.

Denis, Serge. *Lexique du théatre de J. R. de Alarcón*. Paris: Libraire E. Droz, 1943.

Dick, Hugh G., ed. *Albumazar: A Comedy* (Thomas Tomkis). (University of California Publications in English, Vol. 13). Berkeley: University of California Press, 1944.

Doze comedias nuevas de Lope de Vega Carpio y otros autores, segunda parte. Barcelona: Gerónimo Margarit, 1630.

Dozena parte de las comedias de Lope de Vega Carpio. Madrid: Viuda de Alonso Martín, 1619.

Dozy, R., and W. H. Engelmann. *Glossaire des mots espagnols et portugais dérivés de l'arabe. Seconde Edition.* Leyde: E. J. Brill, 1869.

Dunham, S. A. *The History of Spain and Portugal.* 5 vols. London: Longman, Rees, etc., 1832.

Dunn, Peter N. "Honour and the Christian Background in Calderón," *BHS,* XXXVII (1960), pp. 75-105.

————. "Some Uses of Sonnets in the Plays of Lope de Vega," *BHS,* XXXIV (1957), pp. 213-222.

————. "Theme and Myth in the *Poema de Mio Cid,*" *Romania,* LXXXIII (1962), pp. 348-369.

Durán, Agustín D., ed. *Romancero general o colección de romances castellanos anteriores al siglo XVIII. (BAAEE,* Vols. X, XVI). Madrid: Rivadeneyra, 1882.

Enciclopedia universal ilustrada europeo-americana. 70 vols. Madrid: Espasa-Calpe, 1914-30.

Entrambasaguas, Joaquín de. *Lope de Vega y su tiempo, estudio especial de "El villano en su rincón."* Barcelona: Ed. Teide, 1961.

Evans, Bertrand. "The Brevity of Friar Laurence," *PMLA,* LXV (1950), pp. 841-865.

Fajardo, Juan Isidro. *Títulos de todas las comedias que en verso español y portugués se han impreso hasta el año de 1786.* Madrid, 1787.

Farinelli, Arturo. *Lope de Vega en Alemania.* (Translated from the German, *Grillparzer und Lope de Vega,* by Enrique Massaguer). Barcelona: Bosch, 1936.

Fichter, William L., ed. *El castigo del discreto* (Lope de Vega). New York: Columbia University Press, 1925.

————. "New Aids for the Dating of the Undated Autographs of Lope de Vega's Plays," *HR,* IX (1941), pp. 49-90.

————, ed. *El sembrar en buena tierra* (Lope de Vega). New York: Modern Language Association, 1944.

Fitzmaurice-Kelly, James. *Lope de Vega and the Spanish Drama.* Glasgow: Gowans and Gray, 1902.

Flórez de Setién, P. Enrique. *Memorias de las reinas católicas de España.* 2 vols. Madrid: Gráficas Nebrija, 1959.

Fontecha, Carmen. *Glosario de voces comentadas en ediciones de textos clásicos.* Madrid: Consejo Superior de Investigaciones Científicas, 1941.

Gálvez, Ignacio de, copyist. *Primera tragedia de Estephania la desdichada* (Lope de Vega). Madrid, 1762.

Gamayo y Catalán, Angel. *Crónica histórica de los doce Alfonsos de Castilla y de León.* Madrid: Imp. Pérez Dubrull, 1878.

García Figueras, Tomás. *Lo africano en las comedias de Lope de Vega.* Ceuta: Imp. "Africa," 1935.

García Valdecasas, Alfonso. *El hidalgo y el honor. Segunda edición.* Madrid: Artes Gráficas Clavileño, 1958.

G. de Amezúa, Agustín. *Una colección manuscrita y desconocida de comedias de Lope de Vega Carpio.* Madrid: Tip. "Aldus," 1945.

Gili y Gaya, Samuel. *Tesoro lexicográfico.* Madrid: Consejo Superior de Investigaciones Científicas, 1947.

Gillet, Joseph E. *A Study of "Propalladia" and Other Works of Bartolomé de Torres Naharro.* 4 vols. Menasha: Banta Publishing, 1943.

Gilman, Stephen. *The Art of "La Celestina."* Madison: University of Wisconsin Press, 1956.

————. "The Fall of Fortune: From Allegory to Fiction," *Filologia Romanza,* IV (1957), pp. 337-354.

————. "Fortune and Space in *La Celestina,*" *Romanische Forschungen,* LXVI (1955), pp. 342-360.

————. "An Introduction to the Ideology of the Baroque in Spain," *Symposium,* I (1946), pp. 82-107.

González Palencia, Angel. *Historia de la España musulmana. Cuarta edición.* Madrid: Ed. Labor, 1945.

Grandgent, C. H., ed. *La divina commedia* (Dante Alighieri). Boston: Heath, 1933.

Grupp, William J. "Dramatic Theory and Criticism in Spain During the Sixteenth, Seventeenth, and Eighteenth Centuries." Unpublished Ph. D. dissertation, Cornell, 1949.

Hamilton, T. Earle, ed. *El Cardenal de Belén* (Lope de Vega). Lubbock: Texas Tech Press, 1948.

Hanssen, Federico. *Gramática histórica de la lengua castellana.* Halle: Ed. Max Niemeyer, 1913.

Harlan, Mabel Margaret, ed. *El desdén vengado* (Lope de Vega). New York: Instituto de las Españas, 1930.

Herrero García, M. "Ideas estéticas del teatro clásico español," *Revista de ideas estéticas,* II (1944), pp. 79-109.

————. *La vida española del siglo XVII.* Madrid: Gráfica Universal, 1933.

Herrick, Marvin T. *Tragicomedy, Its Origin and Development in Italy, France and England.* Urbana: University of Illinois Press, 1962.

Hill, John M., and Mabel M. Harlan, eds. *Cuatro comedias.* New York: Norton and Co., 1941.

Hoge, Henry W. "Notes on the Sources and the Autograph Manuscript of Lope de Vega's *El príncipe despeñado,*" *PMLA,* LXV (1950), pp. 824-840.

————, ed. *El príncipe despeñado* (Lope de Vega). Bloomington: Indiana University Press, 1955.

Jones, C. A. "Honor in Spanish Golden-Age Drama: Its Relation to Real Life and Morals," *BHS,* XXXV (1958), pp. 199-210.

Keniston, Hayward. *The Syntax of Castilian Prose.* Chicago: University of Chicago Press, 1937.

Kohler, E., ed. *El perro del hortelano* (Lope de Vega). Paris: Société d'Edition: Les Belles Lettres, 1951.

Lapesa, Rafael. *Historia de la lengua española. Tercera edición.* Madrid: Escelicer, 1955. *Cuarta edición.* Madrid: Escelicer, 1959.

Lévi-Provençal, E. *Islam d'occident.* Paris: G. P. Maisonneuve et Cie., 1948.

Ley, Charles D. "Lope de Vega y la tragedia," *Clavileño,* IV (1950), pp. 9-12.

Lida de Malkiel, María Rosa. *La originalidad artística de "La Celestina."* Buenos Aires: Ed. Universitaria de Buenos Aires, 1962.

Lista y Aragón, Alberto. *Ensayos literarios y críticos.* 2 vols. Sevilla: Calvo Rubio y Cía., 1844.

Os livros de linhagens, in *Academia das Sciencias de Lisboa, Portugalliae Momenta Historica, Scriptores,* I, *Olispone,* Typis Academicis, 1856.

Lomba y Pedraja, J. R., ed. *Poesías del P. Arolas.* Madrid: Espasa-Calpe, 1928.

Marín, Diego. *La intriga secundaria en el teatro de Lope de Vega.* Mexico: Studium, 1958.

————, and Evelyn Rugg, eds. *El galán de la Membrilla* (Lope de Vega). Madrid: Anejo del *BAE*, 1962.

Martin, H. M. "Termination of Qualifying Words before Feminine Nouns and Adjectives in the Plays of Lope de Vega," *MLN*, XXXVII (1922), pp. 398-407.

Martín Echeverría, L. *Geografía de España.* 3 vols. Barcelona: Ed. Labor, 1932.

Martínez Kleiser, Luis. *Refranero general ideológico español.* Madrid: Real Academia Española, 1953.

May, T. E. "Lope de Vega's *El castigo sin venganza:* The Idolatry of the Duke of Ferrara," *BHS*, XXXVII (1960), pp. 154-182.

Medèl del Castillo, F. "Indice general alfabético de todos los títulos de comedias, publícalo John M. Hill," *RHi*, LXXV (1929), pp. 144-369.

Meier, Harri. *Ensaios de filologia românica.* Lisboa: Ed. Império, 1948.

Menéndez y Pelayo, Marcelino. *Estudios sobre el teatro de Lope de Vega.* 6 vols. Santander: Ed. "Aldus," 1949.

Menéndez Pidal, Ramón. *De Cervantes y Lope de Vega. Segunda edición.* Buenos Aires: Espasa-Calpe, 1943.

————. *Manual de gramática histórica española. Novena edición.* Madrid: Espasa-Calpe, 1952.

Montesinos, José F., ed. *Barlaán y Josafat* (Lope de Vega). Madrid: Ed. Hernando, 1935.

————, ed. *El cuerdo loco* (Lope de Vega). Madrid: Ed. Hernando, 1922.

————. *Ensayos y estudios de literatura española.* Edited by J. H. Silverman. Mexico: Studium, 1959.

————. *Estudios sobre Lope.* Mexico: Fondo de Cultura Económico, 1951.

————, ed. *El Marqués de las Navas* (Lope de Vega). Madrid: Ed. Hernando, 1925.

Montoto, Santiago de. "Contribución al vocabulario de Lope de Vega," *BAE*, XXVI (1947), pp. 281-295, 443-457; XXVII (1948), pp. 127-143, 301-318, 463-477; XXIX (1949), pp. 135-149, 329-338.

Morby, Edwin S., ed. *La Dorotea* (Lope de Vega). Berkeley: University of California Press, 1958.

————. "Some Observations on *tragedia* and *tragicomedia* in Lope," *HR*, XI (1943), pp. 185-209.

Morley, S. Griswold. *Lope de Vega's Peregrino Lists.* (University of California Publications in Modern Philology, Vol. 14). Berkeley: University of California Press, 1929-30.

————. *The Pseudonyms and Literary Disguises of Lope de Vega.* Berkeley: University of California Press, 1951.

————, and Courtney Bruerton. *The Chronology of Lope de Vega's Comedias.* New York: Modern Language Association, 1940.

————, and Richard W. Tyler. *Los nombres de personajes en las comedias de Lope de Vega.* 2 vols. Berkeley: University of California Press, 1961.

Morris, C. B. "Lope de Vega's *El castigo sin venganza* and Poetic Tradition," *BHS*, XL (1963), pp. 69-78.

O'Kane, Eleanor S. *Refranes y frases proverbiales españolas de la Edad Media*. Madrid: Anejos del *BAE*, 1959.

Parker, A. A. *The Approach to the Spanish Drama of the Golden Age. Diamante series* No. 6. London: Hispano-Luso Brazilian Councils, 1957.

———. "Towards a Definition of Calderonian Tragedy," *BHS*, XXXIX (1962), pp. 222-237.

Peers, E. Allison. "Lope de Vega: Prólogo al Tercer Centenario de su muerte," *Bulletin of Spanish Studies*, XII (1935), pp. 174-185.

Pemartín, José. "La idea monárquica en Lope de Vega," *Acción española*, XIV (1935), pp. 417-459.

Poesse, Walter. *Internal Line-Structure of Thirty Autograph Plays of Lope de Vega*. Bloomington: Indiana University Publications, 1949.

Primera crónica general de España, publicada por Ramón Menéndez Pidal. 2 vols. Madrid: Ed. Gredos, 1955.

Real Academia Española. *Diccionario de la lengua española*. Madrid: Espasa-Calpe, 1956.

———. *Obras de Lope de Vega*. 15 vols. Madrid, 1870-1913.

———. *Obras de Lope de Vega, nueva edición*. 13 vols. Madrid, 1916-1930.

Reichenberger, Arnold G., ed. *Carlos V en Francia* (Lope de Vega). Philadelphia: University of Pennsylvania Press, 1962.

———, ed. *El embuste acreditado* (Vélez de Guevara). Granada: Universidad de Granada, 1956.

———. "Notes on Lope's *El piadoso aragonés*," *HR*, XXI (1953), pp. 302-321.

———. "The Uniqueness of the *Comedia*," *HR*, XXVII (1959), pp. 303-316.

Relaciones de algunos sucesos de los últimos tiempos del reino de Granada, que publica la Sociedad de Bibliófilos Españoles. Madrid, 1868.

Rennert, Hugo A. "Bibliography of the Dramatic Works of Lope de Vega," extrait of *RHi*, XXXIII (1915), pp. 1-284.

———. *The Spanish Stage in the Time of Lope de Vega*. New York: Hispanic Society of America, 1909.

Restori, A. "Obras de Lope de Vega," *Zeitschrift für Romanische Philologie*, XXVII (1902), pp. 486-517.

Roaten, Darnell H., and Federico Sánchez y Escribano. *Wolfflin's Principles in Spanish Drama, 1500-1700*. New York: Hispanic Institute in the U.S., 1952.

Rodríguez Marín, Francisco, ed. *Don Quixote* (Miguel de Cervantes). 10 vols. Madrid: Ed. Atlas, 1947-49.

———. *Mas de 21.000 refranes castellanos no contenidos en la copiosa colección del Maestro Gonzalo Correas*. Madrid: Tip. Revista de Archivos, Bibliotecas y Museos, 1926.

Romera Navarro, Miguel. *Registro de lexicografía hispánica*. Madrid: *RFE* Anejo 54, 1951.

Salembien, L. "Le vocabulaire de Lope de Vega," *BHi*, XXXIV (1932), pp. 97-127, 289-310.

Sandoval, F. Prudencio de. *Chrónica del Inclito emperador de España, don Alfonso VII*. Madrid: Casa de Luys Sánchez, 1600.

———. *Historia de los reyes de Castilla y de León*. Madrid, 1792. Also known as the *Crónica de los cinco reyes*. Pamplona: Imp. B. Cano, 1615.

Sarthou Carreres, Carlos. *Castillos de España.* Madrid: F. Beltrán, 1932.

Schevill, Rudolph. *The Dramatic Art of Lope de Vega, Together with "La dama boba."* (University of California Publications in Modern Philology, Vol. 6). Berkeley: University of California Press, 1918.

Serrano Martínez, Encarnación-Irene. *"Honneur" y "Honor": su significación a través de las literaturas francesa y española.* Murcia: Publicaciones de la Universidad de Murcia, 1956.

Silverman, Joseph H. "El gracioso de Juan Ruiz de Alarcón y el concepto de la figura del donaire tradicional," *H,* XXXV (1952), pp. 64-69.

———. "Judíos y conversos en el *Libro de chistes* de Luis de Pineda," *Papeles de Son Armadans,* XXIII (1961), pp. 289-301.

———. "Peribáñez y Vellido Dolfos," *BHi,* LV (1953), pp. 378-380.

Simón Díaz, José, and Juana de José Prades. *Ensayo de una bibliografía.* Madrid: Ed. Castalia de Valencia, 1955.

Socins, A. *Arabische Grammatik.* Edited by Karl Brockelmann. Berlin: Reuther and Reichard, 1909.

Spencer, Forrest E., and Rudolph Schevill. *The Dramatic Works of Luis Vélez de Guevara.* Berkeley: University of California Press, 1937.

Templin, Ernest H. "An Additional Note on *mas que," H,* XII (1929), pp. 163-170.

———. "The Mother in the *Comedia* of Lope de Vega," *HR,* III (1935), pp. 219-244.

Terlingen, J. H. *Los italianismos en español desde la formación del idioma hasta principios del siglo XVII.* Amsterdam, 1943.

Valbuena Briones, A. "El simbolismo en el teatro de Calderón: La caída del caballo," *Romanische Forschungen,* LXXIV (1962), pp. 60-76.

Van Dam, Cornelis, ed. *El castigo sin venganza* (Lope de Vega). Gronigen: P. Noordhoff, 1928.

Vélez de Guevara, Luis. *Los zelos hasta los cielos y desdichada Estefanía.* Madrid: Imp. de Antonio Sanz, 1745.

Vossler, Karl. *La poesía de la soledad en España.* Translated from the German *Poesie des Einsamkeit in Spanien* by Ramón de la Serna y Espina. Buenos Aires: Ed. Losada, 1946.

Watson, A. Irvine. "El pintor de su deshonra and the Neo-Aristotelian Theory of Tragedy," *BHS,* XL (1963), pp. 17-34.

Wehr, Hans. *A Dictionary of Modern Written Arabic.* Edited by J. M. Cowan. Ithaca: Cornell University Press, 1961.

Wofsy, S. A. "A Note on *mas que," Romanic Review,* XIX (1928), pp. 41-48.

Zamora Vicente, Alonso, ed. *El villano en su rincón* (Lope de Vega). Madrid: Ed. Gredos, 1961.

———, ed. *"El villano en su rincón" y "Las bizarrías de Belisa"* (Lope de Vega). Madrid: Espasa-Calpe, 1963.

Ziomek, Henryk. *A Paleographic Edition of Lope de Vega's Autograph Play "La nueva victoria de D. Gonzalo de Cordoua."* New York: Hispanic Institute in the U.S., 1962.

APPENDIX

Os livros de linhagens, p. 67

Esta dona Exemena Nuniz foy casada com dom Fernam Laindiz irmaão de dom Diego Laindiz padre de Ruy Diaz o çide, e fez em ella dom Aluar Fernamdiz de Menaya. E dom Aluar Fernamdiz porque teue Castro Xarez delrrey em terra, e avia hi huum solar daquelles donde deçendia que fora do comde dom Goterre, chamousse porem de Castro porque era comde e fidallgo assaz. ... E dom Aluar Fernamdez foi casado com a comdessa dona Mellia Anssorez filha do comde dom Pero Anssorez de Catom, e fez em ella huuma filha que ouue nome dona Maria Aluarez. E dona Maria Aluarez foi casada com dom Fernamdo filho delrrey de Nauarra de gaamça, e fez em ella tres filhos ... o terçeiro dom Goterre Fernamdez. E dom Fernam Fernamdez foi casado com dona Maria Aluarez filha do comde dom Aluaro de Fita, e fez em ella huum filho e huuma filha, e o filho ouue nome dom Martim Fernamdez e foy muy boo mançebo e morreo çedo de hidade de xxvi annos, e a filha ouue nome dona Samcha e demandoua o emperador, e ella com medo de seu irmão nom se atreueo, e como aquella que queria fazer mall deu peçonha a seu irmaão e matouo e depois foisse pera o emperador e foy sa barregaã: e o emperador ouue em ella huuma filha que ouue nome dona Esteuainha e foy casada com dom Fernam Rodriguez de Castro.

Sandoval, *Chrónica del Emperador*, pp. 150-52

En esta Era 1188 que es el año de Christo 1150 dizen que vinieron à nuestra España los Moros Almohades, gẽte braua, feroz, y guerrera. En tiẽpo del Rey don Alõso el Sexto, à buelta de nuestro Emperador, vinierõ los Almorauides, y se apoderarõ de todo el Imperio de los Moros Españoles, quedãdo sujetos à Marruecos. Agora en estos dias se leuãto en Africa vn Moro llamado Abentumert, hõbre docto en la Astrologia judiciaria. Sucedio, q̃ viẽdo à vn moço hijo de vn ollero, q̃ se dezia Abdelmon, y considerando su persona y talle, representosele q̃ era moço de grã nacimiẽto, fauorecido de los signos, q̃ le prometian grandes cosas. Cõfirmose mas en ello por sus juizios, y vino à sacar, q̃ segun lo que sus planetas le señalarõ quãdo nacio, auia de ser vn gran Principe. Y como esta ciega gẽte este tan rendida y sujeta à estos juyzios, teniendo por ineuitable, lo q̃ por la judiciaria adiuinã, dixoselo à Abdelmõ. Y como el diablo los guiaua en ello, por el fruto maldito q̃ esperaua sacar, el moço que de suyo era altiuo, aunq̃ hijo de viles padres, luego se le puso en la cabeça lo que despues tuuo efeto, acosta de muchas vidas, q̃ es lo q̃ Satanas pretende en semejantes enredos. Llegosele vn Moro llamado Almohadi, docto en el ciego error, de la secta de Mahoma, y en opiniõ de santo entre ellos, y so color de cierta interpretacion q̃ de nueuo daua al Alcoran, comẽçaron à inquietar aquellas gentes de Africa, siendo ellos de suyo faciles y amigos de nouedades. Llego el negocio à tanto rompimiento, que se dierõ entre si sangrientas batallas. Y finalmẽte preualeciendo los Almohades, que tal nombre tomaron los que seguian al Moro Almohadi, vẽcieron y mataron à Miramamolin Rey de Marruecos, llamado Alboali, q̃ era de los Almorauides, y leuãtaron por Rey de Marruecos y Miramamolin, à Abdelmon hijo del ollero. El Almohadi falso santo, autor destos males, hizo q̃ el nueuo Rey de Marruecos, hechura suya, passasse luego à España cõtra los Almorauides, q̃ por aca auia, y los sujetasse todos, con otros altos pensamientos, de cõsumir el nombre Christiano. Hizo luego su viaje passando con infinitas gentes de guerra, y sin dificultad se apoderarõ de todas las ciudades de la Andaluzia, sugetandolas al imperio de Marruecos. Matarõ cõ grã crueldad todos los Christianos Moçarabes, q̃ siẽpre auiã viuido entre los Moros guardãdo nuestra Sãta Fè, à otros hizierõ renegar della, y à los q̃ permaneciã firmes en su santa cõfesion, martirizauan, y los que no se sentian con fuerças pudiendo escapar, huyã, passandose à la tierra de los Christianos. Fue vno dellos Clemẽte, Arçobispo de

Seuilla, q̃ vino à Talauera, hõbre doctisimo en la lẽgua Arabiga, dõde viuio, y acabo sus dias santissimamẽte.

Otro fue Arnugo santo religioso, el qual vino à la villa de Olmedo, y cerca de sus muros en vna montañuela, al Setentriõ, fundo vna Yglesia à Santa Cruz, que agora es de las mongas Comẽdadoras de S. Iuan de Malta, de la ciudad de Zamora. . . .

Contra la potẽcia de los Almohades acudio nr̃o valeroso Emperador, como lo dizẽ los priuilegios, llamãdolos Muzmitas, y los vẽcio en batalla cãpal, peleando con ellos a vista de los muros de Cordoua, y los vẽcio y persiguio, hasta echarlos de España, y compelerlos à boluerse à Africa, dõde el falso Almohadi murio luego, y le sepultaron cerca de la Ciudad de Marruecos, sũptuosissimamente, y le venerauan y adorauan como à Santo.

J. Censuras y licencias

Examine [e]sta comedia, cantares y entremeses della el S^{ro}. Thomás Gracián Dantisco y dé sus censuras. — En Madrid, a 9 de En°. 1607 años.

Esta comedia intitulada *Estefanía la desdichada* se podrá representar, reseruando a la vista lo que fuera de la lectura se offreçiere y lo mismo en los cantares y entremés. — En Madrid, a 9 de enero, 1607.

S^{ro}. *Thomás Gracián Dantisco.*
(Rúbrica)

Podráse representar esta comedia, cantares y entremeses della, guardando las censuras en ella dadas. — En M^d., a 12 de En°. 1607.

Por mandado de los señores inquisidores y juezes apostólicos de Valld., vi esta comedia, y no ay en ella cosa contra la fe católica ni buenas costumbres, sino ques la historia a la letra de los Conde *(sic)* de Lemos y del S^r. Rey don Alo., y así se le puede dar la liçen^a. de representarla. En S. Franco. de Valld., 29 de abril, 1607.

Frai Gregorio Ruiz.

Los SS. Inquis^{res}. Apostólicos de Vallid., auiendo visto el pareçer de atrás de fray Gregorio Ruiz, lector de Theología de Sⁿ. Franc^{co}. desta çiudad, dieron lisençia para que se pueda representar esta comedia intitulada *Estefanía la desdichada*. En la çiudad de Vallid., 29 de abril de 1607.

Asn. Juan Martínez de la Vega. (Rúbrica)

Por comisión de los Señores Probisores deste Arçobispado bi esta comedia llamada *Estefanía la desdichada,* y con las çensuras que tiene se representará. En esta çiudad de Burgos, en 7 de Set^e. de 1607 años.

El Licen^{do}. (Firma ilegible que parece terminar en López)

Por mandamiento del Arçob°., mi señor, he visto esta comedia de *Estefanía la desdichada,* y digo q[ue] se puede representar, reseruando p^a. la vista lo q[ue] es fuera de la lectura. Así lo firmo en Çaragoça, a 28 de Octubre, año 1608.

El D^{or}. Villalua

Conforme al mandam^{to}. de su S^a. el Ilustriss°. de Plas^a., vi esta comedia, y no ay en ella cosa que se pueda reprouar contra lo dispuesto en los sacros cánones y concilios, y assí la pueden representar. En Trug^{llo}., treze de julio de 1609.

As°. el d^r. A. L. Giménez de Camargo.
(Rúbrica)

No tem cousa (frase ilegible) se não possa representar. Lb^{oa}., a 12 de outubro de 609.

Fr. Manuel Coello.

Por mandado del S^r. Lcdo. Gonzalo Guerrero, canónigo de la S^a. Yg^a., doctoral y prouisor general de su obispado, uide esta comedia llamada *Estefanía la desdichada,* y no ui en ella cosa contra nuestra Fe Católica, y assí podrá a mi pareçer representarse. Dado en Jaem, a 18 de julio de 1610.

D^{or}. Antonio Godoi Checa.

En la ciudad de Jaen, a diez y ocho deste mes de julio de mil y seisci^{os}. y diez años, como el licen^{do}. G°. Guerrero, prouisor general del obispado, auiendo uisto el testimonio de uisita de la comedia yntitulada *Estefanía la desdichada,* h[e]cho por mandado de su m^d., por el dotor Ant. Godoy, prior del arp°., dijo que daua y dio lic^a. y facultad a A°. Granados, autor, a que pueda represe^{se}. en esta ciudad y obispado, y lo firmó de su nombre.

El L^{do}. Gonzalo Guerrero.   A. de mí
Joan de Mata. N^o.

Vi esta comedia y se puede representar en Gr^{da}. 6 de Henero de 1611.

El D^{or}. Franc^o. Martínez de Rueda.

Por mandamiento del Arçob°., mi señor, don Pedro Manrique, he visto esta comedia de Estefanía, y digo q̄ se puede repressentar. — En Çaragoça, a 20 de octubre (?), 1611.

El d^{or}. Villalua.

Podesse representar esta comedia intitulada *Estefanía la Desdichada.* En Lisboa, 8 de outubro, 1611 (?).

(Firma ilegible)

O mesmo me parece. — *J. L. Salazar.*